How Good is David Mamet, Anyway?

Conference of the Birds—The Story of Peter Brook in Africa

The Photographs of William Klein
(an introduction)

The Cameraman, A Posthumous Novel by John Gale
(edited, with an introduction)

How Good is David Mamet, Anyway?

Writings on Theatre— and Why It Matters

John Heilpern

Routledge
New York • London

Published in 2000 by
Routledge
29 West 35th Street
New York, NY 10001

Published in Great Britain by
Routledge
11 New Fetter Lane
London EC4P 4EE

An extract from "Empire of the Stage" was first published in *Vanity Fair* in 1995. The *Observer* of London published "Noël Coward at Seventy" in 1969, "England's Greatest Clown" in 1975, "Tranquil in Connecticut with Arthur Miller" in 1976, and "Lunch with Geilgud and Richardson" in 1977. "In Memoriam Michael Bennett" was published in *Vanity Fair* in 1987. "Peter Brook, Barbra Streisand and Me" is the prologue from *Conference of the Birds—The Story of Peter Brook in Africa*. All the other reviews were published in *The New York Observer*, from 1992 to 1999.

10 9 8 7 6 5 4 3 2 1

Library of Congress Cataloging-in-Publication Data

Heilpern, John.
    How good is David Mamet, anyway? : writings on theater and why it matters /
John Heilpern.
        p. cm.
Includes index.
ISBN 0-415-92547-9 (hb)
1. Theater—Great Britain. 2. Theater—United States. I. Title.

PN2583.H45 2000
792'.0941 21—dc21

                                                                                99-043945

FOR RACHEL, AS ALWAYS.

FOR SHW, MY FELLOW THEATER ENTHUSIAST,

MY LOVE.

viii

I would like to thank two great journalists—David Astor, then editor of the *Observer* of London, and Anthony Sampson, then editor of the *Observer Magazine*, who were the first to hire me and offer much help and encouragement. If you have any complaints about this book, would you therefore write to them personally?

That great American editor, Clay Felker, first hired me in New York and is really to blame for everything.

Arthur Carter, the owner and publisher of *The New York Observer*, has been a consistent, warm friend—not just of mine, but of free expression. My heartfelt thanks to him, as well as to the editor of the paper, Peter Kaplan, and to three editors of the theater column, Mark Lasswell, Bettina Edelstein, and Jay Stowe.

Last, but by no means least, it has been a pleasure to be edited by William P. Germano, Vice President at Routledge, who goes to the theater more than anyone I've ever known, and lives to tell the tale.

Why do we go to the theater? There's a question! Or put it this way: Why, oh why, do we go to the theater? If we go to a movie and it isn't any good, well it's not the end of the world. We're usually quite content just the same, sitting in the cineplex with our Gummi Bears. It passes the time. Though, as Samuel Beckett pointed out, the time would have passed anyway. But if we're disappointed at the theater, everything changes dramatically.

We cannot while away the time at the theater. Time becomes precious. Theater takes place in time present, and Lear goes mad before our eyes. In the "two-hour traffic of our stage," as Shakespeare put it, time is of the essence.

It's live! Sometimes, when irritated by someone eating or talking during a play, I've lost patience and said to them: "Ssssh! This is not a movie." (At which they look surprisingly shocked.) But what can you do? Only moments before the curtain went up on *Art*, the couple behind me were on their cell phone to their child at home.

"This is your mummy, darling. Can you hear me? Go to bed, Sweet Pea," Sweet Pea's mummy was saying. "Yes, we're at the theater, darling. Hang up now, Sweet Pea. Hang up, darling. The show's starting. Yes, I'm with your father. I love you, too."

Theater isn't a church, thank God. But it asks for a certain effort. We enter a theater leaving the real world behind. In this timeless ritual, we willingly exchange reality for the illusion of reality. We collude in a game of pretend the better to understand the world, and to enjoy it more, too. Going to the theater may even be seen as a subconscious rite of passage. We actually travel from light (the foyer) to dark (the auditorium) to light (the stage). There, Artaud's "strange sun," a light of abnormal intensity, illuminates the whole of life, including its convulsive cruelty.

But when theater disappoints, our response can be profound and unholy. We take a bad theater experience personally and might even feel a sense of betrayal. Or mutter disconsolately, as James Thurber did about a play, "It had only one fault. It was kind of lousy." That uncompromising free spirit of English theater, John Osborne, wrote that a critic is someone who would send Hedda Gabler to a marriage counselor. Nicely said, but we are all critics in our own fashion. The expense of going to the theater—"Seventy-five bucks for *this*?"—doesn't entirely account for our disappointment when it lets us down. No, our pleasure in theater is sensual, and our connection to it is deeply emotional. You do not get emotional about a cineplex.

But when theater works—as life at its best can work—how we celebrate then! Perhaps we've just seen an intoxicating performance by one of those kings and rulers of the stage, a great actor. Or a comedy tonight! Or an epic tale of angels in an America lost and found. But we will have experienced something unique and priceless. We will see the world differently. Our hearts are glad And we can say that theater is the one place where all liberties are possible.

In David Hare's *Amy's View,* Judi Dench plays Esme, a well-known West End actress, and theater itself is under siege. Dominic, an ambitious TV producer and future movie director, doesn't see the point of theater, believing it to be dead.

"You know, you go to the theater," he explains amusingly, "A character comes to the door. You think, Oh my God! He's going to cross the room. Jump cut, for Chrissake, just jump cut! And then, the next thing—oh, Christ, you just know it! The bastard is going to sit down and *talk.* [*He shakes his head pityingly.*] And it's so slow. They do it slowly. And the way they act! It's so old-fashioned. In these big barns and they have to shout. Why don't we admit it? It's been superseded. It had its moment, but its moment has gone. Of course, I defer to you, Esme."

"Thank you…" she replies with steely irony. But she makes no formal defense. When her own life crumbles, theater saves her life. It is the only thing that makes sense. Theater is all she heroically has, and, in many ways, all she needs to have.

How I wish, even so, that she had answered the punk. He deserved an answer. He represents a fashionable point of view. ("Jump cut, for Chrissake, just jump cut!") But well-told stories are not to be rushed, a 2,500-year heritage has yet to be superseded. The language and theater of Shakespeare, Chekhov, Brecht, Beckett, and O'Neill has yet to die.

Tell me: What would we lose if we were to lose the theater?

Empire
of the Stage

The rector of St. Giles-in-the-Fields, London, his pink, kind face almost unlined though he's eighty, peered at me hopefully. "Excuse me," he asked. "Are you Alan Bates?"

Now, what was doubly sweet about this is that I'm afraid I look nothing like him. "Oh dear," the stagestruck Reverend Taylor sighed. "I was longing to meet him."

The rehearsal for the memorial service of John Osborne was underway. Osborne, glorious voice of protest and un-English passion, had revolutionized British theater with his 1956 *Look Back in Anger* at the Royal Court Theater (Alan Bates was in the original production). "I have been blessed with God's two greatest gifts—to be born English and heterosexual," the famous dramatist declared in outrageous mischief. He aimed his Swiftian fusillades, John Mortimer wrote in the *New York Times,* at "all those who would turn the world gray in the name of political correctness." And now we had come to celebrate his turbulent, memorable life in the little church that was founded in the twelfth century.

At the memorial rehearsal, the rector was the director. Peter Brook, arguably the greatest theater director England has produced, once defined the mysterious art of directing as "getting people on and off the stage." The rector of St. Giles-in-the-Fields understood this in his bones. "You need to be out of your pew before the Elgar music has stopped. Otherwise it doesn't *flow,*" he was saying to Dame Maggie Smith. "Then it's back to your pew for the hymn."

She nodded respectfully. She would be reading "Mr. Valiant-for-Truth" from Bunyan's *Pilgrim's Progress.* A born worrier, she makes you laugh on sight. She can fill any theater either side of the Atlantic. She's a peculiarly English mix of the suburban and the glamorous. "Enlarge! Enliven! Enlighten!" Maggie Smith exalted as the heroine of *Lettice and Lovage*, the hit comedy Peter Shaffer wrote for her. "That was my mother's watchword. She called them the three Es. She was a great teacher, my mother."

"Really?" says her friend in the play. "At what institution?"

"The oldest and the best," comes the triumphant reply. "The Theater!"

Dirk Bogarde, another of Osborne's friends, was at the rehearsal, looking dapper. He would be reading a moving passage from *Holy Dying* by Jeremy Taylor. "Ooh," said Maggie Smith when he told her that she could park her car in the churchyard. "I don't think I want to park there *yet*." Sir Dirk laughed lightly, enjoying the company of actors. Long before he became a movie star, he was onstage with another young unknown, Peter Ustinov.

Not everyone at the rehearsal was a knight, or a Dame. They'll just have to wait their turn. Michael Ball, a sunny presence, strolled into the church. The young star of Andrew Lloyd Webber's *Aspects of Love* would be singing "If You Were the Only Girl in the World," for Osborne loved the romance and sentiment of Edwardian music hall. The service proper was to take place the following morning, yet there seemed no urgency. Flippancy under pressure—very British. And no one troubled to rehearse their piece—actorly one-upmanship that grew collective. It was a technical rehearsal. "So the rector cues me," David Grant, a West End company manager known as "Mother," was saying to Michael Ball, "and I cue you, dear."

David Hare, one of the foremost playwrights in England, would give the address. The British have a schoolboy weakness for nicknames. He is "the Head Boy." (His frequent director, Richard Eyre, the artistic director of the Royal National Theatre, is "the Headmaster.") "Of course," said Dirk Bogarde, teasing the Head Boy, "you'll have to give the address from the pulpit."

"I'm too terrified," Hare replied, and looked it. "Oh, I *couldn't*. I would have to be ordained."

"Frightful coward," said Bogarde.

"Is it getting ugly?" Helen Osborne asked, giggling. She was grieving, though keeping up appearances bravely. She was John's fifth wife. It was a happy, seventeen-year marriage. She used to be a drama critic.

Enter the earl of Gowrie, an unusual public figure in England and chairman of the Arts Council. Alexander Patrick Greysteil Hore-Ruthven, second earl of Gowrie, had the tragic fate to be born an aristocrat without money. This charming man is therefore compelled to work. Educated at Eton and Balliol College, Oxford, Gowrie has taught English literature at Harvard, was said to be a favorite of Prime Minister Margaret Thatcher, and is the only government minister ever to have been a published poet.

"Good day," the slightly dandified literary lord greeted the assembled cast in church with courteous formality. "How do you do?" He was to read the lesson (1 Corinthians 15, verses 51–59). "So I stand here? I see," he said, eyeing the pews over the formidable Bible on the lectern before him. "Are there microphones?"

The Osborne memorial-play would be unmiked. In the best theater, the pure unfiltered resonance of the human voice is all. "So it's to be good no-nonsense declamation?" he asked the rector, smiling.

"That's it!" the rector replied. "Sound is soaked up like blotting paper when the church is full. So, if I may, speak up!"

"Don't worry, I'm used to it," Gowrie added cheerfully. "Everyone in the House of Lords is deaf."

Trumpeters could be heard from the church balcony—members of the English Chamber Orchestra rehearsing. "What do we wear tomorrow?" Michael Ball asked. (What's the costume?) Nothing too funereal, more the throwaway Gowrie look, was the advice. "Good luck!" they wished one another. "All the best for tomorrow!" "Good luck!"

I had gone to London—"This earth, this realm, this *England*," as the United Airlines commercial goes—to take a look at British theater and how it works. England may soldier on stoically, but its theater seems to rule the English-speaking world like the last colonial outpost of an Anglophile empire. Few would deny, at least, that the American War of Independence has been lost on that oldest established, permanent floating crap game in New York known as Broadway. How come "little" England still rules the waves—and *only* in theater? Who are they? Come to think of it, how dare they?

Shakespeare, like God, is an Englishman. Therefore, the English believe that all theater began in England. They tend to overlook the Greeks. But clas-

4

sical Greek dramatists didn't write in English. The historic continuity of England's theater tradition accounts for the national pride and prejudice. "We have been doing it longer than anyone else," I was often told (too often). But after all, Shakespeare has been performed in England for three hundred years.

"If it's British," goes the saying in New York, where I live, "it must be great!" At which the entire, despairing New York theater community has an understandable wish to jump off the Empire State Building. Anglophilia and prestigious British imports rule Lloyd Webberized Broadway.

Look at just a few facts from the contemporary scene: A quarter of the Broadway productions in the 1995 season were British. There were 52 productions on Broadway; 141 in the West End. Those massive nonprofit theater corporations and power bases, the Royal National Theatre and the Royal Shakespeare Company, between them produced 46 plays. There were a mere 8 new plays on Broadway; the Royal Court Theatre (George Bernard Shaw's old theater) alone premiered 19 plays, with 38 new dramatists under commission. The nonprofit theaters of England are the formidable tributaries to the commercial West End and Broadway. Four recent Broadway transfers were from the National Theatre alone—*Arcadia, Carousel, Indiscretions,* and *An Inspector Calls;* two more were via the tiny Almeida in North London—*Medea* starring Diana Rigg, *Hamlet* starring Ralph Fiennes. Both walked off in successive years with the Tony Award for Best Actor.

"My impressions of Broadway," said Tom Stoppard, "is the less serious theater there is, the hungrier the audience gets. But whatever the state of Broadway, something hasn't changed at all, especially in its sense of community. The experience of having a play produced in New York is unequaled. If you could smoke there, it would be perfect."

Stoppard had just returned to London from the Tony awards ceremony in Manhattan, where his *Arcadia* lost out to Terrence McNally's tour guide to gay weekends in the country, *Love! Valour! Compassion!* "I'm told I came in equal second with three others," he told me cheerfully when we met. (He has already won three Tonys for *The Real Thing, Travesties,* and *Rosencrantz and Guildenstern Are Dead*). "When Terrence McNally won, there was a great outburst of joy. I thought, My goodness, if I'd won, I would have been the most unpopular man in New York."

"It's just that they've had enough of the Brits," I said.

"I don't blame them," he replied.

Stoppard was born in Czechoslovakia and came to England via India when he was eight. "I feel it was a great stroke of good fortune," he explained. "I love England. I love it physically—its landscape, and certainly its language and culture. If I ended up living anywhere else, I'd feel like an exile." The English tend to distrust intellectuals, but not Tom Stoppard. *Arcadia* alone reveals his companiable, essential Englishness: a fondness for carnal embrace, farce, gamesmanship, flippant ironies, scholarly oafs, detective games, smoke screens, crossword puzzles, the poetry of Byron, country houses, and gardens (classical symmetry to romantic disorder).

He writes his plays with a fountain pen. "You have given up the quill?" I inquired.

"My last goose died some time ago," he replied.

The common language that unites and divides us, the sentimental ties that bind us, make for the complex "special relationship" between America and England. As relationships go, we're like a split personality of cultural opposites. In acting terms and style, you could list some of the differing national identities in parallel columns as the late Kenneth Tynan listed the qualities of Olivier (burgundy wine) versus Gielgud (claret):

U.K.	U.S.
Theater	Film
Olivier	Brando
Shakespeare	—
Lyricism	Method
Tea	Psychology
Rhetoric	Emotion
Anthony Hopkins	Dustin Hoffman
Jeremy Irons	John Malkovitch
Emma Thompson	Meryl Streep
Lloyd Webber	Disney

The differences blur—no young British stage actor in his right mind isn't influenced by the film naturalism and awesome method of, say, Pacino—but the division is in the heritage. England is built on a theater culture; America, though it has its great theater, is a film culture. "Theater is our primary way of self-definition, like movies in America," said Stephen Daldry, the punk theater evangelist who runs "the chorus of dissent" at the Royal Court Theater. Daldry's Hitchcockian production of J. B. Priestley's old warhorse *An Inspector Calls* won him a Tony Award on Broadway. "But every time I went through customs, I was stopped," he told me amusingly. "I'd tell them I worked in theater. They'd search my bags as if I were involved in some illicit pornographic activity. I've given up now. I say I work in movies. No problem! 'Welcome to the U.S.A.! Good luck!'"

There is no real British film industry, least of all in the Hollywood sense. (And no American East–West Coast divide, no conflict between a theater career in New York or riches in L.A.) The biggest annual film budget in Britain would scarcely make a single Hollywood movie—TV Channel 4's £16 million, which in turn helps finance eighteen low-budget films, among them *Four Weddings and a Funeral, The Crying Game, Howards End,* and *The Madness of King George.* The successful producer behind them, David Aukin, worked in theater for twenty years and was the National Theater's executive director (his wife, Nancy Meckler, is a well-known avant-garde theater director). Sooner or later in Britain, everything comes back to theater.

"The American way," Aukin pointed out, "is to say, 'Why on earth would you want to do theater when you can be a movie star?' But here, theater is the actors' credibility and calling card. It tells the film world, 'We're not totally beholden to you.' It marks them out as independent and different, because Johnny Depp couldn't do that."

The British are stage actors first and last (not like Johnny Depp). Olivier virtually abandoned his Hollywood career to spend a decade founding the National Theatre. A succeeding generation of leading stage actresses—Vanessa Redgrave, Maggie Smith, Glenda Jackson—won six Academy Awards between them. And today, the roots and heart of virtually every British actor who's made it in Hollywood are in the theater—from Ralph Fiennes to Emma Thompson to Kenneth Branagh, Anthony Hopkins, Ben Kingsley and Jeremy Irons to Judi Dench, Miranda Richardson, Gary Oldman, and Daniel Day Lewis.

When the British stage actor looks in the mirror, he is likely to see a character actor; his American counterpart sees a hero, or antihero. The British at center are great character actors—transferring with effortless superiority from stage to screen into the native *Room with a View* school. In turn, they have a useful sideline feeding Hollywood with superior screen butlers and camp, beguilingly charming villains: Anthony Hopkins's cannibalistic Hannibal Lecter; Alan Rickman's terrorist-aesthete in *Die Hard*; Jeremy Irons's pseudo-cultivated alleged wife murderer Claus von Bülow, his treacherously languid Lion of *The Lion King,* or his terrorist-aesthete in *Die Hard 3.* They earn these born stage actors an honest mil or three.

The English are never quite who or what they seem. They are a nation of actors in disguise.

The higher lunacies of a John Cleese are like a safety valve releasing the English from the pressures of habitual restraint. They are innately understated. "A bit of a set-back last night" means the roof fell in. Traditional reserve, diffidence, insularity, go to the core of the national identity. Outwardly unemotional, the English are easily embarrassed; the rules and riddles of the class system are their containment, irony their greatest defense and smoke screen. The ironist deflects and disguises what he really feels, as if hiding behind an actor's mask.

The British need their theater like oxygen or a fix to loosen up, to understand who they really are behind the masks. I had gone to meet Michael Gambon, in his fifties the finest actor in England (though Ian McKellen might disagree). Albert Finney calls acting "farting about in make up"; Gambon calls it "shouting in the evenings." He was taking a smoke break from rehearsing his Volpone at the National, looking like a tall, avuncular Everyman. I asked him why theater is so essential here.

"I suppose it's because we're so fucked up, really," he replied amiably. "We're such complex liars, aren't we? Constantly deceiving ourselves. Sensitive on the inside, pompous, arrogant bastards on the outside. We're a complex people, putting on disguises and fronts, sidestepping everything. It's just my instinctive response. But that's why we have a real need for theater."

Or, as the director Declan Donnellan put it: "Sex, murder, betrayal, plots and poison, kings, courtiers, damnation and salvation—all the things we really love! A jolly good night out!"

And that jolly good night out takes many potent forms. The English have a perverse taste for the Victorian naughty, or saucy. "Keep your hands off my nuts," went the national advertising campaign for K.P. Nuts. "Carry on nibbling!" Hence all those enjoyably dated West End sex comedies and farces that will not go away. The essential of any West End farce, a uniquely British tradition that came from France, is, of course, that the hero is always caught helplessly with his pants down, like Hugh Grant. The theatrical farce mirrors the farcical reality. Another uniquely British tradition is English pantomime, which came from commedia dell'arte. The productions aren't what they used to be. (They never were.) But every child in the country is reared on the ritual annual Christmas panto whose essential is that the Principal Boy, as he's known, is played by a girl, and the battle-ax Dame is always a man.

So the Principal Boy, who's a girl, is in love with a girl whose mum's a man. The English enjoy a Shakespearean taste for role-playing.

They also love pomp and circumstance. They own the copyright. It was Alan Bennett, an unapologetic monarchist, who showed how the royals are really actors in a national pageant. "Wave! Smile at the people!" the king commands his wayward family in Bennett's *Madness of King George.* "Let them see that we're happy! That's what we're here for!"

I met Alan Bennett for tea midst the faux nineteenth-century French splendor of the Palm Court in the Ritz Hotel. He had chained his battered twelve-year-old bicycle with its little wicker basket to the railings outside. Anyone could snap through that chain with a pair of tweezers. But who would wish to? Bennett is one of England's national treasures, along with, of course, the Queen Mother—not that he relishes the role. "You end up giving a performance of yourself, like John Betjeman. It's easier to go along with—the way people *think* you are. Richard Eyre at the National Theater is always saying how nice I am. But I never go to see any of his productions. Well, that's not nice."

Alan Bennett, as is well known, is on the eccentric side. He is wry and unpretentious, and among the funniest writers in England. "Oh," he said as a Palm Court waiter in white tie and tails hovered with an elaborate menu of little sandwiches and large bills, "I only came for a cuppa!"

The pianist at the Ritz was playing "You'll Never Know How Much I Love You." The ladies who tea had filled the ornate room. "It's like a swimming bath, really," Bennett added incongruously. "Hasn't it turned chilly?" The day was hot. When we sat down, he was recognized immediately. A stranger who turned out to be a representative of the National Summer Fruits Association was so pleased to see him that he invited him to join its annual strawberry tea party in the adjoining room. "Oh, no. I couldn't, I couldn't!" Bennett apologized, turning pink. "Thank you very much, though."

It was as if we were in one of his own plays. What does he appreciate more than anything? "Silliness," he replied, and began to laugh. "It's the saving grace. It's why Mrs. Thatcher is so un-English. There isn't an ounce of silliness in her. Americans have got much more gravity. They get things done more than we do. But they aren't silly. It's not to be confused with foolishness. But I couldn't live without a silly streak."

It was silly, really: even the Osborne memorial made scandalous front page news. Unknown to the rector—naughty!—a notice by the church steps had barred entrance to four public figures. "The undermentioned will NOT be admitted," the notice read like a Lutheran pronouncement. The banned were listed as "Fumanchu," Osborne's nickname for Sir Peter Hall, the former artistic director of both the Royal Shakespeare Company and the National; "The Bard of Hay on Wye," who is playwright Arnold Wesker (who lives in Hay on Wye); Albert Finney, with whom Osborne had feuded over the movie *Tom Jones*, which he scripted; and Nicholas de Jongh, an extremely self-important drama critic.

The fuss! "As for the note on the door excluding four people," Lord Gowrie wrote in the letters pages of the *Times* in reply to those who found the incident un-Christian, "who says the Almighty has no sense of humor?" And as for the old rebel who believed at heart in Edwardian values of honor, John Osborne, Playwright and Actor (1929–1994), rests in his village churchyard in Clun, Shropshire, where, a Christian, he read the Sunday lesson in the church. Carved on his tombstone are the words of Archie Rice from *The Entertainer*: "Let me know where you're working tomorrow night and I'll come and see YOU."

In the headquarters of Cameron Mackintosh, the most powerful impresario in theater history, is a framed scroll. I noted down the following words from the Queen's Award for Export Achievement: "ELIZABETH THE SECOND. By the Grace of God of the United Kingdom of Great Britain and Northern Ireland and Our Other Realms and Territories, Queen, Defender of the Faith, to Cameron Mackintosh Limited—Greetings!"

Sign in Hyde Park: "Please refrain from any leisure activity on this site until new grass has established itself."

Sign in theater lobby: "Due to the indisposition of Miss Stacey Francis the role of Doris Winter will be played by Miss Priscilla Jones."

Music hall expression: "Don't clap too hard, it's a very old building."

The verbal felicities—"Please refrain from," "Due to the indisposition of"—keep up appearances the British way, the old-fashioned way, like West End theater managers in evening dress. The Queen's Award proclamation—"Greetings!"—is pantomime royal. The theaters are old.

Scholars in the field can deduce that the West End theater district began in the seventeenth century on the site of the Theatre Royal, Drury Lane, which isn't in Drury Lane. Drury Lane's round the corner. But the Theatre Royal, Drury Lane, has always been so-called. Built in 1812 (and now home to the Cameron Mackintosh production *Miss Saigon*), it's the fourth historic theater on the site and the oldest in London. West End theater began there, in what would have been an Elizabethan-Jacobean throughway in Covent Garden—a deliberate choice of no-man's-land.

Dangerous places, theaters. They attract all sorts. Un-Disneyfied support groups spring up around them—prostitutes, pimps, bars, bear-baiting. Covent Garden was out of harm's way and sight of Parliament and the City of London, exactly as the turbulent theater world of Shakespeare, south of the river across the Thames, had been kept separate from the seats of power.

The dirt and action of today's Soho and the hub of the West End theater district along Shaftesbury Avenue have a whiff of the Elizabethan. But it's Victorian. What happened was this: as theater grew in popularity, the Covent Garden theaters spread farther west during the Victorian building boom— becoming cozily respectable along the way. West End theaters are basically Victorian, unless they're Edwardian. Anything later is considered new. The "lower orders" preferred their working-class music hall palaces, where the "leisure classes" went slumming and racy Edwardian gentlemen dated the showgirls. The "educated class," the solid middle class (or upper-middle-lower-upper-middle-middle-middle class) had the gold and velvet and cherubs of their Victorian jewel-box theaters of the West End, more or less as today.

The air conditioning within them could melt an iceberg, but one can't have everything. It's for show. American tourists find London theaters quaintly stifling, like convivial smoky pubs. The Pythonesque culture clash comes with the different approaches to waiting on line. In the lobbies of New York theaters, there's a sense of tumult and rush to get the tickets that only adds to the preshow excitement. The English wait on line, silent, uncomplaining, obedient—even when another box office that is open for business *has no line.* They join the line. They love the line. "Ladies and gentlemen," goes the polite announcement. "This evening's performance will begin in two minutes." We are waiting on line. "So that will be two tickets for Saturday night, will it, dear?" the box office lady is saying. "Let me have a look-see. I think you'll do better Wednesday matinee...."

"Ladies and gentlemen, the curtain is about to rise." No rush! We'll all get there in the end. But one night, I broke the rules. I broke the line—it seemed reasonable at the time—going to the box office that had no line. "You can't do that! There's a *queue,*" protested the indignant gentleman, waiting patiently on line.

During my month-long visit to London so pleasant, I saw fifteen productions, for which I shall be receiving an honorary knighthood shortly. We, in America, see the best of British theater. But the reality of the West End is closer to a puu-puu platter—unlike Broadway, there's a little bit of everything for everyone. Some of the marquees might convince you that time stopped in London circa 1949. One half expects to see Shaftesbury Avenue shrouded in fog. There's the revival (or reevaluation) of the shabby gentility and class-riddled British reticence of the Terrence Rattigan oeuvre that Osborne and the new playwrights of social realism were thought to have swept away. There's the ritual fare such as *Don't Dress for Dinner,* a farce about double adultery and gourmet cooking; the *Murder, She Wrote* thriller genre; or the trusty old *Mousetrap,* now in its thousandth glorious year. The oldest theater joke actually happened to me. As the cab driver dropped me outside St. Martin's Theatre to see *The Mousetrap,* he called after me cheerfully, "Enjoy the show, guv! The butler done it!" I'm not saying the butler done it, or that there's even a butler *in* it. But that's what he said.

As always, appearances are deceptive. If there's more pablum in the West End than on Broadway, there's more choice. Among many new and classic dramas to see, there were Tom Stoppard's memory play of Empire, *Indian Ink;* Patrick Marber's poker-playing morality play *Dealer's Choice;*

Arthur Miller's *View from the Bridge;* O'Casey's *Plough and the Stars;* Webster's "House of Blood" favorite, *The Duchess of Malfi;* and Ronald Harwood's *Taking Sides,* his conscience drama of the compromised life of the Berlin Philharmonic's conductor Wilhelm Fürtwangler, directed by Harold Pinter.

Americans, it seems, aren't taken too seriously on the London stage. They are taken seriously at the box office. There was, for example, the earnestly dim American biographer in the Stoppard, the philistine colonel in the Harwood, the crass American scholar in David Edgar's epic *Pentecost.* It reflects an habitual anti-Americanism, or quite harmless jokey snobbery. In a BBC-TV script written and performed by John Sessions, two tourists from Miami are visiting Stratford-on-Avon:

"Lillian, that was really something," says the awestruck Jack after seeing *Hamlet.* "A truly uplifting experience."

"You gotta be out of your mind!" Lillian replies.

There's the Andrew Lloyd Webber empire and the Cameron Mackintosh empire—and there's the rest. Mackintosh's personal fortune is estimated at half a billion dollars. The global earnings of Lloyd Webber's production company, the Really Useful Group, approach $3 billion. *Phantom of the Opera* alone has grossed over $1.5 billion.

Holding court at his 1,350-acre Hampshire estate, Sydmonton Court, with its private chapel (where his megamusicals are previewed before a select audience), Andrew Lloyds Bank, as he's sometimes known, irritates some. "Easy come, easy go," Paul Johnson wrote in the *Spectator* when Lloyd Webber paid $29 million for Picasso's *Portrait of Angel Fernandez de Soto.* The British tradition, known as the Tall Poppy Syndrome, likes to cut uppity success down to size. "At least you know where you are," explained Kenneth Branagh, who's judged as being too ambitious—not a gentlemanly thing, too pushy, in a sense too American.

The egos were always big; it's the theater world that got small. As the world turns and spins, cats and phantoms and trains and helicopters and miserable French people are circling the globe, now and forever. And it all began there, in the land of Shakespeare. Lloyd Webber and Cameron Mackintosh, first in partnership, then separately, beat America at its own game. They invented a new popular culture as powerfully pervasive in its way as

Disney—the global musical.

Broadway traditionalists may not care for Lloyd Webber, but he seized the lightning at the time when Broadway was declining into remembered corn-fed dreams, backstage stories, and uncommercial Sondheimian disenchantment. Look at his early choices: Jesus *(Jesus Christ Superstar)*, the adored wife of an Argentinian dictator *(Evita)*, cats (and T. S. Eliot's cats, at that).

"People hated even the name *Cats*," Cameron Mackintosh, its producer, pointed out. Every other producer had turned it down. He also boldly chose a director who had never staged a major musical before—Trevor Nunn, then the artistic director of the Royal Shakespeare Company. "Global hits didn't exist at that time," he added. "Nobody thought about it, including me. I promise you."

But he saw the opportunity. And when the aging ruling elites of Broadway woke up, it was too late. Mackintosh, the young British impresario, hyped, marketed, and merchandised his musicals in ways that had never been seen before. *Cats* invented the universal musical logo—a neutral symbol, a semiotic sign, a figure dancing in the eyes of a cat, like the white mask *(Phantom)*, the waif *(Les Mis)*, the helicopter *(Miss Saigon)*. The logos transcend language barriers; they're instantly recognized everywhere; they go very nicely on souvenir T-shirts and mugs. When was there ever a Cameron Mackintosh musical that didn't have the biggest advance ticket sale *in the history of the world?* It's a *spectacle!* It's a *special effect!* It's an *opera!* Barnum Mackintosh created Event Theater.

Yet to meet him is to be surprised. His headquarters in North London are within a beautiful eighteenth-century Adams house. He comes into town two days a week from his Somerset home, a restored twelfth-century priory. Another of his homes is a log cabin with a view—12,500 acres on the Isle of Skye. "You look well," I said when we met. "I feel well!" he replied cheerfully. One has the impression he has always been a happy man. He's stagestruck. Ruling the musical world is a bonus. (Fifty Mackintosh productions are currently playing round the world.) He's a likeable man, a tough producer who's also known to be generous, at forty-nine unflamboyant, uncomplicated, clear. "I'm no good at all at coming up with an original idea. I can recognize it. That's my talent. And I can make it work. Anyone who thinks they know what the public wants is an idiot. I'm still surprised and delighted the public likes what I like. I produce absolutely for myself."

He possess the more traditionally American enthusiasm and buoyancy—the vivid, confident *belief* in what he does—that used to be the exclusive territory of Broadway.

I asked him: "What would you say to cultural snobs like me who don't buy your megamusicals?"

He didn't skip a beat. "I'd say you got it wrong."

Although the global musical was born in England, it has taken on the force of a multinational superpower. The unique identity of English theater still resides in its celebrated tradition of great classical acting.

"In England, acting is a heritage passed on through the ages," noted a *New Yorker* profile of Michael Gambon. "From Burbage to Garrick, from Garrick to Kean and Macready, from them to Irving, and on to Olivier, Gielgud, and Richardson—and Gambon and McKellen. As is also true of great clowns, actors learn and borrow from their predecessors, who borrowed from those who came before them."

As befits a king, Laurence Olivier's ashes lie close to where King Henry V is buried in Westminster Abbey. He knew him well. Olivier's plaque is found on the stone floor of Poets' Corner—almost as popular a tourist attraction as Hollywood Boulevard—placed alongside the plaques of two other great actors: David Garrick, from the eighteenth century, and Henry Irving, from the nineteenth. They face the statue of Shakespeare, national playwright.

Olivier (the son of a priest) continued the sanctified theatrical cycle when his astonishing, regal memorial service took place in Westminster Abbey in 1989, attended by two thousand and competing with the battle of Agincourt in patriotic fervor. It was quite a production. The abbey echoed to Sir William Walton's theme music for Olivier's film versions of *Henry V* and *Hamlet*. Paul Scofield, Ian McKellen, Derek Jacobi, Maggie Smith, Dorothy Tutin, "and also starring" walked in stately procession to the altar, carrying what the *Times* of London described as "Olivier's treasury": his insignia of the Order of Merit; a model of the National Theatre and another of the Chichester Theatre, both of which he founded; his Oscar (for *Hamlet*); his crown from the film version of *Richard III*; his laurel wreath from the

Stratford production of *Coriolanus;* his *Lear* crown from the television production that brought him out of retirement; and his most meaningful prop, Edmund Kean's *Richard III* sword, handed on to Olivier by Sir John Gielgud.

Richard Olivier, one of Olivier's four children, at thirty-three now making his way as a well-regarded theater director, was twenty-seven when his father died in his early eighties after a long battle with illness. "There was a strange awareness that I'd seen him die a lot of times," this gentle man told me. "In *King Lear,* in *Brideshead Revisited....* Unlike other children, I saw my dad acting dying. He once told me, 'I've played more than two hundred parts, and I know them better than I know myself. I don't know who I am when I'm not acting.' And when I was young, I would cry at his death scenes. But when his death was real, I couldn't cry." Almost crushed by the legacy of his father, he loved him. "I feel very grateful and proud to have spent that time with him," he said.

Sir John Gielgud is the last of that glittering triumvirate—Olivier, Gielgud, and Ralph Richardson—who, with Dame Peggy Ashcroft, led British theater into its golden age. Gielgud's acting lineage alone stretches back into the nineteenth century: his grandmother was a well-known actress; her sister (and Irving's acting partner) was Ellen Terry—"the most adorable woman ever created by God or man," said a swooning Swinburne. Ellen Terry's illegitimate son—one of a few—was Gordon Craig, the visionary stage designer, and Gielgud's cousin. At ninety-one, and still quite active, Sir John is the most cherished of public figures. His unstoppable "Gielgoofs," or "Gielgoodies," are national collector's items. Here's a favorite:

He had been avoiding a character actor named Clive Morton for weeks on tour, when Morton finally summoned up courage to knock on his dressing room door. "Thank God it's you," Gielgud exclaimed. "For one dreadful moment I thought it was going to be that ghastly old bore Clive Morton."

He is invariably sunny and talkative (and wonderfully tactless). He lives in a seventeenth-century pavilion deep in Buckinghamshire where, he told me, he likes to watch any old rubbish on TV. "I can't keep away from the Simpson trial," he said, laughing. "It's rather bad theater. Too many *interruptions.* Still I can't keep away! I'm sure he did it, aren't you?" He said he acted in "little bits" of films—"quite pleasant, not taxing"—and in radio plays, which he enjoyed, meeting new people. He was too diffident to mention that one radio play, which celebrated his ninetieth birthday, was *King Lear*—his fourth Lear in his magnificent career. The cast—in effect paying tribute to him—included three succeeding generations of leading actors: the knights Derek Jacobi and Robert Stephens, Dame Judi Dench, Kenneth Branagh, Eileen Atkins, Bob Hoskins, Richard Briers, Keith Michell, Emma Thompson, and two new-generation pretenders to imaginary thrones, Iain Glen and Simon Russell Beale.

The entire London picture changes with the power and creative volume of those nonprofit empires, the Royal National Theatre and the Royal Shakespeare Company. "Do the English people want a national theater?" George Bernard Shaw asked fifty years ago. "Of course they do not. They have got the British Museum, the National Gallery and Westminster Abbey, but they never wanted them."

They got used to them.

The spine of London theater—the reason it functions as well as it does—is government subsidy. Virtually every major British import we see in America began life in the nonprofit theater. The arts in America rely mostly on the kindness of patrons—on its generous tradition of philanthropy, sponsorship, and foundation support. Sponsorship hobbles along in England. The financier James Goldsmith was once asked if he would be good enough to sponsor British theater. "I never go to the theater," he replied. "My legs are too long."

Britain's frequently beleaguered arts subsidy has survived cutbacks and assaults, and nuclear attack through the 1980s from Prime Minister Margaret Thatcher. "When can we stop giving money to awful people like Peter Hall?" she pleaded, enraged that the man who was then running the National Theatre should lead the battle against Tory philistinism, as he saw it.

No one has done more to keep alive the theater heritage than the workaholic director-producer Sir Peter Hall, and few powerful public figures in England fascinate and enrage more. He could be Machiavelli, Iago, Coriolanus, Don Juan, or of late, Falstaff—depending on who's doing the casting. Rare for an Englishman, he admits to a complex personal psychology. It's a small claim to fame that I have, briefly entering Hall's published diaries preceded by the words "Last night I dreamed I cut my own throat."

He's the master builder of British theater. At thirty, he founded the modern Royal Shakespeare Company; then, succeeding Olivier, he led the National for more than a decade in its new South Bank empire. And for good measure he ran the Glyndebourne Festival Opera. There's practically nothing left for him to run except his own theater company. Yet this famous man is close to an academic scholar in the privacy of the rehearsal room—tapping out the beat of the Shakespearean verse on a lectern like a conductor.

"What we're all bleating about—as usual," Hall told me, "is the fight against decline. In the 1960s, a young actor would have been marinated in Shakespeare. The easy solution today is the convention of the real—the gritty underplaying of TV acting. It's affected the whole ecology. But Shakespeare's a *verse* dramatist. The reason Shakespeare got longer is because actors play the words, not the *line*. You preserve the sanctity of the line. I reckon there are only about fifty actors left in the country who can do it."

Hall, a railwayman's son, came out of Cambridge University. So did many of the newer generation—Richard Eyre, Nicholas Hytner, Sam Mendes, Emma Thompson, Declan Donellan, Nick Ormerod, and Simon McBurney and Annabel Arden of London's Théâtre de Complicité. The Marlowe Society at Cambridge, under the direction of George "Dadie" Rylands, shaped the undergrad Peter Hall. The heritage was passed on when Hall handed over the Royal Shakespeare Company to Trevor Nunn (who was also at Cambridge), and continued through Hall's years at the National, where the Marlowe torch is now carried by former society president Sir Ian McKellen.

Yet with Shakespeare, of all things, Hall at sixty-four looks more hopefully to America than to Britain. I had put it to him that for too long Americans have been going down on one knee before classical English acting and the god of Shakespeare, when they possess all the skills of dynamic language and physicality—speed, wit, naturalism, daring—to burst through the conventions and make new. "If they could be trained to observe the form and breathe at the right places," said Hall, "they'd knock the shit out of us."

It's extraordinary that Arthur Miller—the founding father of modern American drama with Eugene O'Neill and Tennessee Williams—is produced and celebrated more in England than in his own land. (So is Tennessee

Williams.) Whereas Miller's 1994 play *Broken Glass* closed early on Broadway, in London it was taken under the protective umbrella of the National Theatre, transferred to the West End, and went on to win the Olivier Award for best play. The spiraling cost of producing plays on Broadway is at least twice as much as in London, making the more commercial work a safer bet.

But Arthur Miller goes further: "*Broken Glass* wasn't *Cats*," he points out in his deep, deceptively calm American voice. "On Broadway, it's purely business. But a West End theater doesn't regard a few empty seats as a disgrace. The American system is a commercial, cockeyed, historically determined process where success is everything. Even profit isn't enough. It has to be a *big* profit."

Ian McKellen put it this way: "Americans aren't good gardeners. They don't plant. They're forty-niners. They dig for gold. They're always *mining*. They like it! To get a good theater you plant little seeds and nurture their growing. You should be cross-fertilizing your plants in the hope of producing a black tulip. But in America, they can't wait to be successful. Gold is gold. It's always the *same*."

Same old gold! But look briefly at the route to New York of Tom Stoppard's hit *Arcadia*. It was first produced at the National Theatre. Then it transferred to the commercial West End. Four New York producers wanted it for commercial Broadway. Stoppard chose the nonprofit Lincoln Center Theater instead. "I wanted an axis in New York that would do my plays without picking and choosing the ones that might make money and might not," he explained. He made the nonprofit theater in New York his base, and his uncommercial *Hapgood*—which no Broadway producer wanted—could therefore be produced at Lincoln Center alongside *Arcadia*.

A golden boy of British theater, thirty-eight-year-old director Nicholas Hytner, now lives in London and New York, enjoying the best of both worlds. Hytner understands popular taste, but functions outside the mainstream. After directing the blockbuster *Miss Saigon* (which made him wealthy), he returned to the National to direct the stage version of *The Madness of King George*, then Rodgers and Hammerstein's fabled *Carousel*. "I expect this is going to be another success for you," Princess Margaret told Hytner after seeing *Carousel*. "Mind you, the songs are absolutely *frightful*.

Can't you cut them out?"

In New York Hytner has become an associate director of Lincoln Center Theater, and after all the acclaim for his film version of *The Madness of King George*, when Hollywood was at his feet, he chose the route of modestly budgeted films for adults.

It's his way of keeping control, of "doing good work" unfettered by too blatant commercial compromise. His new film is Arthur Miller's *The Crucible*, with Daniel Day Lewis, Winona Ryder, and Paul Scofield. It continues Hytner's ideal of alternating between films and theater, in the well-founded belief there exist sufficient millions of people on both sides of the Atlantic who take pleasure in the artfully "uncommercial."

The keepers of the nonprofit flame, Adrian Noble of the RSC and Richard Eyre of the National, have this deeply in common: They're both insomniacs. But with the wired Adrian Noble, it shows.

"Terrible, appalling, appalling!" he said when I asked him about his insomnia. What does he do all night? I wondered. "Worry," he answered. He rubbed his eyes, then the top of his head, until his body behind his desk in Stratford bent into the shape of a question mark, as if weighed down by the weary weight of the classical world.

Noble, age forty-four, and married to an actress, is the son of an undertaker. What does that do to the psychology? "Oh," he replied. "Nothing much, really. It gave me certain privileges, actually. I lived in a nice house with a garage full of hearses. We could play in them. There were headstones and stonemason's tools and a woodshop for coffins—a nice playground for a young child. Burying of the dead, passage of the spirit," he added. "It's a ritualistic theater, isn't it?"

Guess so. But for two hours, this tense and feverishly passionate man (who leads seven-hundred people at the RSC) went on to talk animatedly about the classical tradition, and Shakespeare in particular, as if our very lives depended on it.

"It's a *living* heritage," he argued. "For me the English national identity isn't invested in the text of Shakespeare's plays, but in the people who *hear* them. Hamlet said, 'We'll hear a play.' For Shakespeare it was the ear. He made pictures through language. He was the most practical playwright who ever lived. Look at his 'Ohs!' 'O for a muse of fire!' Shuts the audience up if it's *noisy*. He wanted to change life and he was a practical man. So we're very pragmatic and utopian, too. We believe we can affect people's lives, however modestly. We believe you can learn from the past."

How can theater compete with movies? "The movie in America casts such a long shadow that it buries theater—unless theater truly competes with it. We gather in a room to listen to stories. There's a body of knowledge that has been passed on—*voice* and *form* and *verse*. I believe the living heritage contains stories and myth that resonate in life, poetry that can enrich us, an experience that can renew us."

This is the thing: theater people like Noble talk and debate and argue into the small hours as if Shakespeare were still alive. There are leading innovative directors in England who have yet to stage a living playwright. "I *feel* I have," explained Deborah Warner. "I always feel I'm on a new play. Searching for an unfathomable size and depth, it's more likely to be a classic—the enigma that lasts. After all, the Mona Lisa has only got where she is because nobody's *worked it out*."

Shakespeare is alive and well—looking over their shoulders, whispering: "Keep going. I'm better than movies. Find the present in the past and you understand the world."

Let's follow the entrance of the King.

The monolithic scale of the National—where 750 people work—is best appreciated if we follow the actors through its backstage maze as they make their costumed way to the stages of its three theaters. Some actors find their way by following the posters—left at *St. Joan*, right at *Guys and Dolls*. Some have been known to enter the wrong stage, to appear in the wrong play. Gielgud used to tie a ball of string to himself and his dressing room door so he could find the route back.

The backstage entrance itself has all the showbiz warmth of a high-security cop precinct in the Bronx. Beyond, the small identical dressing rooms with identical blue doors wind round the long corridors of a massive civic institution. Number 010 belonged to Fiona Shaw, who was playing Shakespeare's boy-king, Richard II, directed by Deborah Warner. The revolutionary production was on the stage of the Cottesloe, the most intimate of the National's three theaters, all linking backstage. Here's her walk from reality to fantasy:

Exit room 010, crown upon head. Turn left along corridor, past a telephone box. Go through swing doors by the windowless rehearsal room. Turn right through swing doors. Left through next set of swing doors. Left again for twenty-five yards. Past the giant elevator that takes scenery up to the Olivier theater. Do not turn right through swing doors facing you. Turn right, to STAGE RIGHT.

Enter the King.

On the fourth floor of the monolith is the modest office overlooking the Thames of Richard Eyre, the artistic director of the National Theater, described by the New York Times as "the most successful producer in the English-speaking theater." He's closer to a charmingly steely, wry, Christian moralist. The words "community," "group," "society," pepper his conversation like a conscience—words, he said, "people who don't like the theater recoil from, as if from rabid dogs."

The National became royal—The Royal National Theatre—seven years ago, like the royal patronage of marmalade and bespoke Savile Row tailors. Eyre vigorously opposed the change. "Royal and National are a farcical contradiction," he explained. "You can't be simultaneously a subject and a citizen. I think it's an extraordinary declaration of inferiority. At last, from the outer circle of indignity, we were admitted to the center of British culture!"

He casually describes life in the theater as "perfectly suited to the controlled manic-depressive." He is to leave the National in two years after more than a decade of success at the helm. "Let somebody else have the sleepless nights!" he said, and laughed. Fifty-two years old, he's the son of a naval officer turned Devon farmer; his wife is a BBC-TV producer; his daughter is at Oxford. Eyre, who went to Cambridge (where he was taught by Kingsley Amis), has worked in the subsidized theater all his life, and it's difficult to imagine him working anywhere else. He turned down the opportunity to direct Les Miserables, which is like misplacing your winning lottery ticket.

"I don't regret it," he explained phlegmatically. "I didn't think I was cast right. I believe the Faustian bargain is a reality. The others can do musicals like Les Miserables in good faith. But it just won't farm out for me if I do things in bad faith. I know that sounds like a sanctimonious prick, but that's what I feel."

He's a utopian. In his humane and touching autobiography, *Utopia and Other Places*, Richard Eyre sees life and theater as a utopian ideal that can never quite be found. The meaning of the word in Greek, he points out, means "not a place" or "nowhere."

"However sceptical we are of it in public, all of us privately believe in a utopia, in a form of perfectibility, however temporary," he writes. "It may be in love, in marriage, in work, in society, or in religion. Even when the evidence is so strongly against its existence, we continue to seek its tantalising territory."

Today, whispered—and not so whispered—sacrileges are being heard against the heritage of Olivier and Gielgud, as if that tradition belonged more to a pinnacle of nineteenth-century acting. It's an overthrowing, too, of the watered-down legacy of the stiffly rhetorical, the emotionally dead, the British style and voice—the traditional Shakespearean *voice*, which can rip through the back of the stalls and stop ships at sea.

And some of those new, contrary voices come from within, rising up like Calibans against the past. "I never *saw* Olivier, Gielgud, and Richardson," the successful young West End director Sam Mendes told me. "In fact, my generation grew up with John Cleese."

Mendes runs the influential, 250-seat Donmar Warehouse in the heart of Covent Garden. (The Donmar used to be the RSC's rehearsal studio). His bold new production of *Cabaret* would begin life there, before joining the British armies of the night on Broadway.

"There are rules, if only to ignore them," he added. "But the institutionalized *right way* is stifling for the younger generation. Who wants to be told that theater is *good for you*?"

Another of the new generation of international directors is Jonathan Kent, who runs the fringe three-hundred-seat Almeida Theatre in North London. He took Ralph Fiennes and Diana Rigg to Broadway. "The danger of English acting is like one of those beautiful skeleton clocks," he said. "You can see all the cogs go round, it's technically fascinating and in brilliant style. But what time is it?"

Kent took the Fiennes *Hamlet* deliberately outside the English establishment. He subversively staged it in one of the most deprived areas of London, in the crumbling old music hall palace, the Hackney Empire. "It was close to a jam-packed Elizabethan audience," he explained enthusiastically. "I didn't want *Hamlet* produced in a high-art ghetto. I don't want to exhume museum pieces as a cultural duty or a kind of medicine. They were queuing for returns in Hackney! We gave a free show for the neighborhood, and you couldn't get a seat. The only point of doing these plays is because they're terrifically *popular* plays. So it was marvelous that *Hamlet* went to Broadway, down the road from *Beauty and the Beast*."

And so, for the first time in memory, the barricades went up outside the Belasco on Forty-fifth Street and Broadway. *Hamlet* had Ralph Fiennes, of course, which helped. But Kent had talked to him about taking on the unsolvable mystery two years before he became Ralph Fiennes. And the actor, now a movie star, had spent four seasons with the Royal Shakespeare Company.

Our first sight of the Fiennes Hamlet was of a modern antihero standing alone in a trench coat, his back turned on us. He was a prince without the princeliness. Murmurs rippled through the packed Broadway audience, and repressed squeals came from the balcony. "It's *him!*" went the shout. "It's him! The one in black!"

John Osborne's memorial had been a crowded gathering. There were England's dramatists—among them Harold Pinter, Christopher Hampton, and John Mortimer. And there were its actors—among them that patrician, carved, enigmatic face of Paul Scofield, the only actor in England to have turned down a knighthood. And there was the ghost of Olivier, the only great actor in English history to have been made a lord. A recording of Laurence Olivier singing and dancing as Archie Rice in *The Entertainer*, Osborne's music hall metaphor of crumbling postcolonial England, was played during the service, bringing sighs and affectionate laughter. For the most celebrated actor of the century could scarcely sing a note.

And perhaps it was all there in the secluded chapel that morning—in the timeless, formal, expert English ceremony of it all, in those restrained, reedy English voices singing lusty hymns, in the prayers and English music and flawless readings from great actors—the inescapable impression that the best of English life is a play, a show, a pageant even before God.

"It is impossible to speak of John Osborne without using the word 'England,'" said David Hare in his fine and surprisingly emotional tribute. So it is impossible to imagine England without its theater.

Dramatis Personae:

Trevor Nunn succeeded Richard Eyre at the National Theatre; Lord Gowrie left government; Stephen Daldry of the Royal Court Theatre formed his own film company; David Aukin left Channel 4 Films to work for Miramax Films in Europe.

Messrs. Eyre, Gambon, Hare, Mackintosh, Mortimer and Stoppard have now received their knighthoods. Sir Andrew Lloyd Webber was elevated to the House of Lords.

Lunch with Gielgud
and Richardson

Sir John Gielgud and Sir Ralph Richardson, starring in Harold Pinter's No Man's Land, *meet for lunch in a West End restaurant at the request of a newspaper.*

The setting is discreet and grand.

There, the two actors are to be specially photographed for the Observer.

Outside the restaurant, the roar of a motorbike is heard. Enter SIR RALPH RICHARDSON.

He is dressed in a smart brown suit and an enormous cyclist's helmet, like a visor. He offers the helmet to the headwaiter with the aplomb of an English gentleman handing over a bowler hat.

Then he sits at a corner table and orders a vodka martini.

Enter SIR JOHN GIELGUD.

He is tall and elegant, pink and sunny, immaculately dressed. An acquaintance spots him and greets him warmly: "Wish you were lunching with us, Johnny!"

The two actors meet and sit together. Both are very relaxed in each other's company, and fun. Words tumble out of Sir John, whereas Sir Ralph measures them carefully, as if squeezing out every syllable.

SIR JOHN: Come on the motorbike?

SIR RALPH: Best...*way.*

SIR JOHN: The last time you took me on the pillion I practically had a fit. I was a stretcher case.

SIR RALPH: I have been killed several times myself.

SIR JOHN: Shall we have oysters?

SIR RALPH: Good idea! And to follow? Fish and game go rather nicely together.

SIR JOHN: I shall have roast grouse because I love it. I love roast grouse more than anything.

SIR RALPH: Roast grouse is *awfully* good.

SIR JOHN: I remember being taken to the Naval and Military Club as a very young man and being given oysters and grouse for the first time. I thought I really was living it up.

SIR RALPH: Shall we live it up now?

SIR JOHN: Certainly!

SIR RALPH: You're looking very well, by the way.

SIR JOHN: Thank you.

SIR RALPH: I haven't seen much of you lately.

SIR JOHN: We meet in costume.

SIR RALPH: We meet as other people.

A waiter hovers.

SIR RALPH: We're having oysters followed by grouse.

SIR JOHN: You are, too? Oh, *good.*

SIR RALPH: Wine?

SIR JOHN: You're very good on the wine, Ralph.

SIR RALPH: Let's have a small carafe of white wine with the fish and a small carafe of red with the game. I would like to have more, but dare not.

SIR JOHN: We're all much more abstemious with drink than we used to be.

SIR RALPH: I'm *less* abstemious. When I was young I never drank during the run of a show, except on Saturday nights.

SIR JOHN: Oh, I used to drink away like anything. On the first night of *Much Ado* Peggy Ashcroft and I drank a bottle of champagne before going on and we never played so well in our lives.

SIR RALPH: It would have terrified me. The spring wouldn't be there. Lowers the energy.

SIR JOHN: But just think of all those brilliant people who couldn't function without a drink. I'm sure Barrymore couldn't have done it.

SIR RALPH: Kean was the greatest drinker of them all, of course. Hot brandy. When he was playing *Othello* he invented a false exit for himself so he could nip off for a brandy and come on again, fortified as it were.

SIR JOHN: Do you think opera singers have a drop or two between their arias?

A waiter serves oysters. A wine waiter serves wine.

SIR RALPH: A toast! To the *Observer!*

SIR JOHN: May its building never be streaked.

SIR RALPH: Did you see that charming Russian painting in the *Times?* Looked like a Nicholson.

SIR JOHN: With the spires?

SIR RALPH: Curious that Russia has never really produced a great painter.

SIR JOHN: Diaghilev had some very talented people, but they were more designers.

SIR RALPH: I wonder how painting could have escaped a *nation* like Russia.

SIR JOHN: Very baffling country, Russia.

SIR RALPH: And Leningrad?

SIR JOHN: Very bleak.

SIR RALPH: How are your oysters?

SIR JOHN: Marvellous!

SIR RALPH: The strangest thing happened to me when I was coming out of the theatre last night. I was walking down St. Martin's Lane when a man suddenly shouted, "Look! It's Sir John Gielgud!"

SIR JOHN: But in America they always call me Sir Ralph Richardson. Perhaps it's because we've acted together over the years. We're almost like the broker's men in *Cinderella*.

SIR RALPH: But would you say we *look* alike, Johnny? I was in France some time ago. Very peculiar. It was dark and my wife had gone down a little alley. I said, "Mu, it's this way." And a Frenchman appeared in the half-light and cried, "*Mon Dieu!* It's John Gielgud!"

SIR JOHN: I've been stopped twice in London for Kenneth Clark.

SIR RALPH: I should be most flattered to be mistaken for him.

They finish the oysters. Grouse is served.

SIR JOHN: I was so angry with myself at the Garrick the other day. I just couldn't remember the name of an actor I knew. I haven't even remembered it now. Someone like Sybil Thorndike never forgets anybody.

SIR RALPH: *Never.*

SIR JOHN: She even remembers people she met in Australia.

SIR RALPH: She remembers *everyone.*

SIR JOHN: I have to look up the names of actors in *Spotlight.* Emlyn Williams used to turn over all the pages and whenever he saw a photograph of an actor wearing a hat he'd shout 'BALD!' Emlyn could spot them.

SIR RALPH: Pass the Paul Robeson.

Sir John passes over a large pepper mill.

SIR JOHN: A Russian came to see me after the show last night.

SIR RALPH: A Russian! What did he want?

SIR JOHN: He spoke terribly good English for a Russian. He said he was so glad he'd seen the performance because he felt he understood Harold Pinter at last. He said that *No Man's Land* is just a wonderful black comedy. It was such a relief to me. People get rather desperate about what the play means. I'm not so sure I know either. Yet here was the Russian who accepted it simply as a black comedy instead of searching for endless symbolism and implications of every kind. I mean, I'm *sure* Harold's plays always have implications, but I don't think his intention is for the audience to spend the *entire* evening trying to solve them. I'm sure he's quite pleased if people go away and discuss the possibilities.

SIR RALPH: Did you see that man walk out of the performance last night?

SIR JOHN: The only time it's happened.

SIR RALPH: Perhaps he was offended by the language.

SIR JOHN: Yet it's very interesting how the elderly public remains so calm at all the expletives flowing from us on stage.

SIR RALPH: Common parlance.

SIR JOHN: I remember saying to my mother when I was a boy, "Couldn't we go and see Uncle Fred in the Scarlet Pimp?" And my mother replied, "If you ever use such language again I'll turn you out of the house!"

SIR RALPH: There were times when it used to be thought that the legs of furniture were risqué. They used to put little crinolines round piano legs.

SIR JOHN: Like a lady never revealing her ankles. How times have changed! I've never had anyone interrupt a play because of the bad language, except in Brighton, of course. When I was in *Veterans* whole rows got up and stormed out. "Don't use THAT WORD in front of my wife!"

SIR RALPH: Curious, isn't it? Brighton was always the best audience outside London. Very...*dangerous* now.

Suddenly Sir Ralph jumps, pointing to his plate dramatically. Waiters surround him.

SIR RALPH: What is THAT?

SIR JOHN: I think it's a bit of liver, Ralph.

SIR RALPH: Never touch it! Take the liver away. Otherwise, *perfect*. Bear the offending liver away....

SIR JOHN: I hear Peter Brook's coming over from Paris with a new production.

SIR RALPH: Ah, Brook.

SIR JOHN: You've never worked with him, Ralph. But I've done four or five productions and I'm devoted to him. Sometimes I wish he wasn't quite so eclectic.

SIR RALPH: Eclectic? What does that word mean?

SIR JOHN: What *does* it mean? Special, I think.

SIR RALPH: Sounds Greek to me. Greekish sounding word.

SIR JOHN: I suppose it must be Greek. But the only man I've known who had the same quality as Brook was Komisarjevsky. He was an architect, a designer, a painter, a director. *Enormous* talent and knowledge. I think Lindsay Anderson is so brilliant, but he hasn't got the charisma of Brook. Peter's a sort of world figure. I often long for Lindsay to have the same appeal and success. I think he would do marvellous work if he had a little more appreciation. It would give him such wonderful encouragement.

SIR RALPH: What was that *terrible* production Brook did? Of course, he's done such amazing stuff. Parts of *A Midsummer Night's Dream* were among the most brilliant theatre of our time. But that *ghastly* thing. You were in it.

SIR JOHN: *Oedipus?*

SIR RALPH: That's it! *Awful.*

SIR JOHN: Oh, I thought it was extraordinary. I'll never regret doing it. I wasn't very good in it. I didn't know how to do what he wanted. But you know, there were such terrible rows between Brook and Olivier. When Olivier saw this great phallus on the stage of the Old Vic he thought the theatre would be closed down by the police. Brook wouldn't give in, though. They were arguing in my dressing room. So I left them to fight it out between them. When I came back a huge mirror had a crack right through it. It was like the Lady of Shalott. I *long* to know which one of them did it.

SIR RALPH: When I went to see the production, somehow I hadn't got a programme. So I said to Mu, "Leave it to me." And I went down the aisle up to a chap, but he was lashed to a pillar. I didn't know what was going on. It turned out that he was in the show. I think he was in the chorus. But the show hadn't started yet. Mu said, "Did you get a programme?" And I had to say it wasn't possible because all the programme sellers were lashed to the dress circle. *Very* strange.

SIR JOHN: Oh, dear! It's like the old lady who went to Wesker's *Roots* and they cooked a meal onstage during the first act. Onions and a frightful stew. The lady went up to a programme seller and said, "Isn't there a rather *curious* smell in this theatre?" And the programme seller replied, "It's the play, madam." But what did the poor actor who was lashed to the pillar say to you?

SIR RALPH: Well, of course, when I asked him for a programme all I got were these strangled sounds. He was gagged, you see. The whole experience upset me very much. I'm a very *square* man.

SIR JOHN: Yes, you are. But you're also very clever, Ralph. You can be very suspicious, but once you overcome it you're enormously interested and warm. Unlike me, you're cautious. Which is quite right.

SIR RALPH: Very, *very* cautious.

Enter Miss Jane Bown, the photographer from the Observer. *The two actors greet her most courteously.*

SIR RALPH: What do you want us to do, Miss Bown?

MISS BOWN: Forget I'm here, I think.

SIR RALPH: It must be so difficult being a photographer. It's a hobby of mine! But whenever I try to photograph anyone they always look as if they've been hit over the head with a meat ax.

SIR JOHN: I think I'd rather be photographed than drawn. David Hockney did a drawing of me when I was seventy and I thought if I really look like that I must kill myself tomorrow.

SIR RALPH: It wasn't too bad, Johnny.

SIR JOHN: It's awfully difficult to reconcile yourself with your image at any age, I think. I couldn't get over Garbo being seventy the other day. Did you see that photo of her? It really shocked me. Photography is rather a terrifying medium. Look at Richard Avedon's pictures. Merciless! He photographed me once and asked me to cry for him. So I thought of everyone I loved and the tears flowed like mad. But he never published the picture anywhere. Two hours of crying for nothing. I was very cross.

SIR RALPH: The trouble is I can never remember who I am whenever I'm photographed. Who *am* I? I find I'm no one in particular and it tends to emerge in the photos. Is the light all right, Miss Bown?

SIR JOHN: It's strange. I never feel secure whenever I'm photographed in costume at dress rehearsals. You're not yet the character that's being photographed. When you've been playing a part for a little while you get the right face for it. You can *see* it.

SIR RALPH: It's fascinating what part of your body *feels* right when you're preparing a role. I don't know whether you find this but I sometimes find it starts to come to me in my…*feet*. You can feel secure in your feet. The role comes gradually with various parts of the body. It doesn't fill the anatomy at once. Sometimes the voice is behind. Other times, I feel very secure in my…*eyes*.

SIR JOHN: Marvellous grouse!

SIR RALPH: Absolutely wonderful! I went to a restaurant in Hollywood once and had the most frightful lunch. When they asked me to pay I made the only joke I've ever cracked in my life. I said, "The only thing you've cooked here is the bill."

Short pause.
Sir John laughs, a little too uproariously.

SIR RALPH: Aren't you nice, John? The way you laughed at my *only* joke. Jolly nice of you!

SIR JOHN: Have you ever had a really marvellous Indian curry?

SIR RALPH: Nothing like it!

SIR JOHN: I had one in Ceylon. I went to Government House and we had an all-curry lunch. Had to rest for three hours afterwards. It was *unbelievable!*

SIR RALPH: I *know!* I once had a curry in Bombay. There's a millionairess there who lives in a fantastic palace. Talk about food of paradise! Afterwards I said to her, "It must be marvellous to be a millionairess, as you undoubtedly are. And this superb curry! How could you possibly *find* a chef to make it?" And she replied, "There's only one chef in this palace and that chef is me." Imagine it! The Indian millionairess had gone to market at five o'clock that very morning to select the ingredients herself. Probably had bearers to carry her back.

SIR JOHN: How *splendid!* Have you been reading Ackerley's *Hindoo Holiday?*

SIR RALPH: Wonderful! I'm so glad you gave it me.

SIR JOHN: Don't you think it's clever?

SIR RALPH: I savour it sip by sip. What a writer!

SIR JOHN: Don't you find Indians are so extraordinary? When I was in Bombay at the end of the war I was lying naked in my hotel room when the telephone rang. A voice said there was a lady to see me. Well, I'd been flying all week and was too tired to see anyone. But five minutes later the door burst open and an *enormous* Indian lady in a green sari looked at me trying desperately to cover myself with a tiny towel and announced, "My name is Mrs. Sabawala. My house is music in stone. Will you come to lunch tomorrow?" It turned out she had played Madame Arcati in *Blithe Spirit* with the local amateurs. Her house had a huge gate with a cardboard crescent moon pinned to it. Nothing to drink.

SIR RALPH: Nothing to drink!

SIR JOHN: And terrible chairs. As you sat down your back was lacerated by the teak. You had to practically go down on your hands and knees to look out of the windows. The whole thing was absolutely mad! There was a tiny poet in a white suit who read a long poem he'd written in my honour. It once happened with Alan Ginsberg in New York too. I seem to inspire poetry in strange people. But I was so startled by the Indian poet that I stepped back in alarm and fell in a pool covered in lilies.

SIR RALPH: My God, what you suffer! Not that you care, Johnny.

SIR JOHN: Couldn't have happened in England, Ralph.

The two famous actors laugh and finish their lunch.

Noël Coward
at Seventy

It had troubled me at first that I was following in the trail of so many inter-
viewers and critics who had gone to find the "real" Noël Coward and failed
to return with the goodies. What irritation it had caused them! All that nagging away, only to receive a pretty box of witticisms wrapped in tinsel. What
a defeat! Wit is a great asset, of course, and an even greater camouflage. Yet
is it possible that beneath Coward's witty and urbane exterior can be found
a witty and urbane interior? I was soon to find out.

When I met him at his Swiss villa, which is set in four acres of mountains
overlooking Montreux, he looked very friendly, teasable, slightly breathless,
and eager for the fray. "Now tell me," he said in that clipped voice, "how is the
dear old *Observer*?"

He was dressed in a check sports jacket, dark gray slacks, white sweater,
gay cravat, and slippers. On his right wrist was a gold identity bracelet with
his name engraved in capital letters—not that Coward, or anyone else,
needs reminding. He stoops a little now, but it was him all right. He settled
in a high leather chair shaped like a throne, lit one of many cigarettes,
which he holds upright, making them seem pert and alert, and offered
drinks. "I can tell by the quiver of your lower lip that the answer must be yes."

Did he drink much? "Not a lot. It doesn't suit me." What was he like
when he was drunk? "Very voluble—although I can be that when I'm
sober—overaffectionate, not exactly maudlin, but fond."

Fond? "Yes, fond."

I asked if he'd enjoyed Sheridan Morley's biography of him. "Very
much, but of course I was fascinated by the subject matter." He giggled,
which he does often, and it's catching. "But Sheridan has a child called

Hugo who, with a sense of the future, took a great shine to me—flattered me, looked up at me, and laughed at every witticism at exactly the right point. I do love him. He's my latest godson. I shall have to give him some religious instruction." If the number of godchildren a man has is the sign of how much he is loved by his friends, it ought to be mentioned that Coward has eighteen.

He once described himself as looking like a heavily doped Chinese illusionist, and I wouldn't dream of contradicting him. At seventy he tires easily and takes a regular afternoon nap, though I've never met a mind as quick as his. Could he believe his age? "Oh, certainly not! I cannot get out of my head that I'm still a precocious teenager—and *precocious* is the operative word." I reminded him of a line in *Private Lives:* "I hope for a glorious oblivion like being under gas." Did he? "Yes, lovely! Of course one does the most terrible things under gas. I once wrecked an entire dentist's office. I leapt out of the chair, kicked all the instruments in, kicked the dentist in the balls, and was finally chained down by an angry, bearded nurse."

He kept fit? "Do you mean exercise?" He looked genuinely astonished. "It's fatal for me. I'm an immediate stretcher case. Exercise is the most *awful* illusion. The secret is a lot of aspirin and *marrons glacés.*"

I began to wonder if he'd ever been completely thrown. "Yes, I have—literally!" What by? "The king of Siam." One almost said, "Of course." No one could invent the stories Coward tells about himself. The king of Siam had granted him a private audience, and when it was time to go, Coward backed out of the royal chamber, determined to do it terribly well. Unfortunately, he caught his heel on a tiger's head, fell flat on his back, and was carried out by the Grand Vizier. What did the king say? "He didn't seem to mind, even invited me to the ballet—which was deadly."

Coward divides his time between his homes in Switzerland and Jamaica, stopping off in London and New York every year to see friends and catch up with the latest plays. Would he be seeing *Oh Calcutta!* when he was next in America? "I can't," he replied, squeezing out the words, "WAIT."

It's an enviable way of life, though a much quieter one than it seems. Old cronies look him up for a gossip that, one suspects, Coward enjoys enormously, and there are occasional parties with his neighbors who live around Montreux—the Chaplins, the Nivens, Joan Sutherland, and Adrienne Allen, who played in *Private Lives* with Coward in 1930. But his days are spent mostly in a leisured routine of reading and writing. He is slowly getting through the third volume of his autobiography, which is to be called *Past Conditional.* Was it the final volume? "That depends on the Almighty, rather. He's a keen organizer." He wasn't writing a hidden play? "Oh no! Nothing I write is hidden." How much of his work didn't we know about? He paused for the first time: "My *dear* boy . . ."

I had of course meant his writing, and he told me there's lots hidden away, even a novel called *Cherry Pan* that he wrote when he was seventeen. "I was at that time rather influenced by woodland fantasies." Even so, he hung on to his old manuscripts? "I'd never throw away a word. . . ." Coward has also been writing a journal every week since 1939, and this, too, won't be published during his lifetime. "I write sharp little reviews of the plays I've seen. They'll cause a slight flutter. And I write about events that stir the blood." Would I be in it? "Absolutely up to the hilt, God help us all." It was time for lunch.

I doubt if Coward could have changed much over the years. How eagerly those angry young men of the fifties became the right-wing aristocrats of the sixties. Yet this son of a Teddington piano salesman has remained for over fifty years, in or out of fashion, thoroughly himself. "It's sheer endurance," he explained. "By both the public *and* me." Theater is a great leveler of class, and Coward has been on the stage since he was ten. If he is a snob, he's a harmless one. But he's more his own invention, as John Osborne, who acknowledges a surprising debt to him, pointed out.

A friend who knows Coward had suggested I mention any date in contemporary history and watch his reaction. Why not? I asked him what 1930 meant to him. "*Private Lives,* of course!" And 1939? "*Present Laughter.*" But mention of the war years brought an unexpected remark about Chamberlain. "I've never hated anybody in my life," he said. "Except him. Even now I can't bear to look at his photograph." The remark led to the story of how Coward came to hit Ivor Novello in the Tivoli cinema.

They were watching a newsreel together when Chamberlain came up on the screen delivering his "Peace in Our Time" speech. Coward was incensed, but Novello burst into tears of relief, weeping uncontrollably. "Stop it!" yelled Coward. "Stop that immediately!" And hit him.

He scarcely ate any lunch, preferring to chain-smoke. Occasionally he whistled to himself. There was a choice of wine; his Italian cook brought the food in. "Come, dear boy!" Coward said suddenly. "Eat up your meal and stop racking your brains!" I rose above that and mentioned a new film being made that's based on an old Russian fable. "I dread old Russian fables, don't you?" (Slight pause.) "Even new Russian fables…" Had he seen Daniel Massey playing him in *Star*? "Yes, and he was very good except that he made the mistake of singing better than I did. I can't sing, but I know how to, which is quite different." Later, I somehow got on to the subject of Vietnam. Coward didn't say anything—he is known to be uninterested in politics—until he unexpectedly intervened: "They've lost the war. They should get out and shut up."

The lunch continued pleasantly and was highlighted by one particularly amusing story that told a lot about Coward. I had asked him whether, faced with failure, as he sometimes has been, he'd ever despaired. For good measure I threw in the name *Sirocco*, which was booed off the stage as few plays have been since. "Well, if I'm going to have a flop, I like it to be a rouser. I didn't despair at all! What made it much more interesting was that my mother, who was slightly deaf, thought the booing was cheering." Incredibly, Basil Dean, the producer of the play, made the same mistake. "He was ringing the curtain up and down with a beaming smile. I said: 'Wipe that smile off your face, dear—this is it!'"

Coward ordered the curtain to be kept up, went on the stage, ignoring the audience, and shook hands with the cast, which included Novello. Only then did he turn to the audience to take one smiling, regal bow after another. "Well, they booed, and screamed, and roared. Seymour Hicks leapt on to a stall and said, 'Shut up, you swine!' which added to the confusion. I kept bowing. I thought, If they're going to boo, I'll see that they go home with sore throats. Then some idiot shouted for one of the actresses, Frances Doble, so I led her forward. A charming voice cried: 'That's right! Hide behind a lady.' Then dear Frances took her bow. But she was so flurried that when she made her speech, she said: 'This is the happiest day of my life.'"

When he finally emerged from the theater, Coward was spat at. Why did he think it happened? "Very strong personality. Irritating success."

It was time for us to return to the sitting room, and Coward to his leather throne. Scattered around the room are signed photos of the Queen Mother, Churchill, Callas, Nureyev, Olivier, Dietrich, and more. Coward has always enjoyed, perhaps overmuch, the company of celebrities and the glamour and chic that goes with them. It is his kind of showbiz. The world of fringe theater isn't just alien to him, but meaningless. But any soul can sign his visitor's book, which, when I was invited to, I did with a flourish opposite the signature of Elizabeth Taylor: together at last.

I asked him about his public image. "Well, it involves being incredibly witty, you know. I was leaving Australia once when a lady ran up to me and said, 'Oh, Mr. Coward, say something funny.'" What did he say? "Kangaroo."

What else did he think was part of his image? "Well, it's awfully difficult now because it's changed, rather. At one period it was just a series of witty epigrams, which I've never done in my life. In fact, I only used a cigarette holder for a short time. The press have laid off all that now. The public image is largely created by them anyway." True, but Coward gave the press lots to talk about. "Certainly I did! I acted up like crazy. I did everything that was expected of me." Why did he? "Part of the job," he replied, and sounded very firm about it.

Another important part of Coward's image has been fostering the belief that he wrote his twenty-seven plays and two-hundred-eighty-one songs in an absinthe-drenched coma between cocktail parties. Not true, of course! Whenever Coward has been working on a project, he's been up every day at 7:00 A.M. and begun work at 7:45. "Somerset Maugham kept the same hours and told me to do so. I've never regretted it. I don't look upon myself very ardently but I think my technical concentration is something I value very much, and the routine of writing." Did he write easily? "I've always been able to write dialogue by the yard. Prose is different. I sometimes sit staring at the pad for hours." That was very reassuring. But Coward has never made any particular secret of the way he works. It's just that the public prefers his image because it's more fun.

Still, how did he manage to make everything seem so easy? "Critics," he replied, "have nearly always been wrong in the essentials. If I act a part very well, which as a rule I do, the critics mistake the apparent glibness for something casual, which it isn't. It's most carefully rehearsed. I like complete spontaneity on the stage after six weeks' rehearsal."

Shyness isn't part of Coward: he seems a tremendously self-confident man. "Yes, but all that can vanish when one's on the spot, you know—when you're faced with a big and difficult assignment. You can't avoid being shaky." Surely he wasn't a secret worrier! "If I worry, everybody knows it. But I don't worry very often. I prefer to get things settled. I'm much more of a fighter, and I inherit my fighting qualities from my mother. If anything is disturbing I endeavor to deal with it." Was this a warning?

Cyril Connolly, striving for the "real" Coward, once wrote of him: "An essentially unhappy man, a man who gives one the impression of having seldom really thought or really lived and is intelligent enough to know it." But Coward isn't a social reformer or a particularly profound man. When I mentioned Beckett's pessimism to him, he replied amusingly: "He must have read too many of his own plays. It gets him down, I expect." No, he's essentially an entertainer whose crime, apparently, has been to try to cheer people up. I don't suppose Connolly would have minded writing some of the best comedies in the English language. Coward's songs haven't done too badly, either.

The trouble lies in the belief that his notorious "talent to amuse" must be based on shallowness. Yet the Coward I met, and learned about from people who know him, is firmly rooted in disciplined work, a fierce professionalism and pride, the value of friendship, and when it comes to it, the ability to laugh at himself. Did he know that he was recently compared to Michelangelo, no less? "Yes," he replied, "All that chipping away...."

What has helped him to survive has been his love of travel, which he usually does alone. (He wrote *Mad Dogs and Englishmen* traveling from Hanoi to Saigon.) He travels abroad to meet people rather than to see the sights. He was once staying round the corner from the Taj Mahal and refused to go and see it. "I'd seen it on biscuit boxes and didn't want to spoil the illusion." Then, trying to give me a precise reason why he traveled so much, he said, "The best kind of showbiz is making your own point."

Well, I think he's made it. "I've had a long affair with the stage," Noël Coward added. "And it's still flourishing. I can't think of anything more enjoyable than that particular moment when the house lights go down, a glow comes on the curtain, and you know in a second or two that the show will begin. That, to me, is still magic."

Tranquil in Connecticut with Arthur Miller

Arthur Miller, looking cheerful and welcoming like a favorite elderly uncle, met my Greyhound bus at Southbury, Connecticut. At almost sixty-five, this tall and attractive man might have been a local farmer in his worn and battered clothes. His huge hands look as if they would smash a typewriter in two.

He drove me to his home, which turned out to be more of an estate, whistling happily to himself at the wheel of his small Volkswagen. William Styron, Milos Foreman, and other success stories also live in the Connecticut countryside, where wealthy suburbs are a safe distance from the decaying American cities and Miller's hometown of New York. (He was born in Harlem.) "My land begins here," he announced proudly, several minutes before we turned into the driveway of his house.

He lives on 350 acres amid forests and cornfields and great tranquillity. Was he rich? I asked, feeling a bit envious. "Not really. I have enough to live till I die. Compared to New York, there are fewer sewers here to dump your money in."

But how do writers understand life when most of them end up by isolating themselves from it? "Well, I always doubted that writers ever really understand more than anyone else. All you can hope is that maybe you feel a little more." Did he know why he wrote? "Perhaps in the beginning to see if I could. And now, to see if I still can." At which he laughed, knowing it to be true.

His house appeared to be very unpretentious and informal, like its owner. Miller lives there with one of his teenage daughters and his third wife, the distinguished photographer Inge Morath, whom he married in the early sixties after his marriage to Marilyn Monroe. Did he suspect or fear, I wondered, that his visitor couldn't help looking for Monroe's ghost in his home, though it was twenty years since they were married?

Two affectionate Alsatians were slumped asleep on the patio. "They're trained to track sheep," said Miller. "Listen, they've never seen a sheep in their *lives*." His Viennese mother-in-law, an eccentric lady, had made us a simple lunch. Life seemed good there, in the peace and the sun, as if there were all the time in the world.

"Look at that beast!" Miller suddenly exclaimed at the sight of a mysterious green bug. "It's armoured. Its got a great sense of survival." *"Stinky!"* cried his mother-in-law, hurrying to pick it up and throw it away. "It sprays you with stinky, Arthur." "There you are," said Miller, helping himself to another pickle, "you learn something new every day."

Had he read *Death of a Salesman* recently? I asked. "Yes, I read it again two years ago when George C. Scott played it in New York. I had to argue with him about something, so I had to read the play to prove my point." How did he enjoy his play? "It always moves me, I must say. The audience in New York weren't even born when it was first performed, yet it meant something to them. I'm amazed at the cultural continuity of America. I doubt if many people in the audience had even met a salesman selling stuff from a suitcase. It's an antiquated profession, like diving for pearls. Yet it didn't matter. Not much has changed, in the essentials."

This great play, perhaps the greatest in postwar American theater, continues to touch the deepest of chords wherever it is performed. Yet when *Death of a Salesman* was first produced in Britain in 1949, the response was muted and, compared to the devastating effect it had on America, cold. This may have been partly the fault of Paul Muni, who intellectualized the role of Willy Loman, delivering a studied "characterization," whereas Lee J. Cobb, who created the role in New York, understood pathos. But what did Miller think the National Theatre's revival of *Salesman* might mean to Britain this time?

"Well, one *hopes*. When it played in France just after the war it seemed a terribly exotic play to them. It was as if America and American values really were part of a different civilization. But when it was revived in Paris a few years ago, it played with success. The French could relate to it because they now have the same insecurity and problems as America. They could believe in them—as their own."

So, surprisingly perhaps, could Russia. Miller is certain that its excuse for putting *Death of a Salesman* on at first was an exposé of the American Dream. (With deliberate and heavy-handed irony, a Moscow production of *Death of a Salesman* once changed the title to *The Man Who Had All the Luck,* which is in fact the title of Miller's first play.) But Russia has never regarded *Salesman* as easy propaganda. When Miller asked a Soviet critic why it should appeal to the Russians—after all, there are no traveling salesmen in Russia—he received the reply that Russian society is still full of people who keep lying to themselves too.

"The strange thing is," said Miller, "I have no way of summarizing that play, even now."

"Why not?" I asked. "You wrote it."

"Because in many ways *Death of a Salesman* came out of a profound subconscious side of me where the analytic just can't get to. It's not for want of trying," he added, and laughed. "You get *curious.* There aren't many things that are thirty years old and still run, except Rolls-Royces maybe."

He showed me round his place, taking me to his wife's photographic studio, nestling in the grounds, the vegetable patch he cultivates, and the highly professional carpentry shop where he makes furniture for the house. He's quite a craftsman: simple and workmanlike tables and chairs, undecorative. A short walk from the house is his own studio, where he writes each day, looking in every new play, he says, for the feel of walls in a cave—looking for a way out.

The studio is virtually barren, with cheap linoleum on the floor, no pictures on the walls, and no telephone. He works on a thirty-year-old typewriter. Over his desk is a calendar that for some reason has stopped at April 1968. He hoards old drafts and manuscripts like a miser. He told me he has written about fifteen plays that have never been shown to anyone.

At present Miller is at work on two new plays and a lengthy book. Following a recent trip to China, he has written the text to a book of his wife's photos, *Chinese Encounter.* (His first successful play, *All My Sons,* will be the first contemporary foreign play to be translated and produced in China.) Currently on Broadway there's a highly successful revival of *The Price,* which opened to a mixed reception in the late sixties when radical chic critics such as Tynan and Robert Brustein dismissed it as being politically and socially irrelevant. It's as if America and elsewhere have suddenly rediscovered Arthur Miller.

But then, Miller's finest work—*Death of a Salesman, The Crucible, The Price*—have been out of key, it seems, with the spirit of the times as exemplified by Beckett or Pinter. Contrary to their work, which Miller greatly admires (as one might admire an architectural shape), his plays have always been stubbornly rooted in a humanist tradition, characters with a recognizable past, the telling of a story.

Does he feel his work is old-fashioned? "Yeah," said Miller. "As old-fashioned as the latest fashion. I think my work *is* out of tune. But I don't think it's out of tune with the way I perceive people to be thinking about themselves. I can't believe people have simply become concepts. But who gives a goddamn about fashion? The only test of a play does not belong to fashion. The only test should be, do I listen to this playwright or not? Does his play *move* me?"

Later in the day, Miller talked a little about his family—about his eldest son, who makes TV commercials in California, his older brother, who is a business executive, and his sister, who is an actress. She is well known in America, Miller told me, from a TV soap opera—and therein lies a tale and a moral.

The character Arthur Miller's sister played on American TV was killed off. She played Ethel, who unexpectedly finds that she has an incurable disease. But as it dawned on viewers that their favorite was about to be killed off, thousands of protest letters were written into the TV station. Ethel must stay! But Ethel couldn't, because she had an incurable disease.

So, explained Miller, they had to kill her off—but they thought up a bright idea. After a decent pause, his sister returned to the series to play Ethel's long-lost twin sister from South Africa. But whereas Ethel had been a lovable character, her twin sister wasn't. She was different. So the letters of protest poured in again from the nation. Our Ethel would never have a sister like this! So they killed her off.

"I hope that teaches all of us a lesson," said Arthur Miller. "Never mess around with a good thing."

Then he went off for a swim in his lake, swimming at a determined, even pace.

England's
Great Clown

Max Wall, who is related to the Great Wall of China, is a man who came back from oblivion to be hailed a comic genius. No greater justice, none could be as sweet.

At sixty-six, he appears in his outrageous baggy black tights alone for two hours on the stage like an apparition: a ghost of the music halls. "You've heard of the music hall," he says, "it used to be in the newspapers." Perhaps comparisons with John Osborne's Archie Rice are inevitable, particularly as he played him in a recent revival of *The Entertainer*, directed by Osborne. But there's a difference. Unlike Archie Rice, Max Wall has never been dead behind the eyes. He cannot be beaten. Whatever the despair of his wrecked private life, whatever the put-on hopelessness of his legendary act, to watch him perform is to witness one of the greatest clowns the British theater has known. His decline and triumph aren't without irony.

"Frankly, ladies and gentlemen," he announces at the start of a performance, "I don't see any reason, while you're sitting there, I don't see *any reason* why you shouldn't be entertained." The logic of this can be lethal. "Mark you!" he adds, for he's fond of unexpected exclamations: "By the Lord Harry!" Or, for no apparent reason, "Get in there, Arthur." "*Mark you*, I wish I was out there where you're sitting—enjoying a marvelous show." There's danger in him. He plays with the audience, improvising. He's neither the lovable red-nosed clown nor the straight comedian. He's unique.

He always ends each performance with the insane Professor Wallofsky—that timeless, hysterical creation, who discovers one arm growing longer than the other as he attempts to play the piano with the aid of a map. A new generation of admirers are convulsed with laughter. Yet there's a harsh cutting edge about Max Wall that takes the audience by surprise. No one is ever quite at ease, never knowing which way he's going to play it. It's part of his almost perverse appeal.

He can be sentimental and warm. One of the romantic ballads he sings is "I've Never Been in Love Before" from *Guys and Dolls*. Yet he presents a spectacle of human disaster and misery that's disturbing. At times it's as if he despises both himself and the audience that acclaims him. He's a true eccentric, yet the ridicule he invites, feeds off, leaves you more than thoughtful after the lights go down. "Don't laugh," he's been known to say to his audience in a hollow voice, stopping them in their tracks, "it's unkind." Each night, he receives an ovation. "I *know*," says Mr. Wall.

Born in Brixton in 1908, he was christened Maxwell Lorimer, the son of a famous Scottish comedian. His mother, aunt and uncle, grandfather and grandmother were also stars of the music hall; the lineage stretches back to the 1860s. He first appeared on the stage at two years of age, when his father carried him on in a kilt. One of his earliest memories is of seeing Marie Lloyd from the wings. Dan Leno, with whom he's sometimes compared, was a hero. Another was Grock, the great Swiss clown. His eyes light up whenever Grock's name is mentioned. He worked with him in Paris.

Max Wall's own act was what was known as "acrobatic dancing." It's how he learned to contort his body. He's always done deranged funny walks (as John Cleese was to do, in his manic fashion). For some fifteen years he performed without speaking at all. If you spoke in those days, the management had to increase the salary. By the time he was thirty, there was little anyone could teach him about stagecraft. More than anything, he told us, he learned never to give in.

His face looks sad, as if he's churning life over. He is open and honest: without guile. When he smiles, he grins from ear to ear, a clown's smile. Like so many naturally funny men, he was born into unhappiness, and was never to overcome it. His father was an alcoholic who drank himself to death. During World War I, his home was bombed by a zeppelin, which killed a baby brother. Max was buried in the rubble but survived.

Since then, his three marriages have all failed. He was recently declared bankrupt. "Marriage," he says now, "there's no percentage in it. *The lion's den*. I've never understood women, really. No one ever has." He describes himself as a fool in his private life. But there's no obvious trace of self-pity or bitterness in him. He just states it as a melancholy fact.

Twenty years ago, when he was still at his height, one of the most popular comedians in the country, the breakup of his first marriage occurred and almost finished him. By then, he had appeared in two royal command performances; he drove a Rolls. But he fell in love with a former Miss Britain, twenty-six years his junior. They married, eventually. The five children from Max's first marriage, though adult now, still don't speak to him.

Partly because of the bad publicity, some of it vindictive, partly because of the stricter moral climate of the 1950s, his career began to slide. He could never have been an easy man. He had a reputation for independence, moodiness, awkwardness on occasions. But he felt victimized by what happened. He says the impresarios closed the leading theaters to him. Certainly, at a time when music hall was dying, he was forced off the TV screens, only to appear from time to time as a shadow, victim of a few imitators. He received poison-pen letters, which hurt him deeply. Bouts of severe depression followed; guilt, drink, a suicide attempt. He was tempted to top himself, when what he describes as A Voice On High was heard to say: "Don't be a silly sod."

He survived: he worked the northern workingmen's clubs, notorious graveyards. Changing his costume in the gents', competing against the more immediate appeal of booze and scampi—that's where Max Wall has been all these lost years. The act for which he's currently hailed as a genius in the West End is exactly the same as the one he performed in the wilderness. He's married to his craft—and an audience. "Show business is like sex," he announces cheerfully during his act. "When it's wonderful, it's wonderful. But when it isn't very good, it's still all right."

He lives alone now, in a bed-sitter outside the center of London. His only possessions are his props, hundreds of letters, and a thirty-five-year-old typewriter. He thinks, schemes, and writes new material. He's still a hopeful man. Away from the theater he's almost a recluse. He drinks Guinness at his local pub, sometimes gambles at roulette, has supper at Roules in Covent Garden—always alone.

He's pleased by his present success, though scarcely overwhelmed by it. Over the past few years he must have been discovered more times than

North Sea oil. He's a fatalist. "There's a time to be a success and a time to be a failure. Fate decrees it," he told me. "What was it Aristotle said? The will of the masses will prevail. Well, I think he might have had something there! People say I could fill the Albert Hall. I don't think so. But if you put a medium-sized hut in the middle of nowhere and said, 'Max Wall Appearing Tonight,' you might find quite a few people trickling along. Yes, I think that might be true. It's *written*. If the Lord says it, it will be. *Something* will happen. Because the Lord is saying, 'This is the day of Max Wall.' "

He laughed at that. Inside his profession, and outside, he is well loved. Max's signature tune is called "Say It While Dancing."

His Name
Escapes Him

Alec Guinness, the master of anonymity and disguise, is the antithesis of every popular image the public has of actors. He is a man who has always wished to create his own invisibility. Hence the witty title of his enchanting new book of "musings," *My Name Escapes Me.*

Perhaps, at eighty-two, Mr. Guinness's name really does escape him from time to time, like memorizing lines in his reluctant semiretirement (the subtitle is "The Diary of a Retiring Actor"). A self-effacing, dotty, civilized Englishness is his calling card, and this light and charming record of his life from January 1995 through June 1996 should be savored as Mr. Guinness himself enjoys vintage wine.

I can imagine no other diarist opening his remarks, and his eyes, by greeting the New Year with a slightly jaundiced observation about his feet. "As I reluctantly swung out of bed I noticed my feet—never something on which I like to dwell. They appeared to be crumbling sandstone monuments, the soles crisscrossed with ancient, indecipherable runes which probably hold the secrets of 80 years of living and partly living."

England loves actors who are eccentric, which is why Laurence Olivier was merely revered. Alan Bennett, a friend of Mr. Guinness's, can appear to be plain nutty. John Gielgud, Mr. Guinness's youthful mentor, was renowned for his unstoppable faux pas. "I can't think why you want to play big parts," Gielgud once told him. "Why don't you stick to the little people you do so well?"

Mr. Guinness himself is, of course, nicely eccentric, puttering about the place, which is his country home in Hampshire, where he lives happily with

Merula, his painter wife of almost sixty years. He visits London in the manner of an educated Edwardian gentleman—to shop, to have his hair cut, to dine with old valued friends, to visit the theater.

His theater stories are little gems. In typically modest fashion, he recalls Olivier's spikily encouraging remarks about his Malvolio: "Marvelous, old cock! I never realized Malvolio could be played as a bore!" His anecdote about the drunken performance of *Macbeth* he saw in the 1930s in provincial Worthing is priceless. A lush actor-manager of the day, Henry Baynton, presented his Macbeth "on a memorable night of high winds, crashing waves and lashing rain when he decided it was time to battle his way to the nearest pub while Malcolm and Macduff set about their long tedious scene together, which was followed by Lady M prowling about in her sleep."

Unfortunately, no Macbeth appeared again when Lady M left the stage, washing her hands. After a lengthy pause, the stage manager announced to the bewildered audience—who were mostly schoolchildren studying the play for exams—"You can go home now. This is where the play ends." So they all began to leave, doubled up against the rainstorm, when they saw, blown toward them, the drunken figure of Macbeth, like a mad ghost in a Viking helmet. "What!" he cried. "Going home so soon?"

This is no Garrick Club memoir, however. Mr. Guinness is the least theatrical of actors. He has always been a curious chap in more ways than one, possessing the appealing innocence of Charles Dickens's Herbert Pocket. His writing, like his acting, reveals a meticulous, quirky eye for detail. He spots a Hollywood type seated in a Paris restaurant: "He was wearing the smartest navy blue suit I have seen since that worn by Khrushchev's personal photographer, whom I met twenty-five years ago. Tailored by Lanvin, I should think."

He's a watcher. As an impoverished child in London, he used to study how strangers walked, spying on them like a writer. To this day, it's impossible for him to feel at ease in a role until he knows exactly how a character should walk. (By coincidence, Ralph Richardson subscribed to the same method.) He's well read. Lulls in rehearsals and filming make actors quite bookish, but Mr. Guinness is exceptional. He knows his Trollope backward. When he was a captain in the Royal Navy during World War II, he read

C. K. Scott Moncrieff's twelve volumes of Proust, keeping the volumes snugly tucked into a pocket of his duffel coat.

His quiet passion is for books, friendship, dogs of high and low descent, music, art. "The sharply silhouetted black sails of Turner's *Burial at Sea*," he writes, "conjure up a sad nightmare; his way with black smoke is somehow appalling, acrid and choking."

There are moments when, his contemporaries gone or soon to go, he can sum up his feelings in a single, chilling sentence: "My small world threatens to be underpopulated."

There has always been more to Alec Guinness than meets the eye. Kenneth Tynan, borrowing from Shaw on Henry Irving, remarked that Guinness has no face. Little wonder he was so at home playing Smiley, John Le Carré's spy in the BBC's *Tinker, Tailor, Soldier, Spy*. His anonymous looks have enabled him to adopt many brilliant disguises as an actor, as if his face could be molded like clay.

I feel fortunate to have interviewed him twenty years ago when he was but a lad of sixty-two, and remember the meeting vividly. Typically, he wrote to me—rather than phoning back when I contacted him—in careful, cramped ink on a postcard that might have been sent by a jokey secret agent. "O.K. Wednesday," it read furtively. "Would you meet me under the canopy of the Albert Theatre at 12:45. Should I wear a red carnation, or should you? Yours sincerely, Alec Guinness."

He was wearing the carnation, looking both elegant and slightly flamboyant when he arrived on the dot at 12:45, carrying in each hand a box from Fortnum & Mason—one containing cheese, the other, toupees.

He looked like the kind of affable Englishman who might turn out to be the owner of a private zoo. Over lunch in Covent Garden, he did his utmost, with increasingly honeyed charm, to avoid the interview at all costs. Mr. Guinness is a Catholic convert—as Graham Greene was—and life is not plain sailing for him. "He has still found no safe harbors or easy answers," Mr. Le Carré writes in his introduction to *My Name Escapes Me*. So fame has always troubled this reserved, elusive man. But when we went to his modest Westminster apartment, he talked easily enough while deflecting the confessional. *Star Wars* made him unexpectedly wealthy—though God forbid the well-bred Englishman should plead anything but imminent bankruptcy.

Mr. Guinness treads carefully. He's the son of a banker who abandoned his mother when he was less than a year old. His first appearance in the professional theater was at age nineteen when, displaying a versatility that was to make him renowned, he appeared in three acts of the same play as a Chinese coolie, a French pirate, and a British sailor. The play, a classic for its title alone, was called *Queer Cargo*.

He was immensely enjoyable company, slipping into uncanny impersonations, particularly of his mentor Gielgud. Gielgud would arrange various auditions for his young protégé. "Next!" shouted a director at Mr. Guinness. "You're not an actor. Get off the stage, dear."

He is highly unusual in English theater in this backhanded way: he is more famous for his films than his stage work (he won his Academy Award for *The Bridge on the River Kwai*). In a long, successful career, perhaps something within his acting remains unfulfilled. Mr. Guinness tackled some of the great heroic roles in theater over the years—and for many bewildering reasons he failed at crucial moments. In the forties, he took on Richard II; in the fifties, Hamlet, which he also directed; and in the early sixties, Macbeth (with a willful choice of Simone Signoret as Lady M). In each decade, he seemed to return to an unspecified inner desire to conquer the ultimate heights, and each time, whether the outcome was controversial or not, hopes were dashed. It might be that the critical mauling he received for those performances inevitably disillusioned him, forcing his path into safer territory. Perhaps he has always been most at home playing eccentrics or obsessive heroes, more of a miniaturist than a tragic actor with the grand sweep, Lear's fool rather than Lear.

Yet could it be that Mr. Guinness's impersonal, introverted ambiguity, following on the heels of that extraordinary trio of giants—Olivier, Gielgud, and Richardson—made him a modern antihero a generation too soon? Well, such grandiose theories cut little or no ice with him. But when asked, he said simply and honestly this:

"I know my stage career must have been a great disappointment to those who had great faith in me in my younger days. Nevertheless, I think the limits to my talent are very marked. It isn't a sadness to me. I'm just aware of it. I can say that I've never been jealous of any first-class actor in my life. I've had only shreds of jealousy of the second-rate. But it must mean that a large part of my makeup is second-rate, too."

It was a remarkably insecure statement from so great an actor. His eyes tend not to meet yours, except—he pointed out—when he lies. He looked away from me obliquely, offering a cigarette, which he smoked out of the corner of his mouth at a rakish angle.

In Memoriam
Michael Bennett

In happier times, Michael Bennett told me this story about himself: He had been dancing in public since the age of four—he proudly showed a photo of himself in white tie and tails to prove it—and when he was five he danced at his uncle's wedding. But he was too young to remember a sequence of dance steps, so he decided to improvise as he went along. He would dance flat-heel turns round the banquet hall, and take it from there. And instead of turning for sixteen or even thirty-two counts, he made up his mind that he wouldn't stop.

So as the wedding guests crowded nearer, he began to edge them back by dancing closer and closer to them. As he turned and gathered speed, he created his own space—turning and turning round the room until his arms were numb and his body ached. And then he could feel nothing but the vivid sensation that he could turn and dance *forever*—and he tried to, until his uncle dashed onto the dance floor after several minutes and grabbed him up into his arms.

"What do you make of *that?*" he asked me.

I told him he was crazy: a crazed child, crazed on dance. "Still am!" he replied, looking thrilled.

I knew Michael Bennett for seven years, so some people were luckier, because they knew him longer. He was the greatest Broadway director-choreographer of our time, the showbiz heir to Jerome Robbins. (He secretly studied all of Robbins's dances and ballets.) He made people feel that anything, absolutely anything, was possible. "I do not like the words 'You can't,'" he'd say. "They are *not* fun." I never met such an enchanter, in or out of the theater. His favorite expressions were "No problem!" "Go play!" "I'll fix it!" "Have *fun!*" He had his faults, to say the least, but no one could say dullness was one of them.

When Michael bought his mansion in the Hamptons, he called it his "starter home." (David Geffen subsequently bought it.) One day in summer he asked me to lunch there, and when I arrived, there was this *Upstairs, Downstairs* reception line waiting outside, at the end of the long, stately driveway. "This is the chef," he announced solemnly in his new role as Lord of the Manor. "This is the librarian. He will be buying the books later. And this is my spaced-out pedigreed dog." Then he showed off the place a little, hands behind his back, like Prince Philip. "And this is my land, this is my pool, and that is the Atlantic Ocean." But the pool had an amazing amount of pool furniture surrounding it, as if he'd bought out an entire store. "I got it *wholesale,*" he said, looking a bit hurt when I teased him about it.

Well, he was like that. He sent things up, including himself, as if he couldn't quite believe his luck. He was a street kid, born in Buffalo, New York. ("To commit suicide in Buffalo is redundant," as it's put in *A Chorus Line.*) He was born Michael Bennett Di Figlia, the son of a machinist who later became a gambler. He was insecure, highly instinctive, mercurial, egotistical, and generous. When I needed a workplace for a while, he immediately offered a studio in his building at 890 Broadway and, characteristically, didn't charge a cent. He ran the building at a huge loss, maybe a million dollars a year. It was a kind of gift and subsidy from his *Chorus Line* profits to the Broadway and dance communities, who could then rehearse in the best working conditions in New York at peppercorn rents. He built his own workshops and theater there. The theater was to be the home of the American Musical. It was a dream, shattered now.

Michael was the modern Barnum, a child-genius of Broadway. He liked to control events. When he turned forty, there was a huge surprise birthday party for him, but he chose the guests himself. "Well, someone's gotta do it!" he explained, laughing. "I just want to make sure everything goes *well.*" His surprise party turned out to be a children's party for grown-ups. There were hot-dog stands and cotton candy, jelly beans piled in pyramids, and a band playing "Tie a Yellow Ribbon Round the Ole Oak Tree." He loved it. His present was a Porsche wrapped in a bow, like a toy (which was a real surprise—he couldn't drive). There were friends from childhood there, and showbiz moguls overdosing on M&Ms, and more or less everyone he'd worked closely with in the theater. "You see," he said, "they're my family."

He meant it. He was in love with the theater, with its showbiz glitz and excitement and intoxicating possibilities. He felt at home there and safe, creating illusions. "Can I help it if I happen to think the American musical is the greatest thing ever? I mean, I don't know much about *painting*...."

He literally hummed. He was small (five foot seven), electric, and almost always hummed to himself. On the eve of the now legendary gala performance of *A Chorus Line* with 332 *Chorus Line* alumni from a dozen companies—a Bennett production that brought the audience close to delirium—I was going up to his studios when I heard humming along the corridor. It could only have been Michael. "You know something?" he said calmly. "*Chorus Line* is a *good* show." He looked wide-eyed.

He hummed, and he moved. He was rarely still, thinking fast on his feet, pacing the room. It's how he worked. He proceeded with everything rhythmically. He was a dancer! He was essentially nonverbal, feeling out ideas. In turn, he gave out a kind of verbal static, which no stranger found easy to fathom. "Oh, you know what I *mean*," he'd say, despairing of words.

He had to *feel* a scene, and see it, building stage pictures. Cajoling a better song out of a composer, he'd start his own rhythm, and dance, and make up his own song on the spot, usually belting it out at the top of his voice. He'd challenge and push people, deliberately blowing their minds. He always worked in a collaborative group, though he led it. He could be off-the-wall, coming at everything from left field, knocking down conventional barriers. The first time I worked with him, he took a script I'd written and began to reinvent and wreck it—gloriously, I guess. "Let's put page 23 *first!*" "But, Michael—it won't make any sense if we do that." "You *sure?*" he'd insist.

Three years ago, he asked the composer Jimmy Webb and me to write a musical, though neither of us had written one before. He was deliberately going outside the traditional Broadway system. One day, as work progressed, he excitedly said to me, "I got something to show you." He led me to the studio of set designer Robin Wagner, who'd made a scale model of Madison Square Garden. Inside the model were four hundred tiny stick figures. "That's your theater," Michael announced trimuphantly. "And that's your cast!" Four hundred! "You want *more?*" he said when I looked surprised.

Nothing he did was ever small (though eventually our musical was scaled down). He always did battle with the so-called practicalities. He hated the possibility of failure—opening nights terrified him—but he felt compelled to top whatever he had produced before. How could he top *A Chorus Line?* During the opening-night party for the mesmerizing *Dreamgirls,* someone foolishly said to him, "Not as good as *A Chorus Line.*" His face fell, and he quit the party early.

Following *Dreamgirls,* to the dismay of Broadway, he abandoned his raunchy musical *Scandal* after a year of workshops. The show was said to be in trouble—although that wasn't it. (He was a perfectionist, and there was little or nothing he couldn't fix.) He could no longer see the point of producing a musical comedy about sex when people were dying of AIDS. That was the only time I heard him talk seriously for long about anything. Because so many people had died, and were about to die. "And why can't they *do* something?" he said. Several months later, he went to London to direct *Chess.* But he couldn't complete the work. By then he had AIDS himself.

He pretended that he had fallen sick with angina and needed rest. He didn't want to be pitied or, by telling the devastating truth, announce his own death. At the same time, he genuinely believed he could defy AIDS, and beat it.

The day before he withdrew from *Chess,* he asked me to run through our entire musical for him. There were now twenty songs and two and a half hours of material. He was planning ahead, planning on a recovery. His right-hand man and coproducer, the choreographer Bob Avian, attended the run-through with Robin Wagner, and Joseph Papp came along too. Michael looked and seemed okay. "You're *on!*" he said, amused by my stage fright. "Aw, come on! You know you love it really," he'd always add, for who wouldn't want to be in a show?

But about halfway through, the show suddenly went wrong. Jimmy Webb was into a ballad. But the response was out of key: too close to the surface. Michael was in tears, crying silently. The ballad is about a young man who dies young.

Though there would be other meetings and a six-month waiting period, it was over. He couldn't beat it.

No one I know thinks Broadway will ever be quite the same without Michael Bennett. He truly believed, as he had as a kid of five, crazed on dance, that the dancing would never stop.

A few days before he died, he took a call from Robin Wagner, an old friend, who asked him if he could make any sense of his illness. "I'm tap-dancing my way to heaven," he replied.

He died in Tucson, Arizona, July 2, 1987, aged forty-four.

Peter Brook, Barbra Streisand, and Me

Not so long ago, I was at a party and found myself in intense conversation with Barbra Streisand about the meaning of life and the price of fame.

Forgive the name-dropping. But as we talked, Babs asked me about the director Peter Brook and his half-crazed journey through the Sahara Desert and Central West Africa. She was hoping to see a Brook production at the Brooklyn Academy of Music—so what did it all mean?

I replied that everything Brook has done in the last decade links to that incredible African journey a group of us took in the early seventies. In a sense, you can see Africa in Brook's production of *The Cherry Orchard* and in his nine-hour Indian epic, *The Mahabharata.*

"Africa in India? Africa in Russia?" said Streisand. "What's this?"

Though no New York critic has made the connection, when the African journey began in the Sahara Desert, there were two supreme symbols in the work. One was a carpet, which Brook's troupe would ritualistically roll out and perform on for anyone who cared to watch; the other was desert sand, on which the troupe would sometimes form a human ring to create another playing area for their rough improvisations. *The Cherry Orchard* takes place without sets, on carpets. *The Mahabharata* doesn't have sets, either; it is played on carpets and sand.

But Ms. Streisand's close friend at the time, Don Johnson of *Miami Vice*, didn't know *that.* The two symbols link the two productions, so that when—as happened—New York critics respond with raves for the Chekhov but don't like *The Mahabharata*, something is wrong. And I think what's wrong is the critics.

Because, in the crucial essentials, the two productions are the same. I'll risk my neck and go further: every production Brook has done since Africa has been the same production.

Brook, perceived as *the* intellectual figure of theater, is in practice the reverse. He's about accessibility. He wants to make theater, whatever the complexity of the material, accessible to the widest human response without watering anything down. That's what is great about Brook: he trusts audiences.

Where is the theater that addresses itself head-on to the question of its virtual life or death: how to create a genuine alternative to films and television? If it can't do this, why go to the theater? How, in other words, to present theater that will shake its audience out of the everyday passivity that comes from watching films and TV (where, as it were, everything is done for us) into a longed-for, active, imaginative *sharing?* Shakespeare, for one, had the answer:

> *Think, when we talk of horses, that you see them.*
> *Printing their proud hoofs i' th' receiving earth.*
> *For 'tis your thoughts that now must deck our kings,*
> *Carry them here and there; jumping o'er times;*
> *Turning th' accomplishment of many years*
> *Into an hourglass.*

It is the most difficult thing: maximum expression using minimum means. If this magic is successful, the audience can imagine what it actually doesn't see. So those critics who appreciated, or dismissed, Brook's *Mahabharata* as a kind of special-effects Cecil B. DeMille epic were—I guarantee— seeing what wasn't there. Because, as with the Chekhov production, the wonder is that Brook compels us to imagine.

So with Brook, within the Shakespearean tradition (and a different one, the Peking Opera), using almost nothing, you can conjure up a river, an army, a newborn child, or an hourglass.

In *The Mahabharata,* one wheel is a chariot. A silk scarf is a newborn child. A man is an army. In *The Cherry Orchard,* a single chair is a sitting room. A carpet is a forest. A bare stage is earth and sky.

Brook's form of theater is said to be a director's theater. But it isn't. It is an actor's theater, for the actor alone conjures up the magic. But it is also an audience's theater. For the one holds up the silk scarf, and the other imagines the newborn child.

That was one of the things the African journey was about. If one ignores grand theories concerning the collective unconscious of mankind, the experiment was about creating a form of theater from zero. Brook was deliberately throwing away everything he knew, and so were the actors, in order to discover another way of sharing theater.

"How did the Africans react?" Streisand asked.

They were hysterical with laughter half the time. They were good-humored, though. Imagine! A world-famous director and a group of international actors turn up in the Sahara Desert and then the Nigerian bush to perform something they haven't thought of yet. They were always welcomed. But actors and audience couldn't speak the same language.

"What's the bottom line here?" said Streisand, growing a little testy.

The bottom line, I explained, is that I may not have made it on Broadway yet, but I'm very big in the Sahara Desert. I wrote a little play for the troupe to perform there. There was only one catch: it couldn't have any dialogue. "How do you write a play without dialogue?" I asked Brook. And he looked at me and replied, "What is a play?"

As my deadline approached and panic set in, I asked one of the actors what a play is. "A play," he replied in the tones of an oracle, "is anything with me in it." I made sure he had a star part. My play was called *The Shoe Show,* a kind of nonverbal version of *Cinderella.* A pair of shoes—boots belonging to an actor—are placed in the center of a circle. They're magic shoes, capable of transforming kings into slaves, the old into the young, or a one-legged man into a two-legged man.

It was a one-act light comedy with significant undertones. Given time only to glance at my scenario, Brook's actors, living dangerously, began improvising around the story. So the shoes were placed in the desert sand.

The actors, sitting in a circle, stare at the shoes. Who will enter and begin to play? They keep staring. It turns out the actors aren't just waiting for inspiration. They are waiting for an audience.

As a rule, audiences in deserts aren't too easy to come by, deserts tending to be empty. But before long, strangers appear: veiled women with laughing children and exotic men, purple men, on camels. The composer with the group, Elizabeth Swados (then an unknown), strikes a drum. An actor leaps up! He's pointing furiously to the shoes. He's after *attention*. "*Shoes!*" he's screaming, though it is more a sound he makes. "*Shoooooooooooes!*" And more and more strangers gather round to see such fun.

I am here to say that *The Shoe Show* was a hit. It opened in the Sahara and closed in the bush. That's the point. The Tuaregs loved it, but the Nigerians in the villages we came to practically hissed it out of town. Why?

It was the excitement of those first performances that carried Brook's troupe through. But as the weeks went by, it became harder and harder to communicate. Envy those who can break with their past; they will be fearless.

Assuming it possible to begin again from zero, we were blocked. Deadening habits, Western conventions, fear of the unknown, presumed responses—all that and more blocked us. So in the midst of the apparent lunacies of Brook's African journey, lessons were learned and seeds were planted in us, and in Brook.

For example, the mistake with the shoes was to presume, according to Western theater convention, that they could be magic. They do strange things to people, so they must be *magic* shoes! But if you play to an audience that doesn't share the fairy-tale convention—to an audience that may never have seen theater as we understand it—you can't rely on convention. You'd better smash through it, begin again, create a shared convention from zero, and make even a pair of shoes magic in their own right—as a child might.

That's why theater for Brook is the actor who creates magic while showing the audience he has nothing up his sleeve. It is outwardly naive: an artless art. So the actor in Africa faced a supreme test. The Hausa language has no word for theater. Through translators, all Brook could establish was that the troupe would like to "perform" something. An actor enters, playing an old man. Perhaps he stoops and coughs a little, playing old. But the audience looks nonplussed, even concerned.

The audience in the African village didn't see an actor playing an old man. They were receiving a different message. A young actor stoops: there might be something wrong with his back. He coughs: perhaps he's ill. But the African spectator, however sophisticated, doesn't necessarily see an old man. In a sense, he sees a total stranger who isn't pretending to be an old man well enough. Because the actor is relying on his own habits and easy conventions.

So he must begin again. He must stop "acting." And if he can find something fresh and extraordinary within him, he will convince any audience in the world of something very rare: a universal emotional truth. And then theater can become irresistible—a completely truthful, natural event.

That's Brook's achievement, I think.

"Still," said Barbra Streisand, "you could have saved yourselves a lot of problems in Africa if you'd flown out an *old* actor!"

And, of course, we both laughed. She was right. But then, what would Brook have learned? And would an Indian epic and a Russian masterpiece in Brooklyn, New York, have been quite the same?

Angels in America
Parts 1 and 2

PART 1

There can be no doubt that Tony Kushner's *Angels in America* is as great a play as you have heard. Part 1, entitled *Millennium Approaches*, which has just opened at the Walter Kerr, is triumphant—the finest drama of our time, speaking to us of a murderous era as no other play within memory

Its scope and daring, fully realized in George C. Wolfe's superb production, send us reeling from the theater, convinced we must have witnessed some kind of miracle. As with all great stories, it evokes the three most beautiful words in any language: What happens next?

At the end of three and a half hours—and thirty mesmerizing scenes—I'm certain I was far from alone in thinking, "Tell us what happens next! Bring on part 2!" The angel-messenger has arrived, crashing through space and closing part 1. That's some end, some fantastic beginning.

Heralding what? Perhaps hope, or salvation, in this contemporary epic cradled in sorrow. Yet the story within Mr. Kushner's vast apocalyptic canvas is intimate (and often wildly funny). It is ultimately mind-bending. There is one gay couple: a young Jewish self-loathing liberal and courthouse word processor who deserts his AIDS-stricken WASP lover. There is a married Mormon couple: a Republican lawyer and closet homosexual, working in the same courthouse, who deserts his unloved, hallucinating wife. And there's Roy Cohn, Saint of the Right or Antichrist. From that small, unexpected base, Mr. Kushner weaves his glorious tapestry of an entire 1980s era and the collapse of a moral universe.

His specific message is a call to arms to the homosexual community in the AIDS era to march out of the ghettoized closet, as the rabbi in the opening scene reminds us of the heroic journey of persecuted nineteenth-century Jews from the ghettos and shtetls of Europe to the promised land of America. The spectral embodiment of Roy Cohn, mythical witch-hunter and closet homosexual dying of AIDS, offers pragmatic guidance to his prodigal son, the repressed Mormon lawyer. "Was it legal?" he says of his fixing "that timid Yid nebbish on the bench" during the Rosenberg trial. "Fuck legal. Am I a nice man? Fuck nice. You want to be nice or you want to be *effective?*"

Angels in America is subtitled "A Gay Fantasia on National Themes," though I didn't quite see it that way. It is memorably about heartlessness and responsibility during the Reagan years and beyond. Its supreme achievement is its portrait of America Lost, perhaps to be regained. In its richness and pain—"Children of the new morning, criminal minds. Selfish and greedy and loveless and blind. Reagan's children"—I saw *Millennium Approaches* more as a modern morality play, with a debt to the guilt, justice, and iconography of the Old Testament rather than the New. It is, among other things, about good and evil, the disintegration of tolerance and cities and dreams. It asks: Where is God? And yearns for an answer, a prophet, a messiah, or salvation. It is, in its searing essentials, about love.

Mr. Kushner is too witty to be preachy. To the contrary, this near-feverish outpouring of visions and ideas is rooted in an episodic economy of means and a wonderful theatricality. For some years, I have been searching in vain for the new American drama of imaginative ideas, a form of magic realism transcending the bourgeois or the naturalism of movies. *Angels in America* is that landmark drama. It is, on the one hand, painfully concrete; on the other hand, it delights in the theater of magical images. The playwright is good-humored: "*Very* Steven Spielberg," says the dying Prior Walter, an esthete, as the world splits open before his eyes (and ours).

This writer of plays is therefore justifiably playful. The ambitious narrative sweep takes us seamlessly from Manhattan to Antarctica. You cannot second-guess it for a moment. At the same time, the sheer pleasure Mr. Kushner takes in theater itself empowers him to establish his own conventions and take us anywhere he wishes. It seems reasonable and irresistible when, for example, the thirteenth-and seventeenth-century British relatives of Prior Walter visit his deathbed for a chat. Those two cheerful angel's heralds, ghostly survivors of historic plagues, are a theatrical riot. So the ghost of Ethel Rosenberg appears to the dying Roy Cohn to say, "The shit's really hit the fan, huh, Roy?" Actors double in virtuoso walk-on parts; actresses play male roles (not always, let it be said, with equal success). But the delight of a true ensemble is created and with it another dimension, a timeless troupe of traveling players.

I could have sworn that there were fifteen or so actors in the cast. In fact, there are eight. At least four of the performances scale the heights. The reptilian bravura of Ron Liebman as Roy Cohn gets as near to going over the top as all great bravura performances must. Is this the role of his career? It would seem brilliantly so (though watch for his brief reincarnation during the action as a campy Tartuffe). Stephen Spinella's Prior is so transcendentally moving, it is impossible to imagine anyone else playing the role or equaling his mysterious saintly aura. Joe Mantello as Louis, lover of Prior and self-loathing posturing intellectual in search of easy absolution, is exactly right. Marcia Gay Harden as Harper, unloved Mormon in search of escape and a fantasy New World, was first cautious, I felt, in capturing the lyrical (her comic flair is beyond question), but she is a wonderful actress. David Marshall Grant, as her Mormon husband in tortured rectitude—again, terrific. So, too, the immensely gifted Jeffrey Wright as Belize, nurse, ex–drag queen, and conscience, a role that could easily spill over into high camp, but doesn't.

That we have an ensemble as fine as this, and a production as great as this, is due to director George Wolfe and the spare, emblematic poetry of his design team (Robin Wagner, Jules Fisher, and Toni-Leslie James). In one astonishing scene, Mr. Wolfe frees the stage for a quartet of characters, the gay couple and the Mormon couple. They are separate, emotionally explosive scenes happening simultaneously, like a split movie screen. They are about the pain and death of love; both scenes, both worlds, become spellbindingly one. At times, it is just incredible what we see at work and at play here.

I have run out of space and superlatives. Part 1 of Tony Kushner's *Angels in America* has arrived! Bring on part 2! *Save us!*

Part 2

In the history of blind dates, we haven't looked forward to anything with quite so much nervous anticipation as part 2 of Tony Kushner's *Angels in America*.

But the angel that crashed through the ceiling at the close of part 1 turns out not to be the fantasy-redeemer of our dreams. Mr. Kushner's fabulous three-and-a-half-hour *Perestroika* is no sweet fable. It is more uncompromisingly realistic than that, more ambitious than part 1, denser, furious (and therefore funnier), sprawling, flawed, more challenging, a feverishly imaginative achievement. In its thrilling sweep and ambition and chaos, *Angels in America* remains the landmark drama of our time.

"Change! Change!" cries the old Bolshevik, blind prophet of the prologue at the dawn of the new age of perestroika, of the exploding of history and the death of all old orders, Reaganism included. Give the old Bolshevik warrior a new theory and system, and he'll be there at the barricades! Apocalypse or paradise? Doom or change in the AIDS era? Mr. Kushner's answer is that there is no perfect answer—no system, no book of divine revelation, no God, no savior-angels. In the turmoil, there is Truth, if you will, and the hope that humanity can change, confronting the wreckage and lies of our American lives. "Stop!" the angel seems to be saying on orders from above. "Stop, and look around you."

Yet the more painful the message, the funnier Mr. Kushner becomes. Has there ever been a more mesmerizingly comic and ultimately pathetic figure than Ron Leibman's prince of darkness, Roy Cohn? Now dying of AIDS in a Manhattan hospital, cared for by the ex–drag queen Belize (Jeffrey Wright, terrific again), dosed with AZT, symbol of illicit power and money, Mr. Leibman's monumental monster creation can even touch on our sympathy. *"Hold!"* he screams to approaching death, as if pushing the hold button on his third arm, which is his phone—his wire to the outside world, as his deathbed tangle of tubes is his lifeline.

John and that leftish intellectual weasel, Louis (Joe Mantello), are the only characters in part 2 who do not grow and change. We cannot say, then, that Mr. Kushner is "unfair" to both the Left and the Right. But for me, the whining, overtalkative wimp Louis is a case of a dramatic character who has outstayed his welcome. Only once does he speak with blazing conviction. Breaking with his new lover, the Republican Mormon lawyer Joe (David Marshall Grant), he pleads to passionate effect that gays are not a legal technicality but equal citizens. (And for God's sake, *think* and do the right thing.)

How glad we are when Joe's wife and Valium fantasist, Harper, finally leaves him in the dust, hopefully to get her ill-fated life in shape. Marcia Gay Harden has grown wonderfully as Harper, and gives another superb per-formance—as does Kathleen Chalfant, playing, among other roles, the Mor-mon Hannah Pitt, a sensible, generous mother, it turns out, and grace note of the play. The extraordinary Stephen Spinella could not be finer as the dying Prior. He's wickedly comic. "The stiffening of your penis is of no con-sequence," the angel tells Prior, who's at the point of orgasmic ecstasy. "Well, maybe not to *you*," he replies. At the same time, Mr. Spinella brings to his character a heroic dimension, taking the ravaged Prior from terrible fear, and even cowardice, to graceful understanding and courage in the time he has left on earth.

That's a kind of miracle! And, let it be shouted from the rooftops, this is a tremendous production. In its fluent magic realism, George Wolfe and his team have created visions for us. Set designer Robin Wagner and light-ing designer Jules Fisher have achieved their very finest work. The vast, dizzying canvas moves effortlessly from epic fantasy to reality—from mad dioramas at the Mormons' Visitors Center to Roy Cohn ripping his IV from his body in a shattering nightmare image of blood and plague to the ultimate vision of heaven in chaos as a celestial San Francisco at the barri-cades.

Yet I feel in my gut that all concerned would have still killed for three or four weeks more work on part 2. In the heat of Broadway deadlines and Mr. Kushner's urgent last-minute rewrites, there is a looseness to some of the writing within the colliding scenes. The muscularity of the drama dips, for example, in the reunion of Harper and her gay husband; the moving and for-giving kaddish for Roy Cohn, spoken with the help of the ghost of Ethel Rosenberg, is undercut by a graceless "Sonovabitch!" and Louis's amazement at being in bed with a gay Republican would be an easy laugh in underground theater. There can be too many jokes, though not necessarily in the sense of the emperor's advice to Mozart, "Too many notes."

I mean the missing note of the authentically spiritual. The angel—jokey novice—speaking in tongues, is as much an angel of death, offering the potential prophet Prior death. (Die to be reborn as prophet or savior.) In the most moving speech in the play, the dying Prior rejects prophetdom and chooses life: "I want more life." And the heaven he witnesses shows the gods in disarray, and God heartlessly absent. I wish only that Mr. Kushner had brought the leading player onstage. Bring God on! For had there been a genuine debate between them, Prior's choice of life on earth would have been more astonishing, the dice would not have been loaded, and this fantastic drama would have looked into the vision of light.

It is, if you will, the legitimacy of the spiritual that I feel is missing. And God knows how Mr. Kushner might have achieved *that*. But when in the quiet, peaceful, almost wistful end, we are left with the near-blind Prior and his friends by the stone angel of Bethesda Fountain in Central Park, it is his courageous spirit that speaks of longed-for change. In this messy, scintillating, turbulent drama of loss and betrayal, of an entire era of American life and death, his spirit asks for change in all of us, for understanding, commitment, and love. In its entirety, *Angels in America* has been an unforgettable journey.

Janet McTeer-
Up-the-Stage

The great actor and the poor actor share this in common: they both chew the scenery. But the great actor does it gloriously and the poor actor poorly, and Janet McTeer does it very badly indeed.

I'm astonished by her Nora in Henrik Ibsen's *Doll's House* at the Belasco Theater, but for the wrong reasons. She not only chews the scenery, she beats up the furniture. It's said by her admirers on both sides of the Atlantic that you cannot take your eyes off her. But that could also be said by her detractors. She is, if you will, rivetingly over the top.

The famously starched, repressed heroine of *A Doll's House*—a Victorian woman in a patronizing man's world—is played by Ms. McTeer as a wired, modern neurotic who seems to be on the showy edge of a nervous breakdown. The wish to humanize Ibsen's heroine and feminist prototype is understandable. But the star actress proceeds at a manic coquettish frenzy in a performance of extraordinary vanity. There's no nuance in her. For two of the three acts, there's a strident, awfully blatant theatricality.

She's a busy, externalized actress. She mugs, she fidgets, she flutters, she squeals, grimaces, giggles, chirps, and upstages. Described by Torvald as "a little squirrel," Ms. McTeer therefore chirps in a cute approximation of one, with little squirrel hand movements to match. At other times, she flaps her wrists, or tosses her hair constantly like an aerobics chick, or—for some reason—hits herself in histrionic thigh-slapping. She leaves no gesture unturned.

She uses a near baby voice, or tries out what seem to be deliberately silly voices, in order, I assume, to make Nora jokily appealing and "child-like." But there's a difference between naïveté and twittering. For two acts, it seems, Ms. McTeer punctuates every other line with irritating nervous giggles. One wants to clonk her over the head, and shout: "Stop it! Stop it, dear!"

Yet her Nora has received many awards and raves, and she has been compared in London to the young Vanessa Redgrave. They are both *tall*. Ms. McTeer, who isn't petite, is in fact so tall that when she embraces Torvald, she performs the equivalent of the Bunny Dip. There's no period atmosphere in her Nora. The act 3 confrontation with the broken Torvald—and the heroine's fabled emancipation—is thankfully unclut-tered, but her vulnerability is artificial. Ms. McTeer's voice of protest is too strong. She is a Nora who would eat Torvald for breakfast, and does.

Anthony Page's production, which comes to Broadway via acclaim in the West End, is right to see *A Doll's House* as the drama of a wrecked mar-riage rather than a manifesto of women's rights. It's a great play, not a good one. That is, there are more creaky plot devices and coincidences than the dropped handkerchief in *Othello*. Yet in the problem play's ultimate show-down, Ibsen achieves greatness. He anticipates feminism; without reading Freud, he anticipated modern psychology.

Nora isn't a blueprint for women's liberation, however (and Ms. McTeer, obviously, doesn't play her that way). But the claims that this is a new approach to *A Doll's House* are exaggerated. Almost fifty years ago, Eric Bentley wrote that in its theme of the tyranny of one human being over another, "the play would be just as valid were Torvald the wife and Nora the husband." Fifteen years ago, in a celebrated Adrian Noble pro-duction of *A Doll's House* for the Royal Shakespeare Company, the play wasn't seen narrowly as a pioneering feminist tract but as a tragedy of pub-lic and private role-playing.

Nora is the doll in the house: the admired object of desire. But in his stuffy way, Torvald—husband, lord, and master—is a "doll" too: an empty vessel, without humanity or nobility. The sexual heat between Nora and Torvald in the production is overplayed. If Nora is sexually liberated—as opposed to a cautious tease—what's her problem? Only in her tarantella dance is Nora's latent sexuality revealed. In the wild, ecstatic freedom of the dance of life and death, she discovers her true self. She is "uncorseted," free and momentarily liberated. But even there, Ms. McTeer gets it melo-dramatically wrong. Her tarantella is merely angry, ending in violent collapse.

There are other surprising lapses in this admired production: Deirdre Clancy's dull, literal set doesn't suggest Norway, or a life beyond its thin walls; Ms. McTeer's wig is a joke; Torvald's masked ball costume bears a racy resemblance to Michael Flatley's low-cut bolero look in *Lord of the Dance*. The rest of the cast are fine: John Carlisle's quiet and ironic Dr. Rank suavely embracing death in a self-made shroud; Jan Maxwell's dignified widow Kristine yearning to escape loneliness through marriage; the blackmailing Krogstad who, played by the excellent Peter Gowen, we half-gladly see given a second chance in life.

Owen Teale's Torvald is first-rate, too, though Mr. Teale shouts a bit. So would you if you were playing opposite Janet McTeer-Up-the-Stage. This is the only production you are likely to see of *A Doll's House* where you end up on Torvald's side.

Hurry Up Please It's Time

December is the gift-wrapped month, and my mind races and reels a bit. Fiona Shaw's performance of T. S. Eliot's poem *The Waste Land* at the ghostly, derelict Liberty Theater on West Forty-second Street is a spellbinding gift. Directed by Deborah Warner, this is, quite simply, an unreal achievement by the greatest actress you could see either side of the Atlantic.

Let us take no prisoners. I have not seen Eleanora Duse on the boards, but Ms. Shaw is surely up there with the greats. Making her New York debut at long last, she was born in Ireland, and where would the English theater be without the Irish? She injects Celtic blood into Eliot's dry bones and achieves the miraculous with the dense, difficult, haunting poem of terrible despair. In just thirty-seven minutes, she makes the seminal 1922 work—Eliot's "heap of broken images," apocalyptic vision, or crackup mixing memory and desire—seem newly made.

That *The Waste Land* should prove so theatrical and emotionally complex is surprising. Eliot's own recorded reading was famously flat and bland, consciously avoiding any imposed emotion or interpretation. Either that, or he wisely avoided acting, knowing he couldn't act. The poem itself is the anvil of modernism—as its editor, Ezra Pound, remarked, "About enough, Eliot's poem, to make us all shut up shop." But its daunting intellectual rigor can overwhelm if you let it.

The mighty uncompromising poem that will "show you fear in a handful of dust" refers to some thirty-five other writers (including Shakespeare, Ovid, and Homer), spans centuries of cultures like a dizzy collective unconscious, and mixes fragments of six foreign languages, including Sanskrit, into the Babel of poetry glowing in words and savage images.

I think we are in rats' alley
Where the dead men lost their bones.

Thank goodness I first read *The Waste Land* when I was at my academic height, age sixteen. Happy days! Why is it the classics are dutifully and fatally studied in the schoolroom, where we least appreciate them? But there I lusted after Tess (of the D'Urbervilles) and felt sick when opening an exam paper to read "Malvolio and English Puritanism—discuss in no more than 500 words," and heard Eliot's "Bleistein with a Cigar" read before the obedient blushing class by a well-meaning teacher nicknamed Goofy. "Well, boys," Goofy said, boldly encouraging discussion when the poem was done. "Would you say it's anti-Semitic?" And to a man and boy, every Jew in the class, including me, replied a resolute "No, sir!" so as to disguise the hurt and embarrassment.

In our house, T. S. Eliot was banned like Volkswagens. It was much later that I came to see how he could be both a great poet and a flawed human being. I fancy he might have recoiled from Ms. Shaw's raw, jagged performance of *The Waste Land*. She comes too close to plucking out the torment in souls.

Burning burning burning burning
O Lord Thou pluckest me out
O Lord Thou pluckest burning
Burning

This is no sterile academic reading, then. The great actress and her longtime collaborator, Deborah Warner, are the most brilliant theater partnership in England; mundane is not in their vocabulary. (Ms. Warner's recent, revolutionary direction of Shakespeare's *Richard II* had Ms. Shaw in the title role, neither man nor woman, more a boy, asexual as a nun.) In the shadowy wasteland of the Liberty Theater, a ruin filled with ghosts, she enters the bare, dimly lit stage as a ghost. We first hear footsteps in the dark auditorium, walking quite purposefully, it seems, toward the stage. "April is the cruelest month," she begins, as if present for a nice little chat over a cup of tea.

> *He who was living is now dead*
> *We who were living are now dying*
> *With a little patience...*

Samuel Beckett could have written those lines (and did, in his way). The emotional range of Ms. Shaw takes one's breath away. She inhabits Eliot's entire imploding universe in fury, yearning, madness, and quiet lament. Stillness is among her gifts. Her intelligent, angular looks have been often described as Cubist (school of *Les Demoiselles d'Avignon,* obviously). She seems to attack a role perilously on the wing. Yet there isn't a note she cannot hit, including comedy—her Madame Sosostris, famous clairvoyant with a bad cold in der dose; toothless Lil, Eliot's pub habituée, rabbiting on—"What you get married for if you don't want children?"— as closing time is called like death, and the endlessly chatty customers bid their last desperate good nights.

> *Unreal City,*
> *Under the brown fog of a winter dawn*

Ms. Shaw is incredible and "unreal," as I say. Imagine! The limited run of *The Waste Land* has now been extended by popular demand. For a poem! But within those thirty-seven minutes is the beginning and end of everything.

Shanti, which Eliot defined as "The Peace which passeth all understanding," is the last word, repeated three times, that we hear. Ms. Shaw's passion is spent then, and we are left in solitude. But there's an irony in the performance of the poem of such pain: in the ruins, in the wasteland where "I have heard the key / Turn in the door once and turn once only," there lives a spirit that is utterly alive.

The Great Gambon

Michael Gambon, the greatest unknown actor in America, makes his long overdue Broadway debut this month in David Hare's *Skylight*, and one's pulse quickens at the prospect. Anyone who knows the work of this "gentle actor of catastrophic power," as Peter Hall describes him, will think: At last!

Mr. Gambon's anonymity won't continue much longer, though he shies away from all publicity. Here are two or three things I know about this mystery man:

He is the actor most admired by his fellow English actors. Ralph Richardson nicknamed him "The Great Gambon"—a generous tribute giving the impression, possibly deliberate, that the Great Gambon could also be a flamboyant circus performer shot from a cannon.

In a sense, he is. He came from nowhere, bursting into the English theater within the classical tradition of Olivier. Now fifty-five, Mr. Gambon made his breakthrough at the National Theatre in 1980 with a legendary performance as Brecht's Galileo. In a tribute unprecedented in the history of the National, the entire company gathered spontaneously in the courtyard outside his dressing room that memorable evening to give him an ovation.

Unlike many of his contemporaries, his way into theater wasn't through drama school, or Oxford and Cambridge. He's virtually self-taught, not intending to become an actor when young. He left school at fourteen and worked as an apprentice engineer for seven years at Vickers Armstrong. As an actor, he's as precise as an engineer, or a meticulous engraver. He collects antique guns, not to fire but to lovingly restore. He owns about five hundred of them (vintages 1660 to 1820), enjoying their decorative inlays and superb English craftsmanship. His interests are unusual: he likes simulated flying. He climbs into an earthbound cockpit and flies.

He's working class, the son of a factory worker. He has Irish Blood in him. He was born in Dublin, but raised in London from an early age. In 1963 he auditioned for Olivier, hoping to start work at the National as a spear carrier. The audition has passed down into theater folklore, and the story is all the better because what happened is true. He decided to play Richard III, blissfully unaware that Olivier had already made the role his own. He swears to me that he didn't even know Olivier had played the part. One can almost believe him; at the time, he preferred James Dean movies to Shakespeare, and remains unschooled in classic texts, or so he likes to make out. Olivier was incredulous at his choice.

"Which part?" he asked.

"Richard III," young Gambon replied.

"But which part?" Olivier insisted.

"Richard III," he replied again.

"The *main* part?"

"Yes, sir."

And Olivier looked at him and said, "You've got a fucking cheek."

Then, scarcely two lines into his ambitious audition as evil King Richard, he had a hunch, swung round a column—the better to impress Olivier—and caught his thumb on a nail. He carried on nobly despite the blood. "Nurse!" cried Olivier. "A nurse!" According to Mr. Gambon, a good storyteller, his thumb was then bandaged by a nurse or Olivier or both. Thus, his thumb upright and bandaged, he began the Richard III audition again until Olivier said, "Oh, go home."

His cheek paid off, though, and he got his break. His first appearance at the National was as a sentry at Elsinore alongside Peter O'Toole's Hamlet.

Today, Michael Gambon's versatility is without equal. He is—unusually—both a supreme classical and modern actor. Among his generation, Ian McKellen, for example, is more at home in leading classical roles than contemporary parts. Anthony Hopkins's stage career has been lost to movies. Albert Finney (a friend of Mr. Gambon's) pulled back from the brink of the classical theater pinnacles with his Hamlet and Tamburlaine for the National.

When I first saw him act in 1970s London, Mr. Gambon was playing Lear at a Royal Shakespeare Company matinee and that same night was Antony opposite Helen Mirren's Cleopatra. His devotion to the stage is clear, though he's more a great character actor in meaty roles than a conventional leading man. He has never played Hamlet or Romeo. He shines in such monumental challenges as Othello, his recent Volpone, his Galileo, Lear, Antony. In contrast, he has always been known as a born farceur, principally in the comedies of Alan Ayckbourn. He is one of Harold Pinter's favorite actors. And his Eddie Carbone, the longshoreman of Arthur Miller's *View from the Bridge*, was seen as a revelation, as if the British actor had possessed the soul of Eddie, the Italian American.

He's a physically big man with large, elegant hands who's light on his feet, looking jaunty. His shrewd, doleful eyes are hooded, suggesting weariness. He's intensely private, shy, and un-actorish. He has been married for many years to a mathematician. He smokes—tut-tut!—claiming that smoking helps his vocal range. An instinctive, unpretentious actor, he downplays all grand theories of acting ("shouting in the evening," as he says). He is Everyman, as the eccentric Ralph Richardson was often described. He recently described Richardson admiringly to the *Times* of London as "precise and delicate, but at the same time a powerful man who could kill someone." He might have been describing himself.

Frank Rich, then chief drama critic of the *New York Times*, wrote about him, "If Marlon Brando had continued to work in the theater, he might have developed into an American Michael Gambon." Which is quite a compliment. But the American comparison is really with Al Pacino or Dustin Hoffman, character actors who became movie stars almost by accident. Mr. Gambon's Hollywood outings have been in bummers such as *Toys*. He became a household name in England through his bedridden fantasist in Dennis Potter's tremendous 1986 television series, *The Singing Detective*. He has had no luck with movies. It's our good fortune—I don't know about his—that he hasn't been lost to Hollywood. Pacino and Hoffman are stage actors manqué, rarely putting themselves to the fire.

But Mr. Gambon is a dangerous man of the theater, taking dangerous risks.

In David Hare's *Skylight* he plays Tom, a wealthy entrepreneur desperately needing to be reconciled to his ex-lover, Kyra (Lia Williams), who's twenty years younger than he. The blustering, successful businessman and the inner-city teacher; the capitalist pragmatist versus the socialist idealist; the two opposites and the hero's fight to reignite their love. If the piece has a weakness, it is that Mr. Gambon is so persuasively humane and appealing that he ends up winning our sympathy and the arguments hands down.

"Of course, it's only this country, only here in this country, it's thought to be a crime to get on," Tom, the flamboyant success story, protests, nailing the English disease. "Anything rather than achieve!"

Kyra, his ex-lover, now living and working in a slum by choice, indignantly replies: "I'm tired of these sophistries. I'm tired of these right-wing fuckers…. Do you know what social workers do? Every day? They try and clear out society's drains. They clear out the rubbish. They do what no one else is doing, and what no one else is willing to do. And for that, oh Christ, *do we thank them?*"

"All right, very well," says the chastised Tom, a likeable shit in the social conscience department. And here Mr. Gambon looks his most profoundly sincere, even a little hurt. "I do see what you're saying."

He is so masterful that he can make even self-pitying arrogance sympathetic. But his deep disguised agony as Tom makes the performance memorable. The character he plays sweeps everything into his powerful orbit, and so does the Great Gambon. He enters sniffing around the stage and Kyra's apartment to claim the territory—her territory! The big man is giving a big performance, standing at first with his feet apart as if testing the ground like a fighter poised to deliver a knockout.

He delivers one. His performance is cooking in every detail, including his moments of playful theatricality. Just to watch him act embarrassed while grating a slice of cheese—*inferior* cheese—is an unexpected comic bonus, like his lighthearted pirouette in act 2 after Tom gets laid.

He plays it riskily, as is his way. But of all the weapons in his arsenal, his gift of conveying a sense of loss and need beneath the jaunty surface is painfully real. In one wrenching moment, he briefly lets Tom's mask slip, breaking down at the guilty memory of his dying wife. The theater was brought to complete silence. He flickers breezily back to his old self with a joke, a diversion, the diverting, traditionally English game of appearances. But by the play's end, Mr. Gambon's Tom has turned gray, bent in defeat and sorrow.

When I saw *Skylight* in London, a ticket lady was standing at the back of the house with a security guard, and I caught their conversation at the end of the play. "He makes it look so easy," the man was saying admiringly. "He's a bloody good actor, that's why," said the lady.

Mr. Brantley's Torsos

I shall now address Ben Brantley, the chief drama critic of the *New York Times*, personally. This would be a good moment for the rest of my devoted readers to put on the kettle and make a nice cuppa tea. We won't be long.

Dear Ben,

I see you enjoyed *My Night with Reg*, Kevin Elyot's British comedy about six homosexuals living in London. Perhaps it's as good as you say, though the play wasn't for me. I found it all very familiar indeed, a *Boys in the Band* for the less defensive nineties, with the usual gay stereotypes and melodramas of second-rate plays. But I do not think, if I may say so, that the size of Maxwell Caulfield's penis is a decisive factor.

"Well," you begin your June 13 review, a little breathlessly, "at least one man on the threshold of middle age has nothing to worry about when he puts on a swimsuit this summer."

We're very relieved to hear it. But must we? Then you go on to point out that the "impeccably proportioned torso" of the naked Mr. Caulfield, the actor you admired when he played the naked Adonis on the beach in Louise Page's *Salonika* in 1985, is "once again on unabashed display (every inch of him) in *My Night with Reg*."

And now you've gone too far even for me. I regret that I'm unfamiliar with Mr. Caulfield's memorable performance as the naked Adonis in *Salonika*. I have seen him in *Grease* 2 and *An Inspector Calls*.

He was good, though fully dressed. Ben, take my advice, old cockie: You don't want to be known as the critic who writes his reviews with a tape measure. Stop it immediately. Let the impeccably proportioned torso that's once again on unabashed display in *My Night with Reg* (every inch, ho, ho) speak for itself.

It isn't cool to drool. We are more interested in the acting of the good Mr. Caulfield, who I hear has nothing to worry about when he puts on a swimsuit this summer. But there's more: "The flesh of Mr. Caulfield, at least," you continue, "still provides no evidence of a paunch or, despite a catty comment directed at his character, a drooping posterior."

We're very relieved to hear that, too. But I gotta get on with my own review now, Ben. Enjoy the summer.

As I was saying, *My Night with Reg*, which Jack Hofsiss has directed for the New Group at the Intar Theater off Broadway, is an old-fashioned drawing-room comedy in the shadow of AIDS. That it won the 1994 Olivier Award for best comedy proves only that London's gay plays have yet to catch up even with the work of Terrence McNally.

My Night with Reg portrays homosexual men glibly as lonely hearts or bitchy queens, hunks and predators; they are fickle, valiant, promiscuous, or marginally loving. We've seen these facile stage types before: the shy, good-hearted party host, Guy, sometimes known as Gertie, who's lonely and single (and secretly in love with John, who has an impeccably proportioned torso). There's the stud John, aging a bit now, unexpectedly looking for true love; there's the young working-class beefcake, Eric, object of desire; Mr. and Mrs. Bicker, faithful Bernie—poor soul—and unfaithful Benny; and Daniel, the queeny art dealer with a heart of mush and steel who's living with Reg.

Reg never appears, I'm glad to say. The drama's gimmick is that everyone except lonely Guy has had his night with Reg, and the last person to know is the devoted Daniel. The three-scene comedy proceeds schematically to inevitable tears and trauma. The nude scene between Mr. Caulfield as John and Sam Trammell as Eric is one of the more gratuitous in the genre that I've seen in a while. The naked Mr. Trammell is obliged to pose like some nymph in a woodland-fantasy still life, Mr. Caufield is more *au naturel* when naked, or when reclining in a curiously revealing robe. Mr. Caulfield and company are as good as we would expect, with or without paunches or drooping posteriors.

The Ralph Fiennes
Hamlet

Ralph Fiennes's Hamlet is a modern Hamlet for rotten times. Our first sight of the star is of a tragic antihero alone, his back turned on us and the court. Rage is his motif. He is a Hamlet without the princeliness: unregal, unshaven, unkempt, a dark contemporary grunge Hamlet on the precipice. In isolation, he might be a rock star about to explode in smoke and klieg lights, hurling his black trench coat aside to turn and shout to his adoring fans: "Love ya, Cleveland!"

The smoke and thunderbolt lights will come soon enough, with the ghost scene—an unghostly ghost, but an affecting scene for Mr. Fiennes. "King, father, royal Dane: O, answer me!" The note of grace and tenderness—his worship for the murdered father-king—is struck again with his tortured note of violent confusion on the word "mother." The mother-queen, slut and oedipal betrayer: "O, most wicked speed, to post / With such dexterity to incestuous sheets!" Shakespeare wrote quite a drama, didn't he?

A sensational, impossible drama. Which *Hamlet,* and Hamlet, to try to capture? Revenge drama drowning in blood, tragedy of love, political and philosophical discourse, morality play, or cosmic statement about the ultimate meaning of life? "One can select at will," wrote the greatest of drama critics, Jan Kott. "But one must know what one selects, and why."

And who—or what—is Hamlet but an unsolvable mystery and unconquered Everest for every actor, even the greatest, who accepts the challenge? Orson Welles, a wrecked genius, had an unusual insight into Hamlet, claiming the authentic tragic hero is virtually unactable because he *is* a genius. His soliloquies are the poetry of genius, stretching the actor to the outer limits. Hamlet must be a poet, a prince, a scholar, a public figure in trauma, a private man or confused adolescent in grief and wracked indecision, someone driven to madness who feigns madness, a melancholic who is tender, virile, brutal, and suicidal. He sees through the rottenness of the adult world and is consumed by it; he is borne into a princely role and miscast to play the one of avenger thrust on him. "O, cursed spite, / That ever I was born to set it right!"

What Ralph Fiennes boldly "selects," and why, is from the outset dangerously oedipal. He is a Hamlet mad with fury (who in the opening court scene kisses his mother lingeringly, smack on the lips, though he's more the recipient of Gertrude's affections). Jonathan Kent's breakneck-speed, two-hour-and-fifty-minute production at the Belasco on Broadway is not a subtle one. It is a loud and popular one. But Mr. Fiennes rivets us at the start—"Frailty, thy name is woman"—via a rage so deep he gives the impression he'd strangle his mother there and then.

Wouldn't you?

Look at what Hamlet, the adored son, knows and will know: his mother remarried his father's brother, now the king, two months after his father's death. Hamlet's seething suspicion is inevitable: the passionate affair had begun before. A month before? How long before? Was it during his father's marriage? And he worships his father. "I shall not look upon his like again."

Then his worst fears are confirmed by his father's ghost, and Hamlet's young blood is frozen: "The will of my most seeming-virtuous Queen / O Hamlet, what a falling off was there." The "shameful lust" would be enough to set Hamlet on the road to psychological self-destruction. But there is more to come, turning the Renaissance thinker into neurotic avenger. What a story Shakespeare has written! "Foul and most unnatural murder!" The noble prince-philosopher must avenge the murder of his father.

Is there any wonder that Hamlet is sick at heart? His unfaithful mother has married his father's killer, and Mr. Fiennes's Hamlet is a poisoned open wound. But his plaintive, touching stress on the key words "mother" and "father" stands outside his performance as a whole. His prince is a howl personified, a scream of pain and anger and self-loathing. It is a big performance that ultimately reduces his Hamlet in scale. Mr. Fiennes's lyricism, like the mostly garbled verse-speaking of the cast, is better observed in the breach.

He thrillingly and literally beats his own brains out, but the princely thinker and intellectual within Hamlet are absent.

He has thrown down his aces too soon, leaving himself little room to maneuver in reflection. (His vocal power in the steep, awesome climb to the final murderous scene is in jeopardy, and this is the most shouted *Hamlet* production I can recall.) Mr. Fiennes's handsome profile was born romantic. Yet he can memorably play the icy killer, his sadist Goeth in *Schindler's List*, or switch to the transfixing gaze of the Golden Boy, his soft Charles Van Doren in *Quiz Show*. There's a bit of both in his Hamlet. But the arc of his performance grows predictable, externally theatrical. His Hamlet is rarely in repose.

He delivers the "To be or not to be" soliloquy literally on the run, as if anxious to get it over and done with. He enters running barefoot, unhinged, delivering the lines at a manic pace that sets out to break the land speed record. (It does.) Yet if ever there's a Shakespeare soliloquy that asks for the quality of reflective poetry, this is the one.

An easy blatancy sets in, mirroring the broad production. The oedipal connection is overstated: the first kiss between mother and son; Hamlet's violent grabbing of Ophelia's crotch; the smack on the lips between Hamlet and the king; the later near-strangulation of the queen in her bedchamber when Mr. Fiennes flattens her facedown on the incestuous sheets and mounts her—the better position to strangle her, I assume. But we do not call this oedipal; we call this buggery.

The overtheatricalized ideas become imposed rather than felt. Mr. Fiennes kissing Yorick's skull is a nightmarish, wormy moment, but his wearing a dress left behind by the visiting Players vulgarizes the key transition to his longed-for bloody action. The actor *acts*—so indecisive Hamlet then wears the actor's billowing robes and a white mask. It's an actor's disguise or mask of madness, if you like. But *Hamlet* isn't *The Phantom of the Opera*, and we cannot see Mr. Fiennes's eyes.

This broad, unlyrical production received mixed notices when it opened in London. It goes at too much of a gallop, tiring us in a long, noisy act 1, and almost shortchanging us in the cut, fifty-minute act 2. I remain mystified why the action is costumed in the starchy Edwardian era. The sets are dismal—more a dark abandoned mansion in Westchester than the blood-washed stones of a castle. (And neither mansions nor castles wobble, as on occasion the scenery does here.) The popularizing of an already popular play accounts for the special effects of the Darth Vaderish ghost scene, but there are other production lapses: a hammering home of Ophelia's insanity, the king and queen talking throughout the mime in the Players scene, distracting us from the action like talkative members of any audience. The acting of the Player King is so passably skillful that Hamlet's famous advice on how to act becomes superfluous.

The cast is a mixed bag. The usually accomplished Terence Rigby is too similar as Ghost, Player King, and Gravedigger; the Ophelia left me cold; Osric is a blank. I liked Laertes, as well as the pedant, rather than the humor, within Peter Eyre's Polonius, and Francesca Annis's descent and sensual unraveling as Gertrude. James Laurenson's lonely, quiet, conscience-stricken confession as Claudius—"May one be pardon'd and retain the offense? / In the corrupted currents of this world"—was moving and excellent, compelling us to sympathize with the murderer.

Ralph Fiennes's raging modern Hamlet cannot by the nature of things be majestic. It is the selection he has made, and as much Shakespeare's fault as his. Orson Welles was right in the essentials: the heroic poetic genius Hamlet is uncapturable in his entirety. But it is our fault that we expect so much from Mr. Fiennes. The actors who played the Hamlets of folklore returned obsessively to the role and its ultimately impossible challenges two and three times in their careers. Mr. Fiennes, who spent four seasons at the Royal Shakespeare Company before he went on to movie stardom, could, we assume, have picked up a few million smackeroos on another Hollywood movie instead of putting himself to the test here. That's a noble thing to do. If his Hamlet isn't yet fully achieved, a great Hamlet is within his grasp, to be, or not to be, his next.

We Like It a Lot

It's probably sentimental: no matter whether the play has been successful, or the actors at their best, curtain calls always seem so very touching. The evening is at an end; the actors—merely players—have made their exits and entrances. The players bid us farewell with their timeless bow. They always deserve our thanks. But sometimes, on occasions we never forget, we have witnessed a performance of such enchantment that we never want to let the performers go.

Such a moment, the happiest we could have at the theater, happened as the audience at the Brooklyn Academy of Music's Majestic Theater rose to give the cast of the all-male *As You Like It* a standing ovation. Cheek by Jowl, living hand to mouth, is one of the most exciting theater troupes in Britain. Harmony—or the blissful union of apparent opposites—is the outcome of Shakespeare's comedy about the heaven and hell of love. But if ever there was a time when audience and actor were as one, this was it. Declan Donnellan's fantastic production of *As You Like It*, with his co–artistic director and designer Nick Ormerod, is among the finest Shakespeare productions I've ever seen.

It's astonishing that there we all were—howling with laughter at Shakespeare! So fresh and utterly alive was the entire production that we found ourselves responding to Shakespeare as if experiencing him for the first and best time. I caught myself thinking, "He's good, isn't he? My God! Shakespeare can *write!*" And of course, I'm not supposed even to think so—on hallowed, Shakespearean ground.

It cuts deeper. Cheek by Jowl, touring the globe with *As You Like It*, is a popular theater company, and Shakespeare was—or should be—a popular playwright. But the troupe makes Shakespeare more than "merely" accessible. Its *As You Like It* was so natural and spontaneous and full of joy that we actually thought this is how it was in Shakespeare's day. This is how it *must* have been—the Bard before he became the textbook Bard, writing a comedy as a riot, a play of theatrical disguises and sexual ambiguity, a comedy about the reality and illusions of life and theater itself.

"All the world's a stage," goes its best-known soliloquy, a melancholic thought. "And one man in his time plays many parts." A comedy of appearances and role-playing, then. Whatever! As you like it.

Yet the brilliant choices made by Mr. Donnellan in the company's all too brief visit to New York were far from haphazard, and leave us with a few thoughts. One, I guess, is inevitable: If only "we" could do Shakespeare as well as the Brits! Well, New York only sees the best that Britain produces. There is many a lauded Shakespearean production I've seen in London that is stylishly unnatural, declaimed in the English theatrical manner, and emotionally dead.

The sheer wit and irreverence of the Cheek by Jowl production would seem ideally suited for New York's actors and directors. Yet the *merely* accessible is what we usually get, more often than not, with the Public's Shakespeare in the Park. Last summer, someone at the Public had the crackpot idea of setting *Merry Wives of Windsor* in the Wild West. It was meant to be "accessible." That Shakespeare didn't have the Wild West in mind might not matter; the concept itself was mindless, and the audience knew it within five un-merry minutes. The New York audience in the park is, in effect, being patronized by "popularization."

But the *As You Like It* production was popular and enormously successful not just because it's an intelligent reading of an often-performed play but because it respected both the audiences and playwright without toadying to either of them. The British are more at ease than Americans with certain things—among them, it seems, Shakespearean verse and cross-dressing. This isn't the first all-male *As You Like It*. In the 1960s, Clifford Williams staged one for the Old Vic with the young Anthony Hopkins as Audrey the cowgirl. In England, where local bank managers habitually slip into something simple and High Court judges like to relax in tutus, cross-dressing is as normal as it was on Shakespeare's stage.

Boys—or more likely, young men—played Shakespeare's women, actresses having been banned from the Puritan stage lest it corrupt them.

Shakespeare surely saw the joke—and seized the opportunity in his comedies to have fun and games with double and mistaken identities. *As You Like It*, whose core is role-playing, also proceeds from a core of seductive eroticism, beginning with men playing women.

A particularly mesmerizing actor in the *As You Like It* troupe, Adrian Lester, pretends to be the heroine Rosalind, who pretends to be a man named Ganymede, who's all the while head over heels in love with Orlando (and vice versa). But that's not all: disguised as Ganymede, he/she pretends to be Rosalind in order to teach the smitten Orlando a thing or two about the nature of love. So in one supremely ambiguous and hilarious scene, we have a man who's playing a woman, playing a man, who's playing a woman. At the same time, Rosalind's choice of alias is interesting: Ganymede, mythically the most beautiful of all boys among mortals and possibly the Elizabethan slang name for fag. Shakespeare had his in-jokes.

But the point is, not for a single second is this *As You Like It* camp. Mr. Lester as Rosalind (the role that made the young Vanessa Redgrave famous) and his fellow male-female actors—particularly Simon Coates as a censorial Celia in pearls, a future Dowager Duchess—portray the feminine with completely unaffected naturalness. Of course there are laughs—gales of laughter, as Shakespeare intended—and the sight alone of Wayne Cater as that dumpling shepherdess Phebe in her flowered frock was enough to set the audience off. Yet Mr. Lester's Rosalind was no standard romantic portrayal but a miracle of transformations and mood swings, neither quite man nor woman but something beyond: a third force, which cannot be categorized.

The Cheek by Jowl ensemble is itself this compelling power beyond—creating a dazzling life of its own, beyond convention, beyond received response. This was no drag-queen production, and the evening wasn't about gender or facile exercises in androgyny. *As You Like It* is about the complications and comedy of every aspect of love—pure, impure, and very simple; ultimately, it's the transforming simplicity of the Cheek by Jowl troupe that shows the way.

It couldn't have been better that the production was staged at BAM's underused Majestic Theater, the intimate open space modeled after Peter

Brook's theater in Paris. *As You Like It* had the same joyful improvisatory spirit—and almost the same white boxed space—as Peter Brook's landmark *Midsummer Night's Dream*. But in filling the empty space, Cheek by Jowl are among Mr. Brook's heirs to the theater of imagination.

"Well," Rosalind announces. "This is the forest of Arden!" And the audience laughs, sharing the joke. There is no forest—except for the one we imagine. Working with a minimum of means to maximum effect, the production's forest was later suggested simply by green ribbons floating in space. Isn't the play—and all theater—about the nature of illusion? And how better to conjure up a forest against the boringly literal or the antique pastoral grain?

Shakespeare, after all, had no sets. He asked us to imagine them instead, preferring an intimate open space to special effects. *As You Like It* was marvelously designed, even so: with light, with spare emblems and witty costumes. At the prologue to the production, the entire cast came out to greet us, dressed simply in black suits and white shirts. They are players, then, on a bare stage, who say to us in effect: "Let's act a play. You will see the illusion for yourself. Look! He's our heroine, and there's the despised son, and that man shall play the red-nosed clown, and they our lovers, and he our cynic, on the world's stage."

Declan Donnellan and his actors breathed fresh life into each and every part; they reinvented *As You Like It*. But their singular contribution is to turn on a dime, showing us that in empty space they hide nothing, except the wish to perform a Shakespeare comedy with all the love and talent at their command.

The Mayfair Medea

O world! O Anglophilia! And poor old Euripides, too. The award-winning British import of *Medea* on Broadway, with Diana Rigg giving, it's said, "the greatest acting performance of the decade," left me dumbfounded. There's worse. "Come then, Medea," as the lady warns. "Use all your knowledge now. Move toward horror!"

While high-minded custodians of our culture are moaning about the theme-park Disneyfication of Broadway, we ought to note a few low-culture similarities with this *Medea*. It's a theme-park production for the masses, too (though one that makes audiences feel superior). It is a Beauty without the Beast, and, in murderous mood, I shall come to Ms. Rigg shortly. At ninety minutes in length, it is "The Best Moments of *Medea*"—easily digestible, edited highlights of the epic drama for the cultured who make no effort. Its metallic set and theatrical effects are much talked about in the manner of megamusicals (though the sets are familiar). In an unintended Disney homage, it also has cute stage children—the two insufferably glowingly blond sons of Medea with white tunics and invisible halos who are made all the more adorable in case the audience fails to feel something when Mom murders them.

Jonathan Kent's populist production either tries to flatter us via generalized artiness—the wailing "poetic" peasant chorus in black with its foreboding "song-speech" (but can we follow all they are saying? And what are they doing, dancing a Hasidic dance?)—or, obviously meaning to make Euripides accessible, leaves absolutely nothing to chance, hammering home the high drama. Characters literally hammer on the metallic scenery—lest we miss a point or two.

This is a *Medea* simplified and vulgarized for the modern age as a fashionable tract, a Euripides (circa 485–406 B.C.) with feminism on its mind. It is like reducing *Lear* to a ninety-minute version whose message is, Father Knows Best. *Medea* belongs to the savage, irrational underworld of darkest myth, not to tabloid TV. Euripides had his ironies about the cornered role of women, but he was no feminist. The notion that *Medea* is simply a melodrama about a tragic heroine betrayed by an unfaithful husband is a misreading of the play. If not, what are we to feel when Medea mercilessly kills her children?

This is no semirealistic bourgeois drama of a wronged woman's revenge. Medea is a serial killer, isn't she? She killed her brother without conscience and betrayed her own family to help her husband, Jason, steal the Golden Fleece. Her sister in spirit is Lady Macbeth. Is the marriage of Medea and Jason convincing? I wonder. We feel we know couples like the Macbeths. But Medea is a problem (and her marriage is horribly imbalanced). *She is not human.* The devil knows where she came from. She is a poisonous witch, the devil's disciple.

Medea actually has magic powers. When Jason abandons her to marry King Creon's daughter, she sends the happy bride a magic robe that burns her to death. Is this a feminist plea, or an expression of unearthly, terrifying power? The king is also murdered, after which Medea butchers her young children. Infanticide. She murders the living image of their father.

I couldn't sense the barbaric in Diana Rigg's performance. She seemed to me too human and modern, too elegant in her blood-red robes. Perhaps in this popularized interpretation, she must play Medea as a victim. But she appears to be overplaying her, literally and alarmingly, as a Javanese puppet—as if manipulated by godly strings. Except when she is in repose, Ms. Rigg's arms and hands and even her neck are never still, jerking and fluttering theatrically throughout. She is seen to be acting, but an authentic Medea is manipulated by no one, not even the gods. She should be the puppeteer, not the puppet.

Ms. Rigg's center within Medea is coldly intelligent; she is composed within her vengeance. But there's no unearthly mystery in her portrayal, no strangeness. Her tone is more of bitter outrage, a Medea made pragmatic and rational. Of course she dominates and rips up the stage! She is too accomplished an actress not to do that, and this is a star vehicle. Compared to her dominating presence, the "supporting" players are middling. Crucially, Tim Oliver Woodward's workmanlike Jason with his little ponytail lacks the tragic stature to convince us that Medea would marry him in the first place. Ms. Rigg's swooping voice has the fire and range associated with great British acting. But there are some in the cast who do not speak well. The Messenger, Dan Mullane, delivers the news of unspeakable events with the flat unmusical tone of a waiter reciting the dinner specials. Ms. Rigg herself slips into a well-bred Mayfair accent at times, as if she's having a nervous breakdown in Harrod's Food Hall.

What else can I complain about? The line delivered by the grief-stricken Jason, "Unbar the doors," is not sufficient excuse for the set to collapse. Medea's line to Jason, "But in the age-old phrase, let's try to be friends," is a cheap laugh that's typical of the production's clangingly inappropriate attempts to be hip. The House of Horrors sight of those poor, adorable little blond boys painted with stage blood and the sound of their tiny high-pitched screams shakes us all to the marrow of our bones, no doubt. The final image, or nineteenth-century stage tableau, of a statuesque Ms. Rigg posing on high against clouds streaming by her takes the biscuit.

Who Was the Jew Shakespeare Knew?

Who was the Jew Shakespeare knew?

I was reminded of that tantalizing question by John Gross's splendid new book, *Shylock: A Legend and Its Legacy*. Where does Shylock, the most famous, or infamous, Jew in the history of drama, come from? Contra Mr. Gross, I'm convinced Shakespeare knew Jews intimately and that, as a group or individuals, they were the inspirational path to Shylock.

The conventional view was summarized by Wilfrid Sheed in his *New Yorker* review of the Gross book: "Two early clues one comes to are the arresting possibility that Shakespeare never met any Jews at all and the near-certainty that he never met one remotely like Shylock. The only Jews of *any* kind allowed into England during most of his lifetime were a handful of Christianized Marranos on their best behavior and some court musicians (and Shylock had 'no music in himself'); as for the Jews of Venice, Shakespeare would have had to hie himself to the Ghetto, not the Rialto, and preferably speak Yiddish, to meet one properly."

But Mr. Sheed, via Mr. Gross, is mistaken on virtually every point. The Jews of Venice were in Shakespeare's own circle in England; though Shylock had "no music in himself," the supreme metaphor and irony of *The Merchant of Venice* is the healing power and symbolic goodness of music (which was played by court musicians, who were Jews); and though the group of Christianized Marranos, or crypto-Jews from Spain and Portugal then living in Elizabethan London, were no doubt "on their best behavior," they were *known* to be Jews. They weren't Shylocks—who is?—but they were mostly powerful merchants accepted at court. There was generally no oppression of Jews in Shakespeare's London, provided they outwardly conformed. They practiced Jewish ceremonies in private. Shakespeare could have met any one of them at any time.

But that isn't the direction I think he took. My own starting point is this: Why did Shakespeare actually write *The Merchant of Venice*? Let's try to see him as a human being—as a competitive writer, like all writers. In 1594— six years before the earliest printed text of *The Merchant of Venice*—the queen's physician, the Portuguese Jew Roderigo Lopez, was hanged, drawn, and quartered at Tyburn on what was almost certainly a trumped-up charge of plotting to poison the queen. The trial and the fury of the mob—"He is a Jew!"—were notorious, like a Dreyfus case of its day.

Never underestimate the commercial opportunism of the theater. Marlowe's *Jew of Malta*, with its popular, savage caricature of the Jew Barabbas, was then revived with great success on the crest of the Lopez trial. The play was produced at the rival theater company to Shakespeare's, and Marlowe himself was Shakespeare's rival. He therefore decides to throw down an ace. He thinks to himself: "I can top Marlowe, and besides, business will be good." He writes *The Merchant of Venice*.

Shylock isn't a caricature, unless performed as one. Marlowe had already written the parody. Why would Shakespeare, the superior playwright, settle for another? No, he was onto something else, a much richer portrait of the Jew and one that could even arouse sympathy. Shakespeare knew Elizabethan Jews not as mythic devils and heirs to the Antichrist of the medieval miracle plays but as human beings.

The most startling clue is the way Shylock actually speaks. The name Shylock is unique—you will never come across another Shylock—and like the name, Shakespeare's language for him is unique. It is, for one thing, Hebraic in its speech patterns; it is highly naturalistic; there are linguistic lapses, as if on occasion Shylock's English were his second language; the language, outer expression of Shylock's emotional heat and demand for justice, is near rabbinical—the use of the word "and": on the one hand this, on the other hand that, and this, *and* this—Shylock, the disputatious Jew, made flesh and blood.

If he'd wished, Shakespeare could have invented an exotic, glittering language for Shylock (as he did for another renowned outsider, Othello). He made him real instead, based on reality. In his Shylock book, Mr. Gross overlooks that the way Shylock speaks is unique not only to the play but to the entire Shakespeare canon. When Peter Hall was directing Dustin Hoffman as Shylock, I asked him about Shylock's "un-Shakespearean" language. Hall, among the best Shakespearean scholars, said he knew nothing quite like it. "He must have known a Jew!" he concluded, and reminded me that Shakespeare himself went in for a little (illegal) moneylending on the side.

And Shakespeare's route to the more renowned usurer, Shylock? Where is the one safe harbor, the one home through the centuries to the marginalized, to masters of disguise, to outsiders? Theater! If Shakespeare knew a Jew, my strongest hunch is that it would have been an actor—or someone very close to his own theater company.

Enter the Bassanos of Tudor England. They were the musical dynasty who first came to London at the request of Henry VIII (a keen musician who wanted the best). The Bassano family were Jews. They arrived in London *via Venice*. And they originally belonged to a community of moneylenders! Shakespeare could not have failed to have known them—or discreetly heard, if he had wished, their family history of remembered suffering. Shakespeare named Bassanio—suitor to the "merciful" Portia in *The Merchant of Venice*— clearly after Bassano. It's a glorious in-joke and irony. For music is celebrated and played within the play—in effect paying tribute, for those that knew, to the Jews, the court musicians.

Enter, proudly blowing his own fanfare of trumpets, a leading Shakespearean scholar and eccentric, A. L. Rowse, who now transforms the picture. Dr. Rowse, in a brilliant feat of detective work, claims to have discovered the real identity of Shakespeare's Dark Lady of the sonnets. If so, we may conclude that the Jew Shakespeare knew was none other than the Dark Lady herself, who was also Shakespeare's mistress. Can't get much closer than *that*, as we shall see.

In a miraculous scholarly discovery, Dr. Rowse came across the notebooks of Simon Forman, buried for years in the Bodleian Library, Oxford. Forman, a contemporary of Shakespeare, was an astrologer. Everyone visited him in London, including Shakespeare's landlady and the daughters of the Lord Chamberlain, patron of Shakespeare's theater company.

Another of Forman's visitors was a courtesan, described in the notebooks as dark (the Dark Lady?), willful, and musical. She tells Forman of an unhappy affair with, among others, the Lord Chamberlain himself. (She named their illegitimate son, Henry, after him.) There is an implication that she was "passed on" before being married off to a man named Lanier. Emilia Lanier's maiden name was Bassano! The astrologer Forman needed the information for her horoscope. She was the Jewish daughter of one of the court musicians.

Emilia Lanier, née Bassano, lover of Shakespeare's boss the Lord Chamberlain and—A. L. Rowse concludes—of Shakespeare, sets us thinking. In a passing reference in his Shylock book, John Gross thinks that Dr. Rowse's claim to have positively identified Emilia as the Dark Lady is too speculative. I agree. On the evidence, there is no smoking gun. Emilia did not tell Forman, "And there's this talented writer named Shakespeare...." But it makes no difference.

If we go with Dr. Rowse, Shakespeare's mistress of the sonnets who drove him "frantic-made with evermore unrest" was a dark Jewess in disguise. If not, she still existed. As did all the Jewish musicians within Shakespeare's world and theater that he surely knew, speaking their eternal message within *The Merchant of Venice* to hate and prejudice:

> *Such harmony is in immortal souls*
> *But whilst this muddy vesture of decay*
> *Doth grossly close it in, we cannot hear it.*

Anything Goes
with the Professor

To my excitement, tickets to Cole Porter's *Anything Goes* came through, and I took a friend along who would, I was sure, have some interesting insights.

Professor Sir Alfred (Freddie) Ayer is one of the world's great experts on Fred Astaire, soccer, the art of tap-dancing, God, and logic. The hero of Tom Stoppard's *Jumpers*, a dotty logical positivist obsessed with the existence, or nonexistence, of God, is based on Sir Freddie. Considered the heir to Bertrand Russell, the former Wykeham professor of logic at Oxford is a very sprightly seventy-eight and game for anything.

Visiting Manhattan, he practically risked his life by being brazen enough to confront the world heavyweight champion, Mike Tyson, at a party given by Fernando Sanchez, who is, of course, the chic underwear designer. Sir Freddie, a slight figure, had been taken along to the party by young relatives. Thinking Mike Tyson was coming on too strong with a beautiful model, Freddie decided to rescue her.

"Leave this to me!" he announced to his group, who were trying to restrain him.

"But Freddie, he's the heavyweight champion of the world."

"I know that!" he replied, striding toward the champ.

"Look here," he said boldly to a stunned Mike Tyson. "We are both supreme in our fields. I suggest we talk about this like rational men." So it was that, as the beautiful model slunk off, the world champ and Professor Sir Alfred Ayer swapped certain ideas on chivalry, Fred Astaire, soccer, the art of tap-dancing, God, and logic. They became buddies. After the party, as they staggered out of the elevator together, Tyson was playfully shadowboxing with him, and the doorman, mistaking Sir Freddie for his manager, said, "Can't you keep your boy under control?"

He was waiting for me at the Vivian Beaumont Theater, birdlike and eager. "This is a great treat," he said excitedly. "I saw the original *Anything Goes* in 1935. London production, of course. The Ethel Merman role was played by a French lady. *Very* odd, but there it is. No! The French lady was in a musical with the song 'My Heart Belongs to Daddy.' Care for a drink?"

What was the last musical he saw? "*A Chorus Line.* Terrible. Danced well, though. I regard *Les Misérables* as a desecration of the novel and shan't go and see it. I saw *Cats* in Canada. Very jolly! Of course, no songs to speak of. The second musical I ever saw was in Manhattan starring Gypsy Rose Lee, who had intellectual pretensions. She lived in the same building as W. H. Auden. I was taken to see her by e.e. cummings, a great fan of burlesque since his Harvard days. I enjoyed it rather less than I had hoped. It also starred a comedian whose great claim to fame was that he had been knocked out onstage by W. C. Fields with a billiard cue."

Our seats were perfect: center aisle. "Ah!" said Sir Freddie. "I find it very easy to achieve suspension of disbelief in the theater. On the other hand, I find it harder and harder. The plays are less good. In musical comedy, it's a question of *nostalgia.* That's why all the musicals I like are revivals. When I was young I believed musicals were what life was like. I always captured the heroine. Then there was the sheer pleasure of the songs."

How does he rate Cole Porter? I asked.

"Is Cole Porter as good as Noël Coward? *Possibly.* Coward sang Porter's 'You're the Top' in Las Vegas with a new lyric, and it wasn't as good as the original—*true.* Could we agree that Cole Porter is as much a genius as Rossini, almost as good as Gershwin, narrowly better than Gilbert and Sullivan, and less than Verdi?"

We had arrived early so as not to be late. As we were seated on the end of the aisle, we had to keep getting up so people could get by us. "Of course!" Freddie exclaimed with impeccable logic. "How else could people get by us?"

Playbills were studied. "A great mistake to tamper with P. G. Wodehouse, I fear. Oh, dear. There's an understudy on. Major or *minor?*" Minor, fortunately. "Is Ms. LuPone Ethel Merman?" The orchestra was tuning up.

"The important thing in musical comedy is to push all staging to the *back*. More room for dancing, you see."

Curtain up!

"Oh, I say!" Sir Freddie cried with delight at the opening production number. "This *is* a treat." He was singing along to "I Get a Kick Out of You" when the lady in front went shush. "So sorry," whispered a chastened Sir Freddie. "I promise it shan't happen again."

Out of the corner of my eye I could see him struggling to hold himself back, but when it came to "Easy to Love," he cracked. By then, most people around us seemed to be singing and humming along happily to Cole Porter's champagne score, including the lady in front, so it didn't matter. Though his rendition of "Blow, Gabriel, Blow" in act 2 wasn't quite a match for Patti LuPone's, that didn't matter, either.

Anything goes! The night out at the theater had been a pleasure. Only one thing worried the professor of logic. "How," he asked over supper, "did the two Chinese gentlemen escape from jail?"

"I think Patti LuPone secretly rescued them," I replied.

"Yes, but *how?*"

"I'm not sure. But if they hadn't escaped, they couldn't have been in the final number."

"True," said Sir Freddie, "But I still don't know how they did it."

Art Is Good
for You

Art succeeds in more ways than one. Yasmina Reza's ninety-minute inter-missionless comedy famously revolves around a white-on-white abstract painting that almost ruins a fifteen-year friendship among three men. The surprising artfulness of *Art* is that it isn't really about art. In its winning way, it's about the art of friendship.

The pleasures of Matthew Warchus's lean production are underpinned by three super performances from Alan Alda, Victor Garber, and Alfred Molina. We *like* them, though the smug faux-cultivated characters played by Mr. Alda and Mr. Garber aren't always likable. (Mr. Molina's compromising crybaby on the edge of a nervous breakdown and in a miserable marriage is more sympathetic.) But we could say the real star of the play—the fourth character without which there wouldn't be a play—is that pricey, high-status blank, the four-by-five-foot white-on-white painting that soaks up judgment with utter, dominating indifference either way.

The painting has been bought by the pretentious Serge (Victor Garber) for a small fortune. His best friend Marc (Alan Alda), invited to genuflect before it, announces that it's "shit." The third friend, Yvan (Alfred Molina), has no views, wishes only to please, and therefore alienates them both. The contemptuous antimodernist Marc, the upwardly mobile, trendy Serge, and the neurotic amoeba Yvan are brought to the brink by—of all things—a work of so-called art.

This is the first comedy I've seen that revolves around friendship and artistic bickering. The white-on-white painting itself has even been criticized by some for not being truly modern. But the French are invariably behind the times. It's more a classic modern abstract, circa 1975. It isn't one of

Damien Hirst's ultra-chic dead animals. It's just generic modern. But it isn't the dramatist's intention to make too easy jokes at the expense of old-hat targets. She's onto bigger things, I hope.

"You can say, I don't get it, I can't grasp it," Serge protests angrily at his friend's derisive reaction. "You can't say it's shit." In other, pluralist words, you cannot criticize someone else's taste. You mustn't! For to do so would be a lapse of good taste.

As Louis Menand pointed out in a *New Yorker* column, pluralism is the ascendant philosophy of the day. *Art* couldn't be timelier in that sense. "No one wants to get caught asserting that one type of art is better than another," Mr. Menand wrote. For good measure, he reminded us that last fall when the *New York Times* asked seventeen experts, including Philippe de Montebello of the Metropolitan Museum of Art and William Rubin of the Museum of Modern Art, the question "What is art?" they all gave the same answer. They said the question had no answer. Art is whatever people say it is.

But if anything can be art, art no longer exists. Ms. Reza's voice of protest, Marc, might be an envious, condescending middle-aged fossil dismissing his friend's pride and joy as "shit," but he's in favor of a certain standard. He dares to believe that some paintings are better than others.

Over a generation ago, the acerbic Cambridge literary critic F. R. Leavis actually caused an uproar by saying that not all novels are created equal. (Naturally, the novelists dispatched to the lower ranks objected the most.) Today, the highest voices in the art world and other Mad Hatters are saying you cannot judge a work of art. You can say politely—as the offended new art collector Serge advises—that "it's not for me, really," or "I'm afraid I don't happen to like it." But if there's any criticism or judgment, it must be of yourself. It's why, in the *Times*'s laudatory feature on Chuck Close's repetitively pointillist portraits at the Museum of Modern Art, Michael Kimmelman could write that if we feel there's something lacking in the art, "it is really in us." There you are: We're to blame.

No, we are not to blame. Some art is a joke. And some plays are better than others, too. This is one of them. But *Art* isn't about aesthetics. Nor, clearly, is it intended to be a sophisticated Stoppardian mini-lecture about the mysterious meaning of art ("It's shit!"). The white-on-white painting serves as the catalyst to the drama's fun and games about the dodgy art of friendship.

Judgmental Marc—a critic in disguise—breaks the unwritten rules. "I can't love the Serge who's capable of buying that painting," he explains, and means it. (Which reminds us of Kenneth Tynan's renowned "I doubt if I could love anyone who did not wish to see *Look Back in Anger*.") Marc has made the fatal error of taking the taste of his friend *personally*. Worse—he takes it as an insulting betrayal. Personal differences are what spouses and lovers are for—as opposed to the delicate ground of enduring friendship.

The painting—a comparatively minor thing, after all, if expensive— throws them all to the extent that none of them can now be sure what binds them together, or even why they like each other. It's as if you or I visited our best friend's home and wondered aloud, "How can you live in a dump like this?" Or, "How can you live with such an ugly broad?"

Perhaps we fall into friendships. We don't *judge* our friends. It's more tactful and discreet that way, and it's easier, like not judging art. Friends are always there (or they wouldn't be friends). But the moment we analyze the unspoken tightrope chemistry of our friendships, everything can easily fall apart.

Put it another way: What sort of friend are you if you don't think your friends are special? So the white-on-white painting provokes the uncomfortable, amusing question, How can you really care for someone who has awful taste?

The outraged Marc is pointing a finger at the emperor's suit of clothes when he says, in effect: "You are not entitled to find the colors of this painting fascinating. There *are* no colors!" And the opportunistic Serge defends good manners rather than the art. "What I blame him for is his tone of voice, his complacency, his tactlessness. I blame him for his insensitivity. I don't blame him for not being interested in modern art, I couldn't give a toss about that."

Each is a tyrant in his own enjoyably determined way. They approach the tyranny of closed minds—fashionable "good" taste versus "intolerant" critical standards. (Though your intolerance might be my good taste.) Even poor old unpretentious Yvan is a demanding absolute ruler via tearful, pathetic compromise. I'm surprised to learn, however, that the gifted Yasmina Reza has said that her play is as much a tragedy as a comedy. In my view, she is not entitled to say so. Marc would say she's talking *merde;* Serge would say the idea that *Art* is a comedy *and* a tragedy is absolutely fascinating; and Yvan would agree with them both.

I side with the tradition that wisely states one should never believe what the artist says, only what the artist does. *Art* is an enjoyable soufflé— and none the worse for that. In Paris, where it originated, it's in the honorable tradition of witty boulevard comedies. The sparkling translation is by Christopher Hampton. Mark Thompson has designed the highly appropriate, minimalist, white-on-white set of a chic monk. The hangdog Alfred Molina stops the show with his hysterical delivery of the longest sentence ever written in a play, with the exception of Samuel Beckett.

I can't put it any riskier than this: We can't be friends anymore if you don't enjoy *Art.*

A Helluva Musical

We were leaving the Delacorte Theater in Central Park after a night out at *On the Town,* George C. Wolfe's revival of the 1944 musical that amounts to a love letter to New York. This was the first full-length Broadway show for the young Leonard Bernstein and Jerome Robbins (who together would go on to create *West Side Story*), and it was the Broadway debut of two lyricists and librettists, Betty Comden and Adolph Green, who in their turn would become legend. Attending the show in Central Park were Ms. Comden and Mr. Green, and as they quietly got up to leave, looking quite proud and saying hello to a few friends, people began to applaud them.

It was the most touching thing. The audience leaving the theater stopped to say thank you to the two fabled artists who, more than fifty years ago, had written the sparkling book and lyrics to the show we had just seen. New Yorkers know their stuff. The Comden and Green songwriting team has defined the romance of the city for us, and the ovation and thanks from us all were from the heart.

> *New York, New York, a helluva town*
> *The Bronx is up and the Battery's down*
> *The people ride in a hole in the ground*
> *New York, New York, it's a helluva town!*

It's a helluva song! The defining number of *On the Town* that's sung by the three sailors on twenty-four-hour shore leave has us inevitably falling in love with the city all over again, which is the general idea. The bold, dominating emblem of the new production in the park is a replica of the Brooklyn Bridge. (Mr. Wolfe has placed the impressive orchestra on the bridge.) So the physicality of the show itself, with its New York scenes set in the subways and streets, in Times Square and the Carnegie Hall studios, on Coney Island and in the Brooklyn Navy Yard, is mirrored wonderfully by the open-air production in the park.

An act 1 scene, which has a lovely, radiant number, "Lucky to Be Me," is set in Central Park. The script reads: "Scene 9: Central Park." Lucky to be us! We're *in* Central Park. And to top the moment off nicely, Mr. Wolfe opens the backdrop on stage to reveal the park behind, lit on a summer's night. One thinks with pleasure—and can't help but think—"Well, this is fun! This is a *treat.*"

Which is what it is, mostly, and what the exuberant, fanciful, and dopily romantic *On the Town* always was. On the one hand, it's an escapist musical comedy with vaudevillian characters such as Pitkin W. Bridgework, who's a judge; Lucy Schmeeler, who's a Ms. Lonelyhearts with the flu; and Madame Maude P. Dilly, who's a faux-Russian singing teacher fond of Teacher's. There's also an oddity in the Museum of Natural History called *Pithecanthropus erectus*—and try saying that in Danish.

The names of the three fancy-free sailors in search of adventure, love, and dames—"That's the girl for me, fellows!" "Hello, babe, you look delicious!"—suggest a trio of young optimistic buddies from the vintage movies we all love on a rainy Sunday afternoon. (Comden and Green wrote at least one of them, *Singin' in the Rain.*) *On the Town*'s Chip, Ozzie, and Gabey are a neat balancing act. Gabey is the earnest romantic fellow who's fallen for the Miss Turnstiles poster girl, Ivy; Ozzie is the wiseacre gift to women who gets lucky with a loony anthropologist named Claire DeLoone; and Chip is the naive tourist seduced and flattened by Hildy, the lady cabdriver with a heart of gold.

The escapist knockabout comedy grows infectious with Hildy's show-stopping hymn to double entendres, "I Can Cook Too," or with the chanteuse's generic ballad to misery, "I Wish I Was Dead." There's a touch of total insanity in the Neanderthal "Carried Away," performed by "Primitive Man and Woman," among others. Naturally, there's the sentimental (this is, after all, a musical romance in the big, lonely city). But there's also the unusual, unembarrassed delight in witty silliness, a Comden and Green specialty.

> *Hello, babe, you look delicious*
> *You're the answer to my wishes*
> *Let's start buying breakfast dishes*
> *How's about a date tonight?*

On the other hand, the broad comedy of *On the Town* turns poignant. The show was based on the 1944 ballet by Leonard Bernstein and Jerome Robbins, *Fancy Free.* Bernstein wrote a new score for the musical production and brought in his friends, Comden and Green. The story of a day in the life of the three sailors in New York actually takes place during World War II, when time was precious.

> *Where has all the time gone to ?*
> *Haven't done half the things we want to.*
> *Oh, well, we'll catch up some other time.*

The bittersweet "Some Other Time" is more than the wistful farewell of young lovers. In wartime New York, a very real sense of foreboding would have cut much deeper than it does today. The legacy of seriousness that underscored the original is to be found more today in Bernstein's jazzy and jagged urban symphony for Robbins's ballet sequences. The young Bernstein's score for *On the Town* is a junior version of his score for *West Side Story,* and its rich, textured ballet music helped thrust the American musical into a new era.

Eliot Feld, making his belated debut as a musical choreographer, is an intriguing choice to rechoreograph the production. George Wolfe has consciously staged a young version of *On the Town,* which in its day was very young (its creators were in their twenties). Six of Mr. Feld's dancers in the production are graduates of his own sexy company, and among so much fine work from them, the Times Square ballet that closes act 1 with the full ensemble is an urban high in the summer night.

But there are weaknesses. The high-energy production is too eager to please until it settles down to charm us naturally. I felt disconnected at first by all the determined teeth and smiles. There's a danger of pastiche, and Mr. Wolfe's production hovers sometimes on the edge. Kate Suber is currently pushing too hard as the eccentric Claire DeLoone. For my taste, the likable Jose Llana is a little too soft as the romantic lead, Gabey, whereas Sophia Salguero's hoochie-coochie dancer, Ivy, is too knowingly cute. They do not ignite together, and Ms. Salguero's dancing is so limited that Mr. Llana performs a pas de deux with her while she reclines not too artfully on a chaise longue with wheels. She's a cooch on a couch.

The costumes by Paul Tazewell are spiffy, though Adrianne Lobel's admired replica of the Brooklyn Bridge is, in the end, a static backdrop. I wanted it to move and open up. The action invariably focuses on the entrance from the center of the bridge, whereas Mr. Wolfe's work at its fluent best creates many different perspectives and angular playing areas—keeping the stage at its hottest.

But there's a great deal to admire, not least the good-humored vitality of the entire company. There are several appealing performances—Robert Montano's Ozzie, Jesse Tyler Ferguson's Chip, and Mary Testa's cameo as Madame Dilly. An unlikely star may well have been born in Lea DeLaria's show-stopping, belting performance as Hildy, the cabdriver. The practically unknown Ms. DeLaria amounts to sensational casting. I hope it won't be spoiling it when I say that she's well known on the San Francisco stand-up circuit under the name Fuckin' Dyke. The lady is as good as gold in *On the Town*.

It's Big! It's Safe! It's Full of Generic Symbolism!

There has been a sharply divided critical response to the $10 million musical *Ragtime*, and I join the naysayers with regret. I would sooner celebrate the musical's inauguration of its spanking new Broadway theater than damn it, even if the theater is named, in all corporate dullness, "Ford Center for the Performing Arts." With a name as uninspiring as that—the new theater is an advertising vehicle for the Ford Motor Company—you feel it ought to be attached to a shopping mall in Ohio.

Its faux-marble atrium, with gift store attached, could easily be *in* a mall, proudly civic-minded, no doubt. The Ford Center has been built by Livent Inc., the Canadian production company that staged *Show Boat* and now brings the epic, heavily presold *Ragtime* to Broadway. The new theater, built on the ashes of two period theaters, the Apollo and the Lyric, has no sense of the thrillingly new. It is blandly, architecturally safe, as *Ragtime* is big and safe. But this megamusical without any sense of irony ought to be taking real risks—reflecting the turbulent innovative danger of a new age.

A smashing opportunity has been missed with *Ragtime*. The musical version of E. L. Doctorow's 1975 novel about the tumultuous promise and social revolution of turn-of-the-century America held out hopes of a very rare achievement nowadays: the rebirth of the modern, quintessentially American musical. Produced at the close of the century on the eve of a new millennium, *Ragtime*'s panoramic undertow of historic events and colliding themes suggest the exciting promise of the shock of the new as much as the rhythmic, seductive syncopation of ragtime itself. Yet the outcome is uncomfortably similar to the Ford Center for the Performing Arts itself. It is technically smooth, but it fails to excite. It is, when all is said and done, virtuously dull.

Take the first appearance of the mythical Harry Houdini in the big opening number for the entire company. Like Mr. Doctorow's novel, the musical intertwines fictional characters with historical figures (among them, anarchist Emma Goldman, financier J. P. Morgan, and automobile manufacturer Henry Ford). Houdini, the great escape artist, enters descending on a rope, tied dramatically upside down in a straitjacket. My point is, he escapes too easily—without struggle, a breeze. We know he will escape; we have seen the trick many times before. But this Houdini doesn't thrill us. He is simply *there*—a symbol, perhaps, of your huddled masses yearning to breathe free (everything in this musical is a simplistic symbol). But he is a magician without magic.

Too much of *Ragtime* is disappointingly tame. When the leading character known by the generic label of Mother wails in song, "What kind of woman would do what I've done / Open the door to chaos and pain?"—we don't see chaos, least of all pain. (We see smugness, actually.) When another lyric tells us stirringly, "The night Emma Goldman spoke at Union Square / Anger and sweat were in the air," the anger is programmed and sweat has no place in this pretty pageant. Even the rags worn by Tateh, the Jewish immigrant from Latvia, look nice and clean—and unreal.

Ragtime has created a sanitized panorama of an America brimming with symbolic labels. It's why the musical doesn't touch our hearts, though it dutifully touches many bases. Generic types and symbols leave us emotionally uninvolved, like Victorian tableaux. The icons Ford and J. P. Morgan equal Evil Capitalists: Evelyn Nesbit is the All-American Bimbette; Booker T. Washington, the Voice of Reason—and so on. The overcrowded narrative can only scratch the familiar surface of momentous events. But the three central story lines are all generic labels. There's the symbolic white New Rochelle family known as Mother, Father, the Little Boy, Mother's Younger Brother, and Grandfather. As types, these nameless ones are Virtuous, Blind, Curious, Restless, and Irascible. There's the Black American story of the wronged ragtime pianist and future revolutionary outlaw, Coalhouse Walker Jr. His lover, Sarah, and her illegitimate child are taken in by Mother. But Father, returning home from the North Pole (read Spirit of Adventure) isn't pleased. Younger Brother joins black revolutionaries.

The third story line involves the familiar symbolic immigrant success story of the Jew, Tateh, who strives for a better life for his daughter, who's known as the Little Girl. Tateh becomes a successful movie director and ends up—would you believe?—with Mother from New Rochelle. This also means that the Little Girl is now in the same goody-goody family as the Little Boy, as is another youngster known as Little Coalhouse. But let's not go into Little Coalhouse now.

The question is, do these simplistic stories interest us? Are they telling us anything new or fresh? Only the Coalhouse Walker story promises to ignite, thanks to a stunning performance from Brian Stokes Mitchell as Coalhouse. Yet *Show Boat*, created in 1927, has more to tell us challengingly about black and white America than *Ragtime*.

It's a disappointment, as I say. The music and lyrics by Stephen Flaherty and Lynn Ahrens (who also wrote *Once on This Island*) owe a debt to the surging emotionalism of *Les Misérables*. The score is ordinary and repetitive, failing to produce even one memorable song. The book by Terrence McNally isn't his best work. (He is uncharacteristically humorless here.) The "musical staging" by Graciela Daniele—"musical staging" means choreography, I guess—actually reduces the pulse of the show by ending far too many scenes habitually in shadowy, moody slow motion. Eugene Lee's industrial cathedral of Penn Station is splendid—but the intimate scenes can look lost in the monumental setting. The director, Frank Galati (whose work on Steppenwolf's *Grapes of Wrath* was supreme) has managed to hold it all together—but too well, too neat and clean and careful.

We long for *Ragtime* to take flight unpredictably, to be incautiously and wonderfully messy, to be, in a nutshell, as inspired as the new gilded age it yearns to capture. Instead, it could have been produced by committee. There are no individuals in the show. There are types, there are emblems, there are simpleminded, symbolic stories. And humanity—true, dirty, teeming humanity? At the dawn of *our* new age, *Ragtime* and its anonymous new home, the Ford Center, are themselves unhappy emblems of a scary virtual reality—bland corporate culture, mall future.

Whatever Happened to Class?

The hot Broadway revival of *Chicago* at the Richard Rodgers Theater, in which the girls do things to chairs that no respectable chair ought to allow, raises an important question: Whatever happened to class?

The raunchy 1975 Bob Fosse, John Kander, Fred Ebb celebration of cynicism and crotches asks the question in "Class"—the duet between Roxie, the 1920s Chicago broad who gets away with murder and becomes a star, and Matron, the prison warden on murderer's row known as the Countess of the Clink. "Why is it everyone now is a pain in the ass?" they coo. "Whatever happened to class?" The tone is sincerely ironic, of course; the hit song, like the show, gleefully celebrates everything it satirizes.

"Welcome," announces the master of ceremonies at *Chicago*'s start. "Ladies and gentlemen, you are about to see a story of murder, greed, corruption, violence, exploitation, adultery, and treachery—all those things we all hold near and dear to our hearts. Thank you!"

And so the corrupt sluts, or ladies, sing merrily in "Class": "Now no one even says 'Oops' when they're passing their gas / Whatever happened to class?" They have the answer to their own question, with regrets:

Everybody you watch
'S got his brains in his crotch
Holy crap
Holy crap
What a shame
What a shame
What became of class?

Judging by all the critical raves, "class" is this somewhat threadbare production of *Chicago*, though the always classy Ann Reinking and Bebe Neuwirth as the killer sinners, Roxie and Velma, lead an accomplished cast. The revival has been produced on Broadway by Barry and Fran Weissler— revivalist specialists of such old warhorses as *Grease*. The Weisslers are not renowned for their lavish production values. This is the way Broadway will end—not with a bang, but a concert.

The *Chicago* production is virtually a concert party—without sets or period costumes, with the action staged expertly by director Walter Bobbie in front of the onstage orchestra. Not that it seems to matter much to the punters in the $70 seats turned on by the un-shy, seasoned performers in the chorus line. No disrespect, but they all look very well seasoned indeed. This is not a young, fresh-faced show. But the late Bob Fosse was more interested in conveying the sexually seedy, and the roots of *Chicago*'s style are honorably in the suggestive earthiness and fun of burlesque.

Ann Reinking, the former Fosse dancer, has choreographed the show in the slinky style of the master, and it's good to see the real, much-imitated, pelvic thing. This is about as close as we could get to the sexiness, the chic and dirt, of the ragingly heterosexual Fosse. Still, he was never subtle. The girls in the chorus spread their long legs as often as indecency permits, while standing, sitting, lying flat on their backs or in the air. The boys have the biggest codpieces this side of the Royal Danish Ballet. All of which diverts your eye away from the bored lady violinist in the front row of the onstage orchestra.

Chicago, the concert and crotch show, was first produced to acclaim last spring as part of City Center's Encores! concert series. The excellent Encores! musicals are staged readings that are winged wonderfully by our best performers, and there's pleasure in the rough, spontaneous performances of forgotten musicals or a rediscovered gem. In its day, *Chicago*'s vaudevillian satire of amorality was considered ahead of its time. A musical about a celebrity spouse killer who's found not guilty with the help of a smooth-talking, shyster lawyer was apparently considered too cynical only twenty years ago. Who would buy such a dark, jaded view of self-deluding, innocent America? The original *Chicago* had a relatively modest run, overshadowed by the sweeter *Chorus Line*, which had opened two months earlier.

Yet the cynical *Chicago* and the sentimental *Chorus Line* shared the same metaphor: that everything in American life—winners and losers, fame and failure, murderers and saints—is showbiz. *Chicago*'s crooked celebrity lawyer, Billy Flynn, "the silver-tongued prince of the courtroom," says: "It's all a circus, kid. A three-ringed circus. These trials—the whole world—all show business."

Maybe so. But it's a little *easy*. And the Kander-Ebb score has a bit more bounce than bite. Even so, any musical that opens with a showstopper as good as "All That Jazz" knows exactly where it's headed. To glitz heaven. Kander-Ebb (of *Cabaret*) might not be Cole Porter, but their show tunes are catchy. Without knowing the melody, you could almost hum along to the lyric of sleazeball Billy's "All I Care About": "I don't care for any fine attire / Vanderbilt might admire / No, no, not me / All I care about is love."

Bebe Neuwirth and Ann Reinking are an odd couple as the babes of jazz—a vaudevillian duo who might not appear meant for each other. But Ms. Neuwirth has a mad glint in her eye, throwing her pert self into the exuberant, mean spirit of things, and Ms. Reinking, though exaggerating Roxie into a cartoon figure, moves like liquid when she dances. In the star cast—rivaling the 1975 production with Gwen Verdon, Chita Rivera, and Jerry Orbach—James Naughton can do no charming wrong as Billy, the rat. It's good to see Joel Grey giving a relaxed, masterly turn as Roxie's invisible sap, Amos (who's usually referred to as Andy). Why, then, my muted pleasure in the proceedings?

The production—which isn't a real production—borders on camp. The "hard-edged" satire seems pretty obvious today. (The original Fosse production would have been meaner.) *Chicago* no longer shocks, as intended; it confirms and celebrates the cynical. In its showbiz essentials it delivers a sour message: You can fool all of the people all of the time.

The big second-half number, "Razzle-Dazzle," drips with dramatic irony, but its loud message is bitter and unattractive: "Razzle-dazzle 'em / And they'll never catch wise…Give 'em the old flim and flummox / Fool and fracture 'em / Long as you keep 'em way off balance / How can they spot you got no talents?"

"Hello, suckers!" goes the act 2 line that welcomes us back for more razzle-dazzle, more of the old flim and flummox. The audience laughs happily. "Hello, suckers!" It's only a show, I know. But who's being suckered?

Farewell, Carousel

When it was announced that *Carousel* was closing after only eleven months at Lincoln Center, I couldn't have been alone in feeling an awful sense of regret. The celebrated production had been praised to the skies and gave musical revivals a good name. Once or twice every few years if we're very lucky something comes along that is so fine and right, we can't imagine it being staged any other way. Nicholas Hytner's beautiful production of *Carousel* is—was—such a landmark.

Whenever during its run friends asked what Broadway musical they should see, the problem was happily solved. See *Carousel!* I felt then, as now, that no other musical in town could compete with it. And this is the thing: no one was ever disappointed. To the contrary, everyone seemed enchanted by a production of such natural painterly simplicity that it took your breath away. Rodgers and Hammerstein's 1945 *Carousel,* greatest of all romantic musicals, had been reclaimed from its reputation as mere homespun American corn. It became in its honest sentiment moving and very real. When Shirley Verrett and the ensemble sang that enduring secular hymn to hope and survival, "You'll Never Walk Alone," the tragic destiny of the story's two lovers reduced the audience to emotional wrecks. Time and again, audiences dissolved. What an astonishing thing! In the hyped age of megamusical special effects and cynicism, here we had the achievement of this glorious production: it touched people to the core.

The closing performance, like all final curtains, was emotional and celebratory—but this was different. As the audience gathered at the packed Vivian Beaumont Theater, the mood was subdued. It was a natural audience of theatergoers, with a few friends of the cast, director Nicholas

Hytner and some of his creative team, and those of us who wanted a last chance to see the production again. Yet there wasn't the usual excitement. The mood of the audience was tinged with sadness. I could hear the cast members behind the curtain gathering for the prologue. But the sound they made was like cheering.

And, of course, we were soon cheering, too, as one memorable sequence and song after another all but stopped the show. It is an audience's way of saying a heartfelt thank-you to performers who have given us such pleasure. The racing pulse of the cast was at explosion point, as if they would fly off someplace. Easy, easy, one thought. Bring it down a little, if you can, or we'll all be goners. And, of course, they found the right level, which only made things worse. Sitting close to the stage, you could see them checking themselves in midsong, as if remembering this would be the last time. At the curtain call, they were in tears.

"Bravo! Bravo!" went the shouts during the sustained ovation. And as the curtain began to descend, the "bravo" wonderfully became "Don't go!" Don't go, don't go, don't go…

At the Tavern on the Green party afterward, the cast members weren't exactly sad. They were hungry. Have you ever seen an actor eat? It's one of the great theatrical happenings. But there was about them the atmosphere of accomplishment. They had done all they could; the sadness was ours. Why did *Carousel* come off? Or put another way: If *Cats* can still be running after a thousand years, why only eleven months for *Carousel?*

In spite of all the awards and acclaim that came its way, the audience wasn't there for it in the long run. That's a pretty devastating turn of events for those who saw the production as a cut above Lloyd Webber and the usual suspects. And *Carousel* played close to 90 percent capacity throughout its run.

The advance bookings weren't there for January–February—the wintry danger zone for all shows. It was a very large musical in a relatively small house—and therefore expensive to run. Lincoln Center, a nonprofit institution, doesn't operate like a commercial producer. It can't risk high losses and gamble on a spectacular turnaround. Its duty is to produce the best it can—and go on to the next. The production actually lost $1.5 million, though *loss* isn't quite the right word.

"We didn't lose it," said Bernard Gersten, *Carousel*'s executive producer. "We subsidized it to the tune of $1.5 million. That's what we do, that's what we're here for."

It's one of the best arguments for truly subsidized theater in America. Lincoln Center staged a *Carousel* that even had the edge over Nicholas Hytner's original production at the National Theatre in London. But without the subsidy, it wouldn't have been possible.

Then couldn't it have transferred? Apart from the enormous expense of virtually reproducing it in a more traditional Broadway house, the sorry truth is that not a single Broadway producer offered to transfer it. And what does that tell us about the state of Broadway? But when the acclaimed, original National Theatre production transferred to London's West End, its run lasted only seven months.

Carousel isn't *Cats, Crazy for You, Sunset Boulevard,* or even *Damn Yankees.* It was never in its time as big a success as *Guys and Dolls* or any of Rodgers and Hammerstein's later, sweeter work. In today's lackluster, Disneyfied Broadway, it's said that the dark undertow to *Carousel* cannot compete with more "entertaining" Event Theater. It seems that way, I guess, though the disenchantment is palpable.

*Don't go...*Well, at least 400,000 theatergoers saw *Carousel* at Lincoln Center—no small number. And what a treat it was! The production will always be remembered. And as for the rest, what's the use of wondering? As the *Carousel* song goes that touches all hearts:

Common sense may tell you
That the endin' will be sad
And now's the time to break and run away,
But what's the use of wond'rin...

My Blood Brother and Me

You will recall that I had left my life story and portrait of England at the point when Papa, a coal miner, saw me happily off on the train to my new life at Oxford.

"Son," he said, throwing his pickax in the air, "the pits aren't for you. Just show those upper-class buggers at Oxford what you can do, and remember—*Masterpiece Theater* wasn't built overnight. Good luck, son!"

I can still see Papa now, calling after me as the train pulled out of the station, "Well, lads. Gaudeamus igitur, juvenes dum sumus?" ("Pardon me boys, is this the Chattanooga Choo-Choo?")

Happy days! You will no doubt recall, too, that in an effort to keep up all superior British appearances in New York, I had previously invented a somewhat different biography. My artistic family did not, for example, live in a wisteria-clad cottage in Chipping Sodbury. Nor did we have a second home in Tuscany where my father, on leave from the diplomatic corps in Calcutta, was surprised one day to find Mama in carnal embrace with Vita Sackville-West. Nor, indeed, was my long-lost brother a beloved, though grumpy, veterinarian in the west of Scotland. My motives in disguising my background were, however, in a good cause. Namely, myself. It has long since been clear that anglophile New York prefers the easy Merchant-Ivory image to reality, and don't we all? But now I fear the time has come for me to come clean.

I am not, in fact, the proud son of a Lawrentian, socialist coal miner who was befriended by the Bloomsbury set and rumored to be the missing link in the Burgess and Maclean spy scandal. I am the son of a Liverpudlian milkman.

I didn't know Daddy well. Shortly before I was born, he disappeared with a local girl he mistakenly believed bore a striking resemblance to Marilyn Monroe. As you may imagine, my mother was terribly upset. But I didn't know that at the time. You see, I was a twin separated at birth.

What now follows is an English odyssey so touchingly traumatic that I can barely bring myself to describe it. But describe it I must. The fates were kind to me, though less so to my twin brother, Mickey. For he remained working class, while I was reared with every privilege known to the upper classes of England. Or the upper-middle classes, or lower-upper classes, or upper-upper lower-lower upper middle-middle classes. But how could such extraordinary good fortune come my way?

Mummy—that is, my real mother—had nine other children or so to care for when Mickey and I came into the world. She was lowborn, though plucky. I am certain she would not have given me away at birth had economic circumstances and general misery in Liverpool not compelled her to do so. But, of course, I didn't know that at the time. My real mother cleaned house for a childless woman and her remote, wealthy husband, who was, I often suspected, sexually ambiguous. I knew them as my parents.

My twin brother was left to cope as best he could with his fate and the deprived, though invariably stoic, working classes of England.

Poor Mickey remained on the other side of the Liverpudlian tracks with my real mother, while I lived in the house on the hill and attended, of course, the finest prep, speaking the language of the privileged English. It has always embarrassed me a little, speaking this way: "Pahdn meah bores, eez thus thea Chetonugah Jew-Jew?" ("Pardon me boys, is this the Chattanooga Choo-Choo?") But there was nothing I could do about it.

One day, when I was seven or eight, I was walking in the slums of Liverpool, to which I was mysteriously drawn, when I was befriended by a rather loutish child who nevertheless seemed frightfully good, cracking fun to me.

He was Mickey! My blood brother and twin, from whom I was separated at birth. But, of course, I didn't know that at the time. We became close friends from the very beginning. I was enchanted by Mickey's vulgar ways, and he taught me to speak his delightful North Country working-class language. *"Fook!"* he would say. "Fook yerself!" How we laughed! Though, naturally, such coarse language did not go down well at home.

I never really liked the lady I knew as my mother. She was potty. She heard voices, prophesying doom like a Greek tragedy. The least thing would set her off, swinging the carving knife. She was insanely jealous, you see, of my real mother, who still cleaned house for us. But I loved this warm charlady I knew only as Mrs. Johnstone. For some reason, she used to sing a sad song about Marilyn Monroe.

Mrs. Johnstone gave me a locket with a picture of herself, which I always wore even though I was called a sissy at school. You may well imagine how I felt when my mad mother suddenly fired her without so much as a by-your-leave. I was forbidden to play with Mickey *ever again.* And, indeed, we moved far away from the neighborhood to a house in the country where Mad Mum stopped hearing voices, though not for long.

But guess what? It's almost unbelievable. One day, I was walking in the glorious English countryside when I heard the familiar joyful sound of "Fook! Go fook yourself!" It was Mickey! My goodness, what was he doing in the glorious English countryside, when he surely should have been home in his Liverpool slum?

The fickle finger of Fate can be a strange and curious thing. He was our new neighbor. A slum clearance program had rehoused Mickey and my real mother in the countryside where we now lived. What *luck!* Though, I need scarcely add, not so lucky for Mad Mum.

Have I mentioned that Mickey had a rather attractive girlfriend named Linda who was always flashing her knickers? As I progressed into adolescence, and into Oxford, I found myself curiously attracted to the flighty, though warm-hearted, Linda. "The girl in the woman," as the song goes, "trying to get free. Always doing the wash. Always making tea." It loses a little something without the music. But that superstitious trickster known as Fate was to take both Mickey and me to a calamitous end!

While I lived a carefree life of slothful ease at college and was destined, no doubt, to become a member of Parliament, poor Mickey joined the ranks of the unemployed and was involved in a robbery in order to support Linda, now his pregnant bride. But I didn't know that at the time. I thought Linda was free! And, in spite of our class differences, I had asked her to marry me. All right, I admit it. We may have had a one-night stand during this time. It just sort of happened. I was trying to *help*. I still think there was absolutely no reason for Mickey, having been released from prison and now clinically depressed, to come after me with a gun.

In fact, I shouldn't be telling you any of this. Because I'm dead.

My twin brother Mickey shot me dead, and the cops shot Mickey dead. And that's the legacy of the class wars of England for you. That is also the story of *Blood Brothers*, the British musical with book, music, and lyrics by Willy Russell (of *Educating Rita*), now unbelievably on Broadway. O England! Or as the one-man doggerel chorus tells us darkly at the end: "And we call it superstition / For what has come to pass / But could it be what we in England / Come to know as class?"

I doubt it. But forgive me: my true life-story will have to wait until I tell of my early days as an explorer up the Amazon.

Sleeping
at the Theater

Am I wrong, or are people sleeping in unprecedented numbers at the theater? "To sleep, perchance . . ." Of course, it depends how good the show is—but not necessarily. Not necessarily at all. In spite of the limited leg room, the theater has traditionally been a warm and cozy and plush place for a nice little nap. It's said that the worst sound you can hear at the theater is that of polite attention. But the sound of sleep is worse. The lights go down, the curtain goes up . . . Zzzzzzzz.

Don't deny it! I've *seen* you, lolling. I've seen total strangers fast asleep in each other's arms. "What the—" "Sorry!" "Zzzzzzzz." Theater parties making a special pilgrimage and block bookings for a charitable cause are notoriously big sleepers. It has a lot to do with the banquet beforehand. And the cast always *knows.* They can hear the crescendo of light snoring. On the other hand, I've never seen an actor fall asleep on stage—though, during *Hamlet* at the Royal National Theater, I saw Albert Finney fall asleep on his feet. "To be or not to be. That is the question," he began the unforgettable soliloquy, in his tights. But he blanked. He couldn't believe it, either. After a stunned moment or two, it was clear to the audience, and even clearer to him, that the prompter was sound asleep, or in the pub. So the audience helpfully yelled out the next line, "Whether 'tis nobler in the mind to *suffer*," and Mr. Finney continued nobly.

To eat and drink and be merry before or after the show? That is the question. For myself, not before. Because if the show isn't good, there's always something to look forward to, something that might yet save the day. And if the show is terrific, there's reason to celebrate. Let me say now that, out of lifelong respect for the performer and the happy breed who work so hard in the theater, I have never, ever fallen asleep during a performance, except at matinees. Matinees are the perfect postlunch, midday doze, a quiet cultural communion and private moment. Wasn't it Arthur Schnitzler, after all, who said that theater is a refuge from reality?

We, the audience, are actually witnessing a superreality on stage, which is a living dream. Where else do kings and killers, ghosts and relatives, parade before us, except in dreams? We are all the actors and authors of our own dreams, said Freud, though Freud didn't have to see the musical *Five Guys Named Moe*. Critics, in the line of habitual duty, are always falling asleep at the theater, yet they have the last word, which isn't fair at all. A while ago, a leading New York critic fell asleep during an opening night. The following evening, the star actor in the play bumped into him at Sardi's. "I see you're *awake*," said the actor. "True," the critic replied. "But then, you're not on stage."

Sleep is contagious at the theater. During a recent performance of Samuel Beckett's *Texts for Nothing*, John Simon, of all vigilant critics, could be seen discreetly dozing off. Then the lady accompanying him dozed off, too. Then Robin Wagner, the Tony Award–winning set designer, who was seated next to Mr. Simon, joined them. He was sleeping with the enemy!

Theater people, like critics, always fall asleep at the theater, and often during their own productions. This is because they have seen the show a million times. They sometimes have good judgment, too. When Peter Martins of the New York City Ballet choreographed Andrew Lloyd Webber's *Song and Dance*, he asked Lincoln Kirstein, guru to Balanchine, to attend a rehearsal. But within seconds Mr. Kirstein was sound asleep, awakening only when it was over. "What did you think?" Mr. Martins asked him later. "Absolutely terrible!" Mr. Kirstein replied.

It's best to be bold, or vaguely tactful. Years ago, a play of mine was produced in England, and to my immense pride it played in my hometown. But as soon as the curtain went up, my father fell asleep. I tried nudging him, feeling he was missing the best bits, but he slept contentedly throughout the entire proceedings. "Enjoy the show?" I asked with a little edge when he awoke to applaud louder than anyone.

My friend Robin Wagner—John Simon's sleeping partner at the Beckett play—outdid himself recently. He fell asleep during his *own* play.

This is not only astonishing, but proves what a fair-minded democrat he is. Mr. Wagner not only snoozes through other people's plays but his own. He is one of America's finest stage designers, and a secret playwright. To my surprise, he had casually mentioned he was having a reading at the Ensemble Studio Theater of a play he'd written, and would I come? "Absolutely!" I said, though I was looking forward to going to a movie.

Twelve actors were seated in a semicircle for the reading. "We cut thirty other characters," he whispered to me, looking nervous. "We also cut one and a half hours."

It was a rainy Saturday afternoon. "There's going to be more people in the cast than in the audience," he added. But before long, a few souls joined us. The director Randall Sommer and I sat apart from Robin, to be able to hide, if necessary.

His play turned out to be an epic. Entitled *The Straits of Magellan*, it was based on the true story of Ferdinand Magellan, the first man to circumnavigate the earth. Act 1 was a shade too long, to say the least. Still, I was admiring its narrative sweep, its sense of history, its intriguing philosophical questions concerning the symbolism of all voyages, of free will and the divine, when I heard the unmistakable sound of snoring coming from Robin Wagner.

"*Sssh!*" I said to someone who tried to wake him. "How dare you! He's the author!"

Act 2 flew by, however. "Well, you know what's wrong with the first act!" I said to him afterward. "How could I?" he responded cheerfully. "I was asleep." But, of course, he knew it was too long. He thanked the actors, and we went off for a drink. "What do you *really* think of it?" he asked. A very dangerous question.

"Where was the music?" I replied, taking a gamble. "I wrote it to music!" he exclaimed, and looked delighted. He had originally written the entire play to Spanish and Portuguese court music, as well as to pre-Gregorian and Sephardic music. He had written an *opera*. It was there! For the taking. And Mr. Wagner the Broadway designer, who has also designed sets for the Vienna State Opera and Covent Garden, went off to cut and rework his potentially wonderful piece of music-theater. "I'll sleep on it," he said, waving good-bye.

The Killing of
Wonderful Tennessee

Rest in peace, dearly beloved. Brian Friel's elegy to hope and to certain lost horizons, *Wonderful Tennessee*, closed at the Plymouth on Broadway after only nine performances, or one week. One miserable week for this masterly playwright of such generous talent and heart; one miserable week for the great ensemble from Dublin's Abbey Theatre, who were our guests.

What more careless discourtesy could we pay them? How is it possible, when far lesser, feeble dramas are still alive on Broadway, that so tender a play should be so swiftly killed? The reviews were "reserved"; several felt that *Wonderful Tennessee* did not quite match Mr. Friel's *Dancing at Lughnasa*. "It's frustrating if they want us to get like Hollywood now, bringing over *Lughnasa II, III* and *IV*," Noel Pearson, the Irish producer who brought Mr. Friel's new drama here from the Abbey, told the *New York Times*.

The romantic Mr. Pearson is therefore a clairvoyant, sensing the real state of Broadway and the fate of his own production. The death of Broadway has been reported before, of course. But the abrupt closure of *Wonderful Tennessee* is a decisive moment. The play, which is about dreams and reality and the stripping away of all pretense, is pivotal because it confirms the reality. Broadway, if we need any reminding, is no longer home to serious drama. It will produce British imports and the occasional big prestige play *(Angels in America)*. But why pretend anymore? Broadway is an overpriced dead-zone bordello for tourists, producing megamusicals, revivals, and safe bets.

Or flukes. Mr. Friel's *Dancing at Lughnasa*, the story of five Irish sisters living in poverty in 1936 County Donegal, did not seem on the surface to be a safe commercial bet for Broadway. Its success was a gigantic, welcome fluke. It was lucky! *Dancing at Lughnasa* was more easily accessible than the elegiac *Wonderful Tennessee.* I think it was mistakenly compared to Chekhov. But it was a lovely memory play made indelible by the ecstatic dance of the five sisters, dancing disenchantment into dust.

It is written: "A time to mourn, and a time to dance." But whilst almost everyone knows how to dance in happiness, few know how to dance in sorrow. (The Irish know.) And I trust the splendidly drunken cast of *Wonderful Tennessee* danced till dawn at the wake for their play. Yet my memories of *Wonderful Tennessee* are filled with the spirit of Mr. Friel's dance that takes us far beyond "reality" or the power of words. At one point, a character in the play asks the others to tell a story. "Go on," she encourages them. "Once upon a time…" And the professional accordion player, who is dying, tells his story in a minute or so, the entire story of his sad life. How?

His hands dance maniacally over his accordion, expertly playing, of all choices, a Beethoven sonata. The accordion is an odd and comic instrument, and at first we laugh, only to be silenced. Mr. Friel's musician would have been a virtuoso pianist had life turned out differently for him, and his music and story is a dance of death, or of remembered joy. And what of another of Mr. Friel's vivid characters, the comically failed writer Frank, who is entranced by the vision of a dolphin in the ocean near Donegal pier? He *saw* it, like a magic signal, this apparition of a dolphin who *danced* for him, and filled his soul with hope and wonder.

It is a poem and a lament that Mr. Friel has written, brimming with humor and good stories and song. The musical ironies and core of sadness and regret remind one of the dark humor of Beckett, who, after all, was Irish.

Set in the present, *Wonderful Tennessee* is about a birthday outing for three middle-class couples who gather on Donegal pier for a boat trip to a mysterious island. What could be more different from *Dancing at Lughnasa?* The cheerful gathering led by the amiable bookie (Donal McCann, just excellent) might easily be us—the wife who visits a psychiatrist, the unfaithful husband, the dying man, the drinker, the rationalist, the dreamer.

In their way, they could be Irish versions of Chekhov in comic, secret mourning for their lives. Virtually the first line of the play, thrown away, not spelled out in any way, is "Do you know how desperately unhappy I am?" That's Chekhov! But, of course, Mr. Friel, the dramatist also of *Faith Healer* and *Philadelphia, Here I Come!* possesses his own voice, grown darker with yearning.

Who else would tell such a fabulous yarn about the home of Jesus of Nazareth, which apparently flew to Italy in 1294, thereby becoming a mobile shrine to the Patron Saint of Aviation? But that mystical, symbolic island that the group longs to sail to (but cannot reach) has caused difficulty for some. Perhaps it's too blatant a symbol of salvation, though I didn't see it that way. Mr. Friel is far too humane a dramatist to be pretentious, and his yearning for the transcendent, for some living link with myth and spirit—or peace of mind—strikes me as completely and wonderfully natural. The intellectualization of similar needs in the hands of dramatists such as Terrence McNally, John Guare, and Peter Shaffer does not compare.

But what is his island beyond the horizon but our own need for a safe harbor of the spirit, some sense of grace, some undefined home? So his revelers leave behind on the harbor some signs and relics—of what? Their existence, a testament to lives that could yet be saved.

It might be that *Wonderful Tennessee* is flawed; it might be that it is Mr. Friel's "problem play." But one day it will surely be reclaimed. Its very fine cast was Donal McCann, John Kavanagh, Ingrid Craigie, Robert Black, Catherine Byrne, and Marion O'Dwyer. The direction, design, and lighting were by Patrick Mason, Joe Vanek, and Mick Hughes. Their wake on October 31 was, I trust, a merry old wake, with a lot of booze and dancing and song and poetry, and special mention, I'm sure, of their patron saint of the Abbey Theater, one William Butler Yeats.

I have spread my dreams under your feet:
Tread softly because you tread on my dreams

How to Murder
Your Mother

I must offer a minority opinion about Martin McDonagh's raved-over *Beauty Queen of Leenane*. The accomplished director Garry Hynes first produced the play at the Druid Theatre Company, which she founded, and it marked Mr. McDonagh's bright professional debut at the not so tender age of twenty-three. His writing is too self-assured for him to give a damn about his relative inexperience. But I don't think *The Beauty Queen of Leenane* is a good play, let alone the great and memorable Gothic drama we're told it is. To which its many admirers may well respond, "Ah, bollocks to ya!"—as the drama's doomed heroine likes to say.

Mr. McDonagh, now twenty-seven, extravagantly hyped on both sides of the Atlantic—I've been guilty of some of the hype myself—had a phenomenal four plays running simultaneously in London. No dramatist in memory can equal that achievement. *The Beauty Queen of Leenane* is New York's first taste of his work, whose voice, already worn with sorrow and savage humor, has been compared to the J. M. Synge of *Playboy of the Western World*. But his debut remains a comparatively minor drama compared to his maturer, more accomplished *Cripple of Inishman*. *The Beauty Queen of Leenane* is a Grand Guignol yarn told by a born storyteller. But we have serious doubts about the telling. The play is a dark comedy—some call it a spectral tragedy—revolving around an awesomely familiar theme. In retrospect, we wouldn't have been too surprised had the dramatist opened the spooky proceedings with a mighty thunderclap and the foreboding, time-honored, "It was a dark and stormy night…"

Set in Leenane, the dramatist's invented hellhole in Connemara where it pours with ungodly rain and the sight of a cow loping across a field is a major event, strange and terrible events take place in the stifling, rural backwater. Mag Folan, the mother from hell, a bullying old gnarled hag maliciously emptying her pisspot into the kitchen sink, and her daughter Maureen, bone-tired at forty, an eternal spinster eternally trapped, live together in mutual hatred and petty primal feuds about lumpy porridge and foul-tasting biscuits. When poor Maureen's one chance of love and marriage enters her desolate life—the opportunity at last to escape—horrible Mum ruins it. And it will take you about five and a half minutes to guess that Mum won't be around much longer, what with the deranged look in Maureen's eyes and a young local lad saying innocently how the big poker by the stove would make an admirable murder weapon and all.

We know—and can't fail to know—that all will end in bloody disaster. The cheek of this gifted young dramatist! He appears to be sending up Gothic melodramas as much as he expects us to take him seriously. He's assuming—rightly—that we'll want the victimized daughter, who's no sweetheart herself, to deep-six her appalling slag of a mother. Which she gleefully does in the end by throwing boiling fat over the old crone— Wicked Witch Boils in Oil—finishing off the grizzly job with that prized family heirloom, the poker. But what we're watching—surely—is a low-budget horror movie that more than creaks a bit. In another life, it would have starred Bette Davis.

But we aren't unnerved, as we should be. The plot devices are telegraphed at every twist. The entire action—and Maureen's tragic fate— hinges on the conventional melodrama of a crucial letter ending up in the wrong hands—in Mummy's cruel, indolent hands. Maureen's slow-witted suitor, Pato Dooley, tells his younger brother, dim Ray Dooley, *three times* to be certain, absolutely certain—now don't be forgetting or I'll kill you—to be absolutely and unwaveringly certain to deliver his letter *only* into the hands of Maureen. Pato's letter, written from London, asks her to come to America with him. He could have asked her in person when he comes back home to visit, but then we wouldn't have had the business with the letter. *Don't forget to deliver the letter to Maureen—right? Are you listening to me now?*

The plot of Ibsen's *Doll's House* notoriously revolves round a letter, too. So the Irishman's in good company. But he goes a little further than Ibsen. When the unreliable Ray Dooley turns up at Maureen's home to make the delivery, only the ogre is there—casting a greedy, beady eye on the letter he's carrying. "I'm under strict orders now," says Ray defensively. And we're praying to ourselves: *Don't forget to deliver the letter to Maureen.* But— oh no!—the dope hands it over to the mother-witch, saying, "And may God strike you dead if you open it!"

God does just that. And we are not surprised. At the play's end, Maureen—who, we learn, spent some time in the nut house during her youth— is now destined for a life of delusional, rotting loneliness in her mother's threadbare shoes, stuck forever in her rocking chair in front of the depressed, unending dull glow of the telly.

The Beauty Queen of Leenane—said to be ushering in new-wave Irish drama—is an old-fashioned potboiler and power play. It isn't well made; it is splendidly acted. The Irish actors play off each other so well: they are authentically, unaffectedly real in ways we don't often see. In particular, Marie Mullen's beaten, bitter, fleetingly exultant Maureen is an extraordinary model of naturalism. But we aren't happy with Martin McDonagh's over-praised drama, failing to see it even in terms of a rattling good mystery tale. In his hard-edged reality and absence of sentiment, he's distancing himself from the elegaic memory plays of Brian Friel and the older generation of Irish dramatists. So are the ghostly monologues of Conor McPherson. But so far, both have created quirky tall tales of Ireland compared to the enduring substance of Sebastian Barry's devastating *Steward of Christendom*, with the mad bliss of its hero, saint or betrayer, a relic of savage history lost in its crossfire.

Mr. McDonagh's love of Ireland—he lives in London—is born with gallows humor out of affection and disaffection. An Irish friend of mine is troubled by how much the play unconsciously reinforces the patronizing myth of an Ireland that's home to backward yokels living in squalor and ignorance, as if Ireland, with its stormy nights and goblins and Guinness, were still locked in turn-of -the-twentieth-century backwater blarney. As if Ireland had never become our contemporary. And to that I say: Don't forget to deliver the letter to Maureen. Mr. McDonagh nevertheless mocks the Irish postcard stereotype in *The Beauty Queen of Leenane,* but he does it to more satisfying effect in the superior *Cripple of Inishman.* His first play led to greater things, better tales.

Brave
New World

I report with joy that the watershed achievement of George C. Wolfe's *Tempest* is to throw off the weary weight of Europe and break with all English styles. For the first time in my experience of Shakespeare in the Park, we have a glorious, unapologetically American production. In its blazing, inventive energy and melting-pot cross-culturalism—the vision of the Brazilian stilt walkers, the heat of the very un-English percussionists, the Indonesian puppets and timeless shadow plays—this is a *Tempest* utterly free at last of the traditionally English Shakespearean.

For too long—it seems like a century—American producers of Shakespeare have been bending on one knee before England as if America were still colonized. The superiority of the British in stiffly poetic, mundanely staged Shakespeare productions is an illusion breeding inferiority complexes among the former colonies. And what is *The Tempest* really about but lost illusions and freedom?

Prospero has "colonized" his found island and New World, teaching the natives—his enslaved Caliban—how to speak proper English. He gets no thanks for that:

> You have taught me language; and my profit on't
> is, I know how to curse. The red plague rid you
> of learning me your language!

So the bold, if flawed, new production frees us from the colonial curse of how to do Shakespeare, and reinvents the language of production from an uninhibited American perspective. On the other hand, Mr. Wolfe may also be suggesting, in a sly aside, be careful or you may end up speaking like Patrick Stewart's Prospero.

No one declaims like Patrick Stewart. The former Royal Shakespeare Company stalwart, now captain of the starship *Enterprise*, has "the voice." When Miranda says to him, "Your tales, sir, would cure deafness," you better believe her. Mr. Stewart as Prospero, like every other role I recall him playing during his RSC years in London, has two acting styles: rhetorical loud and rhetorical louder. He has no need of the body mike he casts off in Prospero's frail last words. Mr. Stewart will never give a bad performance; he's an accomplished actor, but greatness eludes him. He is a Prospero without magic.

Perversely in so spontaneous a production, some scholar's idea of correct Shakespearean pronunciation has Mr. Stewart pronouncing Milan as "Millen" (as in "millinery"). Mr. Stewart's Prospero is the deposed duke of Millen. "Alas, poor Millen!" and there, in all its declamatory glory, is the British style and *the* voice! But it cannot make us feel. It is remote from real, live action—the Shakespearean actor as flesh and blood.

No one in this *Tempest* touches us more than the utterly natural Carrie Preston as Miranda. She's a wonderful young American actress—a discovery. Ms. Preston abandons the traditional way of playing Miranda as a lyrical English rose with pretty daisies in her hair. She's a tomboy! And one thinks, with a sense of revelation: Of course! The only men Miranda has known on the island until the arrival of her love, Ferdinand, are her dad, Prospero, and the hag-monster Caliban. Wouldn't she be a tomboy, then? Well, why not? Ms. Preston is so alive and real, and fun. She's the best Miranda I've seen. But, alas, the Ferdinand of Kamar de los Reyes is at sea: a stock romantic juvenile lead mangling the verse. And here we begin to hit trouble. Whereas Mr. Wolfe has reimagined his Miranda, whose lyricism is effortless, he has taken his Ariel (Aunjanue Ellis) too far in the wrong direction. He has made Ariel human.

Ariel, a spirit, an angel who is Prospero's avenging angel, may be played by a man or a woman. But he, she, or "it" must be a third force, a power beyond the human : "to dive into fire, to ride / On the curl'd clouds." This unpoetic Ariel is too obviously a woman, and worse, costumed like a modern cabaret star. In reversing the conventional rules—Ariel as an ethereal abstraction, perhaps in tights or wings—Mr. Wolfe has given us a taut, stylized, earthbound human, whereas Ariel must be electric and light as air. The lapse creates an imbalance with Caliban (well spoken and acted by Teagle F. Bougere). But this Caliban—"not honour'd with a human shape"—is almost too recognizably the exotic "native," and a little too lightweight to be the central tragic figure of the play. Bill Irwin has brought a familiar bag of tricks with him as Trinculo—and strangely for him, he isn't always amusing. But his partner in comic crime, John Pankow as a drunken Stephano, compelled here by Mr. Irwin to go it alone, carries the day.

We remember, then, the staggering visual sweep and beauty of George Wolfe's production: a brilliant storm sequence; the breathtaking "masque" scene performed on stilts; the puppet underworld of Devil's Island; the betrothal party that explodes like a Brazilian carnival. If we are going to have a party, Mr. Wolfe is saying, let's do it. So the visceral magic and rhythm of this *Tempest* truly reflects the world, as Shakespeare intended—Old and New World, on a stage, which is the world.

And here the stage is a globe of sand. The magic that takes place isn't of the refined English kind, but cosmic "rough magic"—again as Shakespeare intended. "Trouble, wonder and amazement inhabit here," though not "torment." That is the crucial missing element. Torment is absent from Mr. Wolfe's production. In spite of the lapses, it is almost too infectious. The percussionists play on when the production ends—and we want to dance along with them. Should we?

Shakespeare's *Tempest* is severe and dark at center, but not so here. And Prospero's farewell to us is in despair: "Now I want / Spirits to enforce, art to enchant / And my ending is despair...."

It was Shakespeare's farewell to the stage, too. Prospero has forgiven his entrapped enemies, reclaimed his dukedom, and set Ariel and Caliban free. Yet his closing words seem desolate. Divested of all magic, now merely mortal, Prospero still looks to spirits to enforce, and art to enchant. He despairs, but within his struggle he sees a new world and a new beginning.

Safe Pedophilia

There's a new confessional theater we'll call Oprah-Drama. The Oprah-Drama phenomenon, like Kathryn Harrison's memoir of incest, *The Kiss*, ranges from Paula Vogel's highly regarded drama about incest and pedophilia, *How I Learned to Drive*, to a sweet little musical about a horribly scarred young woman in search of an Oklahoma preacher with healing hands, *Violet*, to John Patrick Shanley's *Psychopathia Sexualis*, which is about the troubled life and times of a sock fetishist.

The hero of Mr. Shanley's unexpectedly sparkling comedy is unable to make love to his future bride without his father's argyle socks. He doesn't have to wear them. He has to touch them. "Therapy's not so great," he confesses forlornly to his best friend. "I've been going six years. I still need the socks."

Would that the earnest Paula Vogel possessed the good humor of John Patrick Shanley—or any humor. Though *How I Learned to Drive* is described—and sold—as both a comedy and a tragedy, it's hard to see the comedy in child molesting. What's Ms. Vogel's message? Relax with incest? Pedophilia, the tragicomedy? I couldn't see the humor in her taboo-breaking drama, though others do.

"A wonderful new play," the *New York Times* hailed it. "Both wryly objective and deeply empathetic; angry and compassionate; light-handed and devastating…." To the contrary, I think that Ms. Vogel has written a bland, ingratiatingly poor drama. The dramatist—whose most popular play is *The Baltimore Waltz*—has a reputation for writing on the dangerous edge. But she would have to be a genius to convey the lighter side of pedophilia. She would have to be Vladimir Nabokov.

In fact, Ms. Vogel has said that *How I Learned to Drive* was inspired by Nabokov's *Lolita*, her favorite book. "I read that book over and over again," she told the *Times*, fascinated by the Humbert Humbert character and how "the eroticizing of children is so prevalent in the culture yet so seldom acknowledged." But the Nabokovian irony of *Lolita* isn't meant to convey the eroticizing of children, as Ms. Vogel assumes, or to prophesy a culture of Calvin Klein ads. The brilliance of *Lolita* surely resides in its metaphor of old crumbling Europe (Humbert Humbert) being seduced by the lollipop charms of young, irresistible, uncultured America (Lolita).

In comparison, *How I Learned to Drive* is literal and bourgeois in its tale of Uncle Peck—as in "pecker"—and his reluctantly complicit niece with the somewhat crude name Li'l Bit. It is good that Ms. Vogel is as tired of stifling political correctness as most of us, but what exactly is she trying to do?

"I want to seduce the audience," she told the *Times*. "If they can go along for a ride they wouldn't ordinarily take, or don't even know they're taking, then they might see highly charged political issues in a new and unexpected way." Fair enough. She would like us to see both sides of the argument, with no clear-cut villains and victims. But why would she like us to be "seduced" by the pedophile charms of Uncle Peck? Because, she says, she would like "to see if audiences will allow themselves to find this erotic." In other words, Ms. Vogel would like us to be turned on by child molesters like Uncle Peck.

Now, Uncle Peck is an extremely *charming* pedophile. His perversity is virtually secondary, a blemish. Whether Ms. Vogel would like us to find him erotic if he were more obviously a vile human being, or a child murderer, is another question. Uncle Peck is presented as a sweetheart, a caring man and a good husband (who even washes the dishes after meals, being so thoughtful). He is therefore meant to be appealing to us. Ms. Vogel presumes too much. There is no such thing as a sympathetic child molester, any more than there are good racists.

Would it be dreadfully old-fashioned of me to ask: Whatever happened to right and wrong? Why does no one at the *Times* at least question the moral premise of the play? Uncle Peck, we learn, began molesting Li'l Bit when she was eleven years old. Ms. Vogel has written a discreet scene showing him briefly aroused when she sits on his knee as he drives a car. (Driving lessons are the running gag and suggestive emblem of the play.) But think about it. Ms. Vogel wishes us to be turned on by a pedophile aroused by an eleven-year-old child.

That isn't quite how she presents it, however. Far from being openly daring or dangerously provocative, Ms. Vogel is actually quite timid. She hasn't written the provocative drama she claims; she has neutralized the issues, making them more or less harmless. The outcome is dishonest. For one thing, she has made incest "tasteful," and pedophilia "comfortable." She notes about Uncle Peck in the script of How I Learned to Drive: "Despite a few problems, he should be played by an actor one might cast in the role of Atticus in To Kill a Mockingbird." As for the casting of Li'l Bit: "If the actor is too young, the audience may feel uncomfortable. With this particular play, the more we can make folks feel comfortable, the better...."

Come on in, folks! See the safe pedophilia! But making us feel comfortable isn't the business of radical dramatists. It's more the business of musicals. The face of the young heroine in the Off-Broadway musical Violet is severely disfigured. Its creators, Brian Crawley and Jeanine Tesori, have written a lovely musical—but we never see Violet's scars. We must imagine them—lest the reality, the entire raison d'être of the piece, prove too discomforting. It probably would (which is why the iconic mask of Phantom is so clever). Ms. Vogel has it both ways, though. She is radically comforting.

Uncle Peck, the charming pervert, is the only "decent" man around. Men in general are parodied by the sexist Ms. Vogel; they "only want one thing"; they give women pain; they cruelly mock Li'l Bit's large breasts (but kind Uncle Peck doesn't). Mary-Louise Parker plays Li'l Bit from the age of eleven to damaged adulthood at about forty. Looking about twenty-two throughout, Ms. Parker conveys childhood by turning her toes and knees inward, alas. But what do we actually see on stage? We see two adults at different stages of a doomed relationship in a car together. Uncle Peck isn't related to Li'l Bit by blood, but by marriage. (Comforting. It isn't really incest.) And Li'l Bit, played by an adult, passes for one. (More comforting.) Ms. Vogel didn't intend it this way, but How I Learned to Drive takes a leaf out of the heading in the driver's manual: "Idling in the Neutral Gear."

Paula Vogel's How I Learned to Drive went on to win the 1997 Pulitzer Prize for Drama.

The Sad Tale of Jack the Cat

The biggest drama this week has been the night my cat tried to strangle me. It's true we hadn't been getting along. I also realize I'm not always too easy to live with. I'm not ashamed to admit it. It takes two to tango, you know.

True, my previous experience with pets has been less than ideal. When my daughter was two, I had to explain why, after only twenty-five minutes, Goldie the Goldfish was lying absolutely still on its back in the fish tank. "It's dreaming of the ocean," I explained, but she didn't believe me. Tim the Tortoise—not a vibrant presence—didn't last long, either. It's the only tortoise I know who actually left home. Then came Brenda the Bulldog, a *pedigree* dog purchased for a colossal sum, who terrorized the entire family and ate the furniture. We became a postmodern family, dining off three-legged tables while seated on one-legged chairs. Or so it seemed. Eventually, we gave Brenda away to a good home of future minimalists who had a big garden, which would soon be a wreck, where Brenda could *romp*.

The curious thing is that my wife, who was to go the way of Tim the Tortoise, blamed me for all this. It's true we hadn't been getting along. But why blame me for the pets? We had just replaced Brenda the Bulldog with a designer dog, a shih tzu from Harrod's named Tommy. He was a depressive. "Well, he wasn't when he arrived," my wife said indignantly. Tommy jumped out of the car window during a family trip to the Cotswolds, I'm afraid.

My pet days were long since over when Jack the Cat, as I lovingly named him, arrived as a cuddly kitty in my apartment in New York. Jack was a gift. Now, anyone who knows me well would not give me such a gift. I'm so easy to please in other ways—a Cartier watch, two or three Turnbull & Asser shirts, money, a book. Anything but a pet. Jack the Cat was a stray who had been found in the countryside by a girlfriend. "You've no need to keep him, if you don't want," she said sweetly at the time. Well, what was I to do in the flush of a new romance? "What a lovely little kitty he is!" I heard myself cooing. "We must buy some cat litter immediately."

Gentlemen, a word of advice: When a beautiful girl looks at you with her dark melting eyes and offers you a little pussy, just say no. Make up an allergy, as cabdrivers do with cigarette smoke. Say anything, but do not fall for it. Because you do not know what that kitty will become. Because before you know it, your girl will have taken a powder and you will be left with Jack the Cat.

This is what my life has come to. I live with a cat. We are the Odd Couple. Oh, I'm not saying it wasn't fun at first. How we laughed! "Fetch the ball, Jack!" I'd call out, throwing the bouncing ball especially made for cats across the living room. Jack would fetch the ball. "Good boy! Now fetch the ball again, Jack." And Jack would fetch the ball again. "Good boy, Jack!"

This began to pall a little after two years. "Here's the ball again, Jack." He wasn't moving. "Look, Jack! String! You like string." Nothing. "Paper bag trick, Jack?" But poor Jack wasn't even up to that. Not that I didn't invent other fun and games for us both, such as hunt the slipper, hide and seek, and let's see who can destroy the apartment the most. But I sensed that the bloom was off the rose.

Even so, he has always been a beautiful cat, if I say so myself. And the neighborhood folks know him quite well. "How's Jack the Cat?" says Harry the Butcher while reluctantly walking his dogs. "He's been a naughty boy, Harry." But at least Jack and I have always talked to each other. "Well, here we are again, Jack. Another busy day!" Or: "Up for Zabar's smoked salmon, Jack? Who's a good boy?"

Let's face it. You're just a meal ticket to a cat. Jack lives for the Fancy Feast. Each morning he strides into the kitchen with the purposeful air of the ravenous. Then he has a catnap for three or four hours. Then he wakes up and bites me.

This is the thing. He began to bite the hand that feeds him, and for *absolutely no reason whatsoever.* "Catnip, Jack?" And Jack would go, "Yippee!" And bite me. I refuse to blame myself. That cat lives in luxury. He lives in better circumstances than I do. He has his own bedroom en suite. I'm a door-mat to him. You know my problem? I'm too good. You give and give until there's nothing left to give. He doesn't even use his bedroom en suite. He sleeps with me.

He doesn't give me any choice. He sleeps at the end of the bed, then he crawls in. I'm sleeping with a cat! "Jack," I say desperately. "Do me a favor. I'm expecting a stopover. Sleep in your room tonight, okay?" Then he purrs and I think, "You're not a bad old sausage, really. Who's a good boy?" Then he bites me again.

I sought help, principally from *How to Get Your Cat to Do What You Want*, by Warren and Fay Eckstein. "Signs of Depression—What to Look For: Is the normally sweet kitty more aggressive, or is the normally friendly, sociable cat hiding under the bed every time your visitors come by?" I've tried everything the Ecksteins recommend, including kitty calisthenics and throwing dinner parties so Jack the Cat will be suitably entertained. Nothing seems to work. And you know why? Jack the Cat hates me.

Not that blood isn't thicker than water. When I'm away—and, oh, to be away from Jack for even a day—ten-year-old Kate Blumm from upstairs looks after Jack. Kate's a kind of Salingeresque genius, and she used to love cats before she met Jack. "Boy," said her dad, Harvey the Postman, "is Jack the Cat *neurotic*." "I don't know what you mean, Harvey," I replied immediately. "He's never given me a moment's trouble." Though I was thinking of a sep-aration at the time, we must always defend the ones we love.

It was shortly afterward that Jack tried to kill me. It happened at 3 A.M. We were both asleep, Jack by my side as usual. "Nighty-night, Jack," I'd said, and dozed off, glad to be out of it, frankly. When all of a sudden—I didn't know what it was at first—Jack landed with a frightening thud on my chest. It was quite a shock, as you can imagine. But what was doubly shock-ing in the panic of the night was that he had his paws around my throat.

Good thing I'm a light sleeper, or I wouldn't be here to tell the tale. Cats just don't leap up in the air and go for your throat by accident. Well-mean-ing friends have suggested various theories: He had a nightmare, or mistook me for a pigeon. But he's never had a nightmare *before*. And I've seen him with pigeons. It's the only time he moves nowadays, chasing the pigeons outside the window where they gather. One day I'm going to leave that window open. But he *knows* what pigeons look like. And he knows they don't look anything like me.

Besides, he looked guilty, though not exactly remorseful. "Your days are numbered, buster," I told him in no uncertain terms, and I banished him from the bedroom forever. "You're grounded!" I called after him. "There are going to be new rules in this house! One more bite, one more…incident and it's *over*. Finished! You hear me?"

The next night, I lay awake in bed reading *Medea*. I was waiting for a sneak attack. "Nighty-night, Jack," I called out the room. "I'm just going to sleep now. Sleep tight." Two hours later, I heard him charging down the hallway. "My God," I thought, "I'm living with a werewolf."

You might wonder why I didn't close the bedroom door. I did. He battered it down. Jack charged through the door, obviously to make another attempt on my life. But I was ready for him this time. *"Hah!"* I cried in triumph as he took a flying leap at my throat. "What do you take me for—a pigeon?"

Mankind's grip on sanity can be tenuous at the best of times. But this was the state to which Jack the Cat had brought me. I decided there and then that he would be given away to one of those societies where a custodian with a voice like Boris Karloff's says, "Ah, yes. Jack will be more than happy here. Why, your Jack will be the happiest little cat he's ever been in his life."

I couldn't do it. Cats sense things. I know that Jack does. Ever since I told him that it was completely over between us, he's been as good as gold. It's still not perfect, of course. But he hasn't bitten me in a week now. I've allowed him back into the bedroom, having learned to sleep with one eye open. Things take time. Who knows—right, Jack? He's curled on my desk under the warmth of the lamp as I write this, staring at me.

Brilliant
Blues

August Wilson's *Seven Guitars* is a great, bluesy achievement. We would feel lucky in any season to see anything to equal this chronicle of a death foretold. Lloyd Richards's supreme production at the Walter Kerr Theater not only does the sprawling drama proud: it gives us an ensemble of seven actors, riffing brilliantly together like seven blues guitars.

The drama, which is set in Pittsburgh in 1948, is August Wilson's seventh play of his epic dramatization of twentieth-century America and the black experience. *Fences* and *The Piano Lesson* have each won the Pulitzer Prize, and it wouldn't be surprising if *Seven Guitars* gives Mr. Wilson his third. For me, however, it isn't the dramatist's admired poetry and lyricism, as such, that touches us so deeply. It is the utterly unaffected humaneness at his core that makes his stories complete and universal.

The blues are central to him. He has spoken eloquently of the legacy, born of oppression and yearning and, perhaps, the devil, as in "the devil's music": "One day in my stack of records I saw this odd-looking, typewritten yellow label. I put on this song called 'Nobody Can Bake a Sweet Jelly Roll Like Mine,' by Bessie Smith. And I heard this woman's voice that was so strikingly different than anything I'd ever heard. I was stunned, and I listened to it again. And I listened to it again. I listened to it twenty-two straight times. And I said, 'This is mine.' I knew that all the other music I'd listened to wasn't mine. But this was the lady downstairs at the boardinghouse—she could sing that song. And I began to look at the people in the house in which I lived in a new way, to connect them to the record, to connect them to some history. I claimed that music, and I've never looked back."

He does look back, though, to the boardinghouse of *Seven Guitars* that's run by a lady who could sing that song. *Seven Guitars* "sings" in that thrilling sense of the drama's sweep and cadence, as well as the naturalism and vitality of its fine cast (some of them accomplished musical performers). But the play itself—the stories it tells, from the fate of a rooster to the ritual combat of guns and knives—springs from the rage and raunch and love and lament of the blues.

In one sustained scene, the note struck ignites the stage with music, as three characters break out into song. They are all broke musicians:

Lawd, when I get back to Chicago
Gonna turn my ol' blues into green
Move over Muddy Waters
Make room for the meanest guitar man you done seen!

And the improvisatory joy on stage then is something to see: *Seven Guitars* is a tragedy, but it is not solemn. To the contrary, it's often funny. The incandescent outburst of the blues musicians sings disenchantment into the dust as the women of Brian Friel's *Dancing at Lughnasa* famously danced their grinding poverty into the ground with a spontaneous Irish jig. But August Wilson goes even further. In the midst of the blues sequence, the elderly half-mad Hedley, the play's bitter black conscience, crazed like a mad prophet in the wilderness, enters to hammer into place a single string of chicken wire.

"What's he gonna do with one string? He can't do nothing with one string."

"Watch!"

So the old man, who's a West Indian chicken slaughterer, begins to play "a simple tune for a simple instrument"—as if it might hold the secret to life, summoning spirits. "One string make plenty plenty music," he says. Then in a moment of such daring and simplicity that we could scarcely imagine a wise dramatist risking it, the hero reflects in quiet reverie: "If I could hear my mother pray again, I believe I'd pray with her...."

Seven Guitars is an epic blues song in words that tell the tale of Floyd, a musician and ex-jailbird whose death is mourned in the opening scene. The flashback narrative is like an extended improvised riff of duets, solos, and full ensemble, which takes place in the yard of the Pittsburgh boardinghouse where the seven characters shoot the breeze, with moonshine and roosters. Floyd (Schoolboy) Barton (Keith David) returns home to get back the girl he abandoned, Vera (Viola Davis). A record he made in Chicago has become an unexpected hit. Floyd, the sweet talker fated to have bad luck, has dreams of fame and fortune, and perhaps that seems a slender narrative device. But it's enough of a springboard for this great playwright to bewitch us with Floyd's world. From the outset, imagining funeral-parlor men as angels, Ms. Davis's Vera rivets us. Her early speech about the loss and betrayal of the abandoned is among the compelling reasons why this play proves so moving.

"After I had walked through an empty house for a year and a half looking for you," she tells Floyd, and one wants to avoid her outraged, tearful eyes. "After I would lay myself out on that bed and search my body for your fingerprints. He touched me here. Floyd touched me here and he touched me here and he touched me here and he kissed me here and he gave me here and he took me here and he ain't here he ain't here he ain't here...."

And there's good humor. As the common-sense, witty lady of the house, Louise (Michele Shay) advises Vera: "What I'm trying to tell you is don't let no man use you up and then talk about he gotta go. Shoot him first."

And there is an old madman (Roger Robinson) who dreams big dreams of fathering the Messiah and of owning a plantation so the white man won't tell him what to do. There's a pregnant young woman in trouble (Rosalyn Coleman) with her "little fast behind," who is capable of acts of miraculous, saving grace. There are sidekicks like Canewell (the terrific, cool Ruben Santiago-Hudson), who can talk of love as if it were an unembarrassed, tender confession: "I always did believe in love...." And there's a sunnier sidekick, the drummer Red (Tommy Hollis), who remembers this childhood rhyme:

One bright morning in the middle of the night
Two dead boys got up to fight
Back to back they faced each other
Drew their swords and shot each other
A deaf policeman heard the noise
And came and killed those two dead boys.

August Wilson makes the mundane world—the everyday world of living and of getting through—extraordinary, like a gift or a poisoned chalice. By the final curtain of *Seven Guitars*, sane dreams have ended in desperation and death, and big, mad mythic ones have burnt to ashes. You should see this memory play of bluesy, proud, humane love. As with all stunning blues songs, Mr. Wilson's rich drama of struggle and the black experience ends movingly where it began, as a memorial to imagined angels and faith, or as an elegy to life enduring in silent tears.

Holocaust Denial

The new, improved version of the *Diary of Anne Frank* has opened on Broadway, packaged like any commodity. It's better! It's different! It's more Jewish....

Why, forty years after it was first produced on Broadway, has it been revived? The question is far from frivolous. We ask it all the time about revivals of classics. Let me say from the outset that, whatever the so-called improvements to the original, a Broadway potboiler is a Broadway potboiler. It never was a great play; it still isn't. We have no need to be defensive or apologetic because its subject is the Holocaust. To the contrary, we should be put on red alert. Is the Holocaust an appropriate subject for a commercial venue thriving under the festive banner of Entertainment?

Why revive *The Diary of Anne Frank* today? You would think that theater, at least, had moved on. Do we need another old-fashioned drama, another good cry? The original tearjerker was created by hacks from Anne Frank's iconic diaries. The Hollywood screenwriters Frances Goodrich and Albert Hackett had previously worked on *It's a Wonderful Life* and *Easter Parade*. Little wonder they managed to turn the already censored diaries into a near secular song to life. Anne Frank's most famous line could have been written for them: "I still believe, in spite of everything, that people are truly good at heart."

As the Holocaust survivor Bruno Bettelheim pointed out about the "truly good at heart": "If all men are good, there never was an Auschwitz." The safe, sentimental play and Otto Frank's doctored version of the diary on which the 1950s drama was based subverted and trivialized history. In her blistering condemnation of the Anne Frank industry in the *New Yorker*, Cynthia Ozick wrote that the mythic story has been "bowdlerized, distorted, transmuted, traduced, reduced; it has been infantilized, Americanized, homogenized, sentimentalized, falsified, kitschified, and in fact, blatantly and arrogantly denied."

The lady, obviously, is scandalized (and she forgot to mention "vandalized"). At times, her zeal is overdramatized. But who would deny her the agony that she feels and her outraged sense of betrayal? She is protesting, loud and clear, against the Holocaust amnesia actually caused by cheap, quite comforting Broadway fare such as *The Diary of Anne Frank.*

"Cheap sentimentality at the expense of a great catastrophe," Hannah Arendt wrote of the original play. And Ms. Ozick concludes at one point, "Almost every hand that has approached the diary with the well-meaning intention of publicizing it has contributed to the subversion of history."

Why the new production? James Lapine, its director (and the overpraised Pulitzer Prize–winning playwright of Stephen Sondheim's *Sunday in the Park with George*), explained in a recent interview, "The play had to be made stageworthy for 1997. That is not to cast aspersions on the earlier production. It's just a different era now. The war is not as present in people's lives as it was then. Plus, there will be hordes of people coming…who know nothing about the Holocaust."

Mr. Lapine appears to be saying, firstly, that when the Holocaust was more present in our lives, it was therefore okay to have a hackneyed play about it. But will "hordes of people" who today, apparently, "know nothing about the Holocaust" now go to Broadway to learn all about it?

Has it come to this? Our memory and unending nightmare is now bequeathed to Broadway and Steven Spielberg. If there are "hordes of people" who know nothing about the Holocaust, they are ignorant people. It's difficult to accept that any home proud to be called civilized—and any Jewish home in particular—could be so ignorant. How will they be helped by a Broadway version of a Holocaust tragedy? We have been reared on the harrowing, indestructible testament of documentaries such as *The Sorrow and the Pity,* and *Shoah,* and the books of Primo Levi and Elie Wiesel, among others. Go, or be dragged, to a Holocaust museum. But do not tell us that dinner and a Broadway show are the answer.

"We wanted to deepen the Jewish themes, to confront the Holocaust more directly," explained David Stone, one of the producers of the new *Diary of Anne Frank*. It's an honorable enough intention, though it reveals the original play to be nonsensical. It *avoided* the Holocaust; it neutralized Jewish themes. The new version has been adapted by Wendy Kesselman from the uncensored diaries, published in 1995. Otto Frank cut passages describing, for example, his daughter's adolescent sexual awakening and her resentment of her mother, as well as references to "the cruelest monsters ever to walk the earth."

The outcome is solemn and dutiful (as if Cynthia Ozick were hovering menacingly over the entire proceedings). Mr. Lapine has never been an inspired director. His notion of making the Holocaust "relevant" is to punctuate a scene with a loud recording of a Hitler rally or the sound of a train thundering over tracks in menacing red light.

The adapter, Ms. Kesselman, is so conscientious that one senses the B student, anxious not to risk offense. The Holocaust is now more present, but the play remains a safe potboiler. "No one is leaving! If we panic, we are lost!" "I will make the best latkes you ever tasted." "Stop! I can't bear it!" "I'm sorry about Mother. We just don't get along." There is some new material, yet there is nothing we don't already know, nothing we haven't already seen in second-rate dramas elsewhere or a TV movie of the week. Yet some in the audience were in tears as if on cue, as if attending a pious empty ritual or a soap opera, in which only the monstrous end is too terrible for words.

Does the new, improved *Diary of Anne Frank* subvert history—as Ms. Ozick convincingly said of the original? Maybe so. But it's hard to see the play itself as that important to history. The new production is just a marginally better version of a mediocre play. Ms. Ozick herself has written a poor Holocaust play. *The Shawl,* her stage adaptation of her own novella, was produced at the Jewish Repertory Theater two seasons ago. Starring Dianne Weist, directed by Sidney Lumet, her prestigious, well-intentioned first play about Holocaust denial and memory turned out—frankly—to be a forgettable mediocrity.

Was she, therefore, subverting history? No, we would say of Ms. Ozick, the dramatist, what Henry James said following the failure of his play *Guy*

Domville: "I may have been meant for the Drama—God knows!—but I certainly wasn't meant for the Theater." No one, except lunatics and Hollywood hacks, consciously subverts history. For all kinds of reasons, many of them misguided, *The Diary of Anne Frank* has been revived on Broadway. The production stars sixteen-year-old Natalie Portman as Anne, with a solid cast that includes George Hearn, Linda Lavin, Harris Hulin, and Austin Pendleton doing their stuff, doing their honest best.

The Amazing Vanessa Redgrave

If I were an actress—heaven forbid—I would avoid playing Cleopatra. In her bewildering, magnificent entirety, she's virtually unplayable. In her "infinite variety," Cleopatra is too much—and too much for mere mortals. I've long been convinced, however, that Vanessa Redgrave was born on another planet. Her God-given talent isn't of this world. There's no one like her, no one quite so glorious and so gloriously unhinged. Now sixty, beautiful and at the peak of her powers, she is a near-mythic actress playing a myth.

Cleopatra, Queen and Serpent of the Nile, magics and consumes the world, and spits it out as if the world were a paltry thing and "kingdoms are clay." No heroine is more baffling, no whore more seductive, no goddess less divine. Arguably the most challenging female role of all, Cleopatra seems to mesmerize and bewitch and infuriate her own creator—as if Shakespeare, like Antony, had fallen wildly in love with the unfathomable.

It surprises us to realize that his heroine is no longer young. Cleopatra might be knocking forty or more. Her hair is described as graying. Antony is described as "grizzled," a battle-scarred general, knocking fifty and a day. *Antony and Cleopatra* isn't, then, the story of the young, innocent love of *Romeo and Juliet*. It's a tragedy of mature and immature love, a desperate romantic obsession, and very dangerous. Antony and Cleopatra are half in love with death, or eternity. The shifting, mercurial, murderous moods of Cleopatra transform Antony, "the triple pillar of the world," into "a strumpet's fool." But no mere strumpet, she.

"She is vain. She is vulgar. She is cruel. She is cowardly. She is a born commander. She is a born slave. She is innately faithful. She is innately deceitful," wrote critic and playwright Herbert Farjeon, and one senses his frustration. Cleopatra is all things, and all things to all men. "She is at once Rosalind, Beatrice, Ophelia, Gertrude, Cressida, Desdemona, Cordelia and Lady Macbeth," wrote Shakespeare scholar G. Wilson Knight, who had already compared her to Helen of Troy.

Vanessa Redgrave's Cleopatra at the Joseph Papp Public Theater—she also directs the production—is her third Cleopatra. (Her first was in 1973, directed by Tony Richardson, her late husband.) She touches greatness this time around. She miraculously plays every note and some that aren't in the book—except for the Lady Macbeth within, the poison within the snake. The serpentine venom—as opposed to capriciousness—is absent. Yet Ms. Redgrave astonishes us, all but pulling off the impossible.

She goes for broke from the start—literally dancing onstage with the company. Why not? This radiant Cleopatra has just fallen in love (again)! Ms. Redgrave is so open and luminous it's extraordinary. She giddily conveys Cleopatra's narcissism in her opening line to the dazzled Antony: "If it be love, indeed, tell me how much?" In other demanding words: "How much do you love me?" (To which the true response would be, "Never enough!")

She is a Cleopatra who would compel kingdoms to be kissed away. The serpent may be missing from Ms. Redgrave's memorable performance, but not the opulent, reckless love, the imperial power and romantic destiny. You believe that she could be fire and air in a vile world. (And, let's face it, Antony is a lovesick dope, anyway.) Cleopatra, in turn, is in love with a romantic myth. The unadorned lyricism of Ms. Redgrave's tribute to the memory of Antony is staggeringly beautiful and moving. "His legs bestrid the ocean; his rear'd arm crested the world…." Her death scene, played with utter tragic naturalness, is simply magnificent. "Give me my robe, put on my crown; I have immortal longings in me…." To be in Ms. Redgrave's company at such transcendent times is a gift.

But yet…or, as the Queen of the Nile herself warns the poor messenger bringing bad news: "I do not like *but yet*." But I must come to a few of them before the day is done, though this is a far superior production to the 1995 version I saw in London with the Moving Theatre, the company Ms. Redgrave founded with her brother, Corin Redgrave. The British critics howled at the apparent loopiness of it all—a politically relevant production that seemed to be set in Bosnia, an apparent allegory of imperialism, a real snake for the asp, an avuncular Antony who was so dozy that when he killed him-self everyone thought he was taking a nap. The new incarnation, which comes to the Public via the Alley Theater in Houston, has firstly given us a decent, sexy Antony played by David Harewood costumed like a revolu-tionary in a red hat. But Mr. Harewood blows his death scene by verging on dark comedy and is too likably young for "grizzled" Antony.

A young Antony commits youthful folly for love of Cleopatra, whereas the middle-aged Antony, great warrior and ruler of the world, is dishonored and cannot go back to what he once was. The tragic pathos of the lovers is therefore thrown off balance here. But I was intrigued by the casting of the actress Carrie Preston as Octavius Caesar, though it seems off-the-wall. Having seen Fiona Shaw play King Richard II, anything is possible. For one thing, Ms. Preston is a terrific, gutsy young actress. I wrote of her tomboy Miranda in George Wolfe's *Tempest* that she was the best Miranda I've seen either side of the Atlantic. She cut through all the pretty English rose ver-sions. Her Octavius Caesar is an uphill battle, however. The gifted actress brings out the boy in her boy king, though she's playing St. Joan.

I'm uncertain about Ms. Redgrave's view that *Antony and Cleopatra* is essentially about the death of the Renaissance (symbolized by the death of the two lovers) and the onslaught of repressive puritanism (symbolized by the triumph of Octavius Caesar). It narrows the play, and the love story, into a political statement. Who is responsible for Antony's death but himself? Is it imperialist war that does the lovers in, or—as I tend to think—their unstoppable, disastrous passion for each other? "Eternity was in our lips and eyes…."

For all Ms. Redgrave's scholarship as a director, the style of her pro-duction is, I'm afraid, an overfamiliar grab bag of references. When is there ever a Public Theater production of Shakespeare that isn't performed amid scaffolding, with Elizabethan costumes and urban graffiti, iambic pen-tameters and video screens, batteries of microphones and press confer-ences, parties and guns? The mishmash setting is by now so familiar that it neither offends nor disturbs. It actually neutralizes everything, including us. The Public Theater Shakespeare style is even comforting. We know what to expect. Whereas the glory and alchemy of Ms. Redgrave, the actress, is that we've never been able to anticipate her for a second.

The Still Subversive Joe Orton

If I had to name my favorite comic playwright, I wouldn't hesitate. It would be Joe Orton—though "comic" doesn't quite cover the subversive bite and anarchy of his work. He can make us laugh more than anyone, and he can gleefully disturb us more than most. I don't think there's been a comic dramatist before or since his death in 1967 who can match him.

Orton's enduring, savage comedy remains unique and is still a near un-American activity. *Entertaining Mr. Sloane,* now receiving a first-rate production at the Classic Stage Company, was booed off the Broadway stage in its 1965 American premiere after thirteen performances. Its psychosexual frankness and violence had also been dismissed as filth by upright citizens of England, but *Entertaining Mr. Sloane* utterly changed the possibilities of comedy and farce (and it was a hit in London). At the time, Puritan America was not amused.

"We know over here there are two American neuroses—Communism and Homosexuality," Orton wrote without bitterness from New York after the blisteringly negative response to the first Broadway production. "Americans aren't sane on those subjects. I touched off number one neurosis. It would be interesting to put out a questionnaire: 'Would you rather your son grew up to be a Communist or a Homosexual?'"

Could we honestly say the question is irrelevant even today? If Orton were alive, and earnestly following the primaries when not glued to *Baywatch,* he would surely laugh and reply, "You must be joking." He nails society's deadening bourgeois conformists and hypocrites, and has us convulsed with laughter at the same time. The amoral anarchy within his scintillating work is actually built on the classical tradition of drawing room dramas and conventional farce. Within the disciplined forms—the shabby gentility of middle-class drawing rooms, the coincidences and timing and sexual absurdity of farce—anything could happen in an Orton play. He invented his own genre that received the high honor of a name: "Ortonesque," which passed into the language like "Thatcherite" or "Churchillian."

Here's Orton himself describing the plot of *Entertaining Mr. Sloane*, from an interview quoted in John Lahr's biography, *Prick Up Your Ears:*

> It's about a young man, 18 or 19, who wants a room and comes into this house. He's met the woman of the house in a public library. He comes to the house and she shows him around the house. Then within about eight pages, I suppose five minutes of being in the house, she attempts to seduce him. A bit later on, she actually has the trousers off him, and then her brother appears, and we see that her brother also would like to have the trousers off him. As the play goes on, one finds that Sloane has murdered a man in the past who was going to take pornographic pictures of him, it was just accidental. The man happened to be the boss of the woman's father, and the old man knows that Sloane murdered his boss. Sloane finally murders the old man, which gives the woman and her brother the opportunity of blackmailing Sloane into bed with them.

The seductive, ambivalent young hero, Sloane, is a double murderer. Orton appears to be matter-of-fact about it; so does Sloane. "You must accept responsibility for your actions," says Ed, the landlady's brother, a man of principles, a businessman and leather fetishist. Sloane replies that he does. "Fully."

"Good," replies Ed. "Remove that hand, will you?"

Sloane is a psychopathic Zelig (and possibly Orton's version of himself). We can't be certain who exactly "Mr. Sloane" is: thug, orphan, son, lover, or innocent. He is what you want him to be, and an object of laughable desire. "Kiss my hand, dear, in the manner of the theater," says pretentious Kath, the overseductive landlady and frump, as Sloane kneels graciously before her. For Orton, sex, like violence, is no laughing matter and therefore couldn't be funnier. The moral center of *Entertaining Mr. Sloane* is the triumph of the amoral, or the victory of desire and selfish pragmatism over principled outer appearances—a typically English double standard, it's said, but universal. The end justifies the means, which is why he's such a contemporary playwright.

The play was Joe Orton's first major breakthrough, coming before the superior onslaughts on farcical respectability, *Loot* and *What the Butler Saw*. Each is a comic masterpiece. But Orton's career was famously too brief. He was bludgeoned to death by his jealous lover, Kenneth Halliwell, who then killed himself. The mythology of the death can overshadow the achievement of the plays, and the plays aren't easy to get right. The forlorn garden-gnome gentility of *Entertaining Mr. Sloane*'s suburban London is usually staged more naturally by the class-conscious English. Its rancid atmosphere of heightened, faux refinement is a peculiarly English specialty known as "piss elegant." (It's a lower-middle-class art form.) How good to report, then, that the Classic Stage Company's production of *Entertaining Mr. Sloane* has got it right in every suggestively sinister, farcically piss-elegant detail.

David Esbjornson's four-member ensemble is perfect and hugely enjoyable. Ellen Parker's Kath, the middle-aged landlady coyly conforming behind lace curtains to the standards of the cowshed, is a delight. "Poor boy," she coos to the homosexual Sloane. "All alone in the world. Like me." In one of her more girlish seductions of Sloane, which is preceded by strawberry-scented air spray, the hideously bold Ms. Parker must be seen to be believed. "I want a very young boy for Sloane. Someone you'd like to fuck silly," Orton suggested. Wishful thinking. Neil Maffin gets the troubling, sinister undercurrent of Sloane right, as well as his low-rent narcissism. "We had a nice little gym at the orphanage," he confides to Kath's salivating brother, the closet homosexual Ed. "Put me in all the teams, they did. Relays...Yes, yes. I'm an all-rounder. A great all-rounder. In anything you care to mention. Even in life."

Is there ever a production with Brian Murray when he's anything less than fine? He consistently delights. Mr. Murray played nine roles, expertly and full of good humor, in *Travels with My Aunt;* more recently, he was the vulnerable, touching Reverend Henderson in David Hare's *Racing Demon*. His righteous, blustering, weak, and dangerous Ed of *Entertaining Mr. Sloane* is another super performance. The beat he takes before asking Sloane,

"Ever wear any leather?" is priceless. "You're pure as the Lamb," Ed says, smarmily drawing a biblical analogy to Sloane, who becomes his chauffeur. The smallest role is the doddering codger known as Dadda, pervading the happy home with surly silence and imminent death. George Hall couldn't be bettered, playing the role as the kind of near-senile blackmailing old fart that lively young lads like Sloane would disrespect and kick occasionally and possibly kill sort of by accident.

The set, which is a house not on a hill but on a garbage dump—is designed in all its tacky glory by Narelle Sissons, and the costumes are by Michael Krass. The director, Mr. Esbjornson, has given us such timely, perverse pleasure in the comic evil of *Entertaining Mr. Sloane* and the hypocrisies it demolishes, we hope he'll now go on to stage *Loot* and *What the Butler Saw*. Joe Orton was not a respectable dramatist. He remains unsafe, and we need him more than ever.

Theater Thingie
of the Year

As we tiptoe into the New Year while thinking of the Old, there can be little doubt that in theater it has been the year of the wee-wee.

Male flashing on stage has reached monumental proportions. It's a sensitive issue and, as always, I shall be bending over backward to be fair. The penis, thingie, wee-wee, dick—however we wish to describe the darling—has been on the ascendancy all season. We need only recall a few examples of the extraordinary trend:

The skinny-dipping scenes of Terrence McNally's smash hit concerning gay weekends in the country, *Love! Valour! Compassion!* The male shower scene in the gay boxing saga, *Blade to the Heat.* Stephen Spinella stripping for his medical exam in *Angels in America.* The downtown production of something called *Prosthetics & the $25,000 Pyramid,* which had an ex–All-American football star as a closeted gay cross-dresser forced to strip at gunpoint. There's no end in sight: the London production of Cocteau's *Parents Terribles*—retitled *Indiscretions* for Broadway, lest the French title frighten the horses—has the usual naked young man, this time in an *après-bath,* or after bath, scene.

We must set the record straight. The buck-naked male on stage isn't exclusively a gay phenomenon. The theater does not discriminate; heterosexual characters have equal stripping rights. There was, for example, the Shakespearean skinny-dipping scene for the boys in the Shakespeare in the Park summer production of *The Two Gentlemen of Verona.* Now, you may ask, "Why were they all splashing about starkers in Verona?"

The integrity of the moment and the bold esthetics of the production were clearly revealed on the cover of the *Playbill,* which showed an 1883

Thomas Eakins painting of bare-assed Victorian gentlemen bathing. And there you have it. It is all a question of Art.

And it all began earlier this season with a heterosexual swan. Elizabeth Egloff's drama of desire, *The Swan*, the big daddy of the genre that played to enormous interest at the Public Theater, has now passed into folklore. No one had seen anything like it. One night, "somewhere in Nebraska," a nurse called Dora, played by Frances McDormand with a very straight face, is woken by a swan crashing into her front window like a meteor. She rescues the injured swan, carrying it inside in a wicker basket. At length, in one of the season's most riveting coups de théâtre, a naked man emerges from the basket, emitting cries of yearning for Dora.

Dora, in turn, finds herself strangely attracted to the naked birdman, whom she names Bill. Well, what can I say? It quickly dawned on everyone in the hushed audience that the Swedish actor, Peter Stormare, as Bill the Swan, was perfectly equipped for the role, having previously played Hamlet in Ingmar Bergman's memorable production. It was just swan of those things. But clearly the artistry of *The Swan* could in no way be compromised. Swans don't wear clothes. You can't have a swan strolling around the stage in his Calvins. It would look ridiculous.

Swans, however, are monogamous. But Bill wasn't. He was a horny, heterosexual, uncircumcised swan who got the girl. So let us have no talk here of exclusively gay flashing on stage. Or as the congressman so felicitously put it, "I've nothing against homosexuals, but do they have to ram it down our throats?" As George C. Wolfe, who directed *Blade to the Heat*, told the *New York Times*, "Nudity can disarm an audience. That's the idea, not to assault. In *Blade*, you see Paul out of the shower after he's just lost his title. It's a stripping down. It reveals the frailty in the human flesh."

Quite so. My goodness me, we all thought to ourselves at the time. There's the naked ex-champ center stage in the shower revealing the frailty in the human flesh. Mr. Wolfe went on to explain enthusiastically, "What's fascinating is that now men are nude in these innocent situations, while for the women it's only in sexual ones." And here was I, earnestly believing that actresses have stripped only for art's sake since the beginning of time.

There's obviously more to penises than meets the eye. But from my point of view this trend of entirely innocent male nudity distracts us from the sacred texts. I ask you in all candor: When an actor drops his pants, what is the entire audience looking at? Do the playwrights, the directors, the actors themselves, imagine for a single gloriously naked second that anyone in the audience is listening to even a word? No, siree. The audience is understandably transfixed by the actor's pecs.

True, the peckers on display throughout *Love! Valour! Compassion!* draw our attention like lighthouses at sea, but it's the pumped-up pecs and abs of the supremely conditioned stud Ramon that send us scurrying back to the gym. Joe Mantello, the director of *Love! Valour!* keeps all in proportion, while pointing out a typical hypocrisy. "The real double standard is in film," he argues, most innocently. "It's routine for an actress to be asked to bare her breasts for movies. But you can count on one hand the male actors who appear nude."

May I first wish Mr. Mantello and his partner, the dishy dramatist Mr. John Robin Baitz, a belated hearty mazeltov on being named "Couple of the Moment" in the Sunday *Times* Arts & Leisure section cover story earlier in the season? May their moment never pass. But the talented Mr. Mantello, by concentrating on the routine nudity of actresses in movies, is surely forgetting the entire film oeuvre of Mr. Harvey Keitel. Good old Harvey, that's what we say. But do we wish to count on one hand, or otherwise, the male actors who appear nude?

Doubtless, principle is at stake. And so is the casting couch. The civil rights of male actors now compelled to strip while auditioning for a role is an issue, however, for Actors Equity. But Mr. Mantello reveals, alas, a short memory. Male actors have been appearing on stage in their birthday suits for years—from *Equus* to *Six Degrees of Separation.*

The 1968 *Hair* of beloved memory is said to be the historic first to show naked cast members, coyly lit in shadows. But actually, I vividly remember a naked Julian Beck sitting on my knee during an earlier Living Theater happening in London. "You are not allowed to travel without a passport," he whispered in my ear. "Be that as it may," I stammered in response, "just get off my knee, okay?" Those were the days! Those were the days when Lindsay Anderson's production of David Storey's *The Changing Room* proudly revealed an entire rugby team in the nude at a stunned Royal Court Theatre. You couldn't get a ticket for love or money.

So the current bimbo penis trend isn't new, if I may say so. It is merely the latest special effect. Regular readers of this column well know my aesthetics on the matter. Special effects, the ruination of theater, have only one place to go. Bigger and bigger and bigger. My New Year's wish to the happy theater community is this: We've all seen it now. Remember the Swan. Grow up, boys, put it away, and get on with the play.

Slumming with Sam Shepard

Buried Child, Sam Shepard's 1978 Pulitzer Prize–winning drama, is enjoying acclaim and masterpiece status at the Brooks Atkinson Theater, and it celebrates Mr. Shepard's belated Broadway debut after all these years. Still, I'm uncertain why whorish Broadway should be seen as the ultimate seal of approval and homecoming for this essentially alienated downtown dramatist.

There's too much slumming going on. Within the plush, cozily bourgeois Brooks Atkinson, Mr. Shepard's white-trash scumfest dissolves the solidly middle-class intelligentsia into gales of laughter (or compels Serious Thought concerning the Breakdown of the American Family). The brain-dead family in *Buried Child* is a source of hilarity that evokes the easy, patronizing mockery of the midwestern simpletons of *Fargo*. It's an unattractive trend: the more stupid the characters, the more entertaining; the more squalid the circumstances, the more Meaning.

Sam Shepard's territory is a fixed—though not always fashionable—part of the dramatic landscape, and it's been mythologized as much as his American "true West" of open roads and rootless motel dwellers, of emotional murders, dislocation, flight, and solitude. "Aloneness was a fact of nature," goes a line from one of the short stories in Mr. Shepard's new collection, *Cruising Paradise.* "He'd learned to not look beyond it; to avoid the trickery of the mind where women were concerned: to avoid the imagery of seduction altogether."

"Aloneness" as a fact of nature accounts for his cultivated cowboy myth—the hip rock 'n' roll writer as reluctant movie star, the American as romantic, the manly *goyischer* loner amidst the "green lush wet dripping corn...bacon and tomatoes the size of your fist...."

"What's happened to the men in this family?" cries Halie, the mother-slut of *Buried Child*. "Where are all the men?" The matriarchal witch surely nagged them all to death, or caused them to flee the happy home. Or drove them to the safe, domestic sanctuary of silence and the bottle, like Halie's grizzled old husband, Dodge, rotting on a flea-bitten sofa.

Mr. Shepard's "trickery of the mind"—self-deception, a lie of the mind—is the near-surreal psychic need for some kind of home that will suffocate you just the same. He paraphrases Samuel Beckett: You can't go home again, but you must. No character in *Buried Child* is comfortably at home, including the one-legged idiot son and crybaby thug, Bradley. Dodge's father disowns him—or refuses to recognize him. In the drama's opening, the unseen Halie savages her couch-potato husband, Dodge, for what must be a miserable, ongoing lifetime of petty abuse. They do not love or "recognize" each other. Another son, the former golden boy, Tilden, is a shell, a quiet lost madman. He cannot even recognize himself.

After six years in the city, Tilden's son Vince returns home (with saxophone and girlfriend) to see the folks. His father doesn't know who he is; nor does Dodge, his grandfather, nor anyone else. In a sentimental search for roots, Vince is curious about his past. "Jesus Christ! What do you know about the past?" asks indignant Gramps, the drunken old cuss. "The past is past." There is no memory, then; no identity. And the message is clear—too clear. No, you can't go home again. Even Vince's well-meaning girlfriend Shelly isn't acknowledged. She's an outsider, like him. "I am alive!" she protests. "I am speaking. I exist. Do you see me?"

This is some dysfunctional family—and one with a dark secret, too. (A buried child.) Perhaps we see ourselves in this family at war. We're certainly meant to. But this is a family of grotesques. Mr. Shepard wants *Buried Child* every which way: Gothic comedy, spooky mystery tale, absurdist farce and metaphysical statement. "I'm trying to figure out what goes on here," is one amusingly defensive line. "Good luck!" comes the response. "What's the meaning of this corn, Tilden?" the zombie Tilden is asked when he brings in an armful of corn from the fields that haven't seen any since 1935. "It's a mystery to me!" he replies.

It's a mystery to most of us. Maybe not. Bountiful corn—a fertile land of plenty, now barren. Aha! A metaphor. Mr. Shepard's humor tends to be wry and deadpan. The appropriately slummy setting has an incongruous moosehead hanging comically askew on the wall. It's too high to adjust without effort, but no one in this family of ghouls troubled to get it right in the first place. It's a neat, light touch that's mostly absent in Gary Sinise's Steppenwolf production and, from this dissenting point of view, in the bloated symbolism of *Buried Child*.

The House of Wax thunder and lightning—followed by wailing saxophone—that open the play signal both a melodrama and a parodiable jazzy soulfulness. Mr. Shepard takes no symbolic prisoners: the mysterious appearance of those armfuls of vegetables from the wasteland; the crumbling farmhouse, or madhouse, an America literally trashed; the ugly, dysfunctional all-American family of freaks who acknowledge only their mirror image, the American Dream gone all too blatantly wrong.

There's too much "mystery," and not enough. When the one-legged bully-boy Bradley enters, what happens? A pratfall, a cheap laugh (similarly, Dodge's business with phlegm and fleas). What's that nagging granny and mother Halie doing when she enters in neat pious black with gray hair in the first act, yet returns from church later with messed-up red hair? Well, the old broad *might* have had a tumble with Father Dewis, the decrepit local cleric, and been brought symbolically back to life, as it were.

And what of the family secret of torment, the buried child? Does it exist? Possibly. Is the dead child Dodge's? He denies it. Is the child the outcome of incest? Possibly. Was that why it was killed? Possibly. Was that why Tilden turned into a zombie bringing in armfuls of corn that shouldn't exist? Who knows! Is the buried child a symbol? Is he—could he be—the Buried Child Within?

Sam Shepard's fabled drama has grown familiar, or time has caught up with it. Or perhaps I just don't appreciate metaphysical Gothic comedies. But this is a wonderfully acted production. Lois Smith—the memorable Ma Joad of Steppenwolf's *The Grapes of Wrath*—is superb as the damaged Halie with her absurd pretensions and pieties, and she's a perfect partner in family crime to James Gammon's Dodge. We expect physicality and realism from Steppenwolf, but Mr. Gammon is awesomely real. His raspy, near-terminal Dodge is so squalidly authentic that one actually worries for his health.

But among the fine ensemble—which includes Jim True as the wrecked Vince, and a very welcome Broadway debut from Kellie Overbey as Shelly—the actor who seems to have the fewest lines is outstanding. Terry Kinney, a cofounder with Gary Sinise and Jeff Perry of Steppenwolf, appears to be doing little or nothing as Tilden, yet he quietly achieves everything in his shell-shocked silence and grief. He shows us Tilden's frightened broken heart, silently pleading.

No Tony for Julie

We've known for some time that the Tony Award nominating committee is completely and wonderfully nuts. It never lets us down, and neither does Charlton Heston.

"I applaud the courage Julie Andrews displayed in refusing the Tony nomination she deserved," Mr. Heston wrote recently to the *New York Times*. "The committee's rejection of her show, *Victor/Victoria*, and of the artists and technicians who made her performance possible, reflects outrageous bias."

Good old Chuck. This is what the whole mess needs—an aperçu from Charlton Heston. "I've found over many years," his letter went on, "that critics are repelled by success, unless they themselves first anoint it." A little off the subject there, but never mind. Chuck, writing from the theater capital of Los Angeles itself, knows what's at stake in the courageous decision of Julie ("I Stand with the Egregiously Overlooked") Andrews. "Her challenge to the Tonys," Chuckypoo concluded, "will force a re-examination of the process and certainly a new committee. Don't back down, Julie. Bravo!"

I stand with the egregiously overlooked. I stand with Patrick Stewart. I didn't particularly do so when I reviewed his performance in *The Tempest*, but I stand with him now. He's been overlooked, egregiously. Almost every other critic across this fair land raved over his Prospero. He has therefore not been nominated for a Tony. What short memories we all have! It's only two seasons ago that Joan Rivers was nominated for best actress. The shocking thing is that she didn't win.

But who can forget the play she starred in, *Sally Marr . . . and Her Escorts*? True to its long-standing tradition of reversing all known logic, the nominating committee solemnly asked itself: "Who is an actress who isn't an actress?" So they nominated Joan Rivers for leading actress in a play that wasn't a play. Because *Sally Marr* was a monologue. That's why Jackie Mason returned his honorary Tony and sued the committee. Because he believed that his monologue had been egregiously overlooked as best play.

It's *normal*. Only last season Nathan Lane, unanimously raved over for his performance in Terrence McNally's *Love! Valour! Compassion!* was egregiously overlooked. Yet three of his fellow actors were all nominated. Did they all do a Julie and tearfully announce from the stage to their stunned audience: "We do not choose to run. We stand by our man, Nathan"? Nah...They did what brave Julie would not do. They proudly turned up for the awards in their best bib and tucker.

The Julie Andrews uproar, however, has distracted attention from another thoroughly sensible decision by the nominating committee. Nominated as best new play, as opposed to best revival of a play, is Sam Shepard's seventeen-year-old Pulitzer Prize–winning *Buried Child*. How on earth is it possible?

The producers of *Buried Child* appealed to the committee, followed by Gary Sinise, the director of *Buried Child*. "You may think this play is seventeen years old," they argued. "And there, you would be wrong."

Precedent was on their side! Last season, Jean Cocteau's fifty-seven-year-old *Indiscretions* was nominated for best new play. It wasn't a revival because, the committee decided, it had never played on Broadway before. A revival is a play or musical that has been staged before on Broadway, or it's a classic. A classic is something the Tony administrators say is a classic. *Indiscretions*, after fifty-seven years, wasn't considered a classic. It was therefore nominated as a new play. Don't ask.

Buried Child, on the other hand, is half a new play. The half that counts got the Tony nomination. In fact, the entire oeuvre of Sam Shepard has never played Broadway before now. All his plays—including his work from the 1960s—would therefore be new. If it's new to the Orwellian Tony nominating committee, it's new—unless it's half-new, in which case that will do. The producers and Gary Sinise of *Buried Child* pointed out to the rapt committee that there were 1,151 lines in *Buried Child*, but the dramatist had cut or rewritten 519 of them. Well, obviously, *Buried Child* must now be a new play. And so it was.

It's still the same Pulitzer Prize–winning play, unless we say it's now half a Pulitzer Prize–winning play. The half a Pulitzer clearly applies to the 632 lines left over from the original *Buried Child,* which strictly speaking no longer exists.

Where does that leave David Merrick? Mr. Merrick is the legendary producer of Rodgers & Hammerstein's *State Fair,* which has been nominated for best original score. But the Tony voters will be allowed to vote for only four of its songs. That's because eleven of the *State Fair* songs have been heard before, rather like the 632 lines from *Buried Child.* They had been borrowed from other Rodgers & Hammerstein musicals on Broadway and from the original movie of *State Fair.* On the other hand, the *entire* score of *Beauty and the Beast* was nominated two seasons ago, even though its hit songs were lifted from the original movie. Now Mr. Merrick is understandably upset, too, and is handing out cotton balls to the Tony voters so they'll stuff them into their ears during the eleven egregiously overlooked songs.

And none of this would have happened if it hadn't been for Julie Andrews. As I said at the outset, the Tony Award committee is nuts, and has invariably proved it. This season's uproar only confirms the farcical image of an industry that needs to get its house in order. How can they run a billion-dollar-a-year industry like this? Does anyone seriously imagine that come the Tony telecast on June 2, millions of Americans will be saying excitedly: "Ooh, the Tony Awards. Let's stay in!"?

At the same time, I don't agree that the Tony nominating committee, bless it, should vote according to Julie Andrews's say-so. If that were the case, the Tonys would be called the Julies. "And the winner *is*…everyone who has ever worked with Julie Andrews!" The gracious lady has a point, though. By nominating two short-lived, long-gone musicals and ignoring other worthy artists, the Tony establishment makes worse its habitual muddle. I'm with Charlton Heston: sweep away the current committee and reexamine the entire, laughably devalued Tony process.

What Is the Sound of One Hand Acting?

I am not in the giving vein today. Or, as Sir Ian McKellen as Richard III puts it: *"Eeey em nawt een thah geeving veyun todayah."* Ah, the common language that divides us—again! But it's never divided us quite as much as Mr. McKellen's aristocratic English accent in *Richard III* (by *Willem Shake-speah*). Therein lies but one of the major problems of the Royal National Theatre's ballyhooed production, which is the setback of being unable to understand what is actually said, or *wort eez sayud*.

Now, it is true that at the Brooklyn Academy of Music, where *Richard III* is playing, sound echoes and reverberates through the theater like a shotgun in Death Valley. The cast is pushing and straining to be heard, which is bad enough. But heard it is! Deciphering what we hear is the remarkable challenge. My neighbors during the performance—generous New Yorkers, all—confirmed for me, after the standing ovation, that they could hear Mr. McKellen but would have appreciated a simultaneous translation, as at the Italian opera.

It would be no loss to this production if Mr. McKellen dumped his pseudoaristocratic pronunciation in favor of free speech. Shakespeare, I believe, didn't instruct his actors to speak the speech "clippingly on the tongue." Mr. McKellen's choice of accent, based on the Duke of Windsor's, is a star actor's "concept," just a trick, or effect, that characterizes his externalized performance. But it isn't too difficult to understand, once you get the hang of things, like tuning into the BBC Foreign News Service. For example, in the near-Chaucerian pronunciation of the English upper classes, house is pronounced "hice." Nice is pronounced "naice," really is "rairly." Hence:

"What a rairly naice hice!"

"Niow eez tha wintah awf our deescontent / mayud glorious summah..." ("Now is the winter of our discontent / made glorious summer...") It is not just a silly accent affected by certain silly Englishmen. It is drooled, dawdled, and dribbled by the English upper classes in order to exclude the bemused and confused lower classes. It is clever that way. It is loud and languid in delivery, a noise uncluttered by intelligence, a self-assured aristocratic style submerging language itself. It is about as appropriate an accent for the tale of Richard III as it would be for Shakespeare's gravediggers. Mr. McKellen's showy and fatal choice of vocalization confines and defeats Richard's murderous intelligence. It is a parody. Your guess is as good as mine why Mr. McKellen pronounces Richmond in Anglo-French, *"Richemonde."*

Then again, why doesn't Richard's family speak with the same accent? They would, wouldn't they? (As the royals do today.) But what is the usually intelligent director, Richard Eyre, up to—or think he's up to? Having set the play in the 1930s, he explained how he was hit by a revelation during the reading of the play. "Good lord," he said. "Isn't this exactly analogous to what happened under Hitler, Stalin, and so on?" And hasn't this been noticed before, by one or two others, such as Brecht and Alfred Jarry and so on? Hasn't it been *done* before? (Though *Coriolanus* and *Julius Caesar* are usually the Shakespeare plays of choice for modernistic fascist interpretations.) Very well; what does the director do with his concept? He reduces Shakespeare's early drama of elemental amorality and ambition to a muddled political cartoon. Hitler, for one thing, wasn't upper class. The Duke of Windsor, for another, was no Richard III. The future, and brief, King Edward VIII spent World War II happily sunning himself with Wallis Simpson in the Bahamas. Let that pass, too. The crucial specifics of the production—its 1930s English reference points—are mistaken.

The Director hammers his "revelatory" metaphor home—the pseudo-Nazi uniforms and rallies; Mr. McKellen's Nazi salute during the coronation scene, accompanied, lest we miss the point, by the lowering of a backdrop of monumentalist Nazi art. The admired production doesn't dare audiences to imagine, so anxious is it to popularize an already popular play. But even its blatancy is inconsistent. The coronation takes place in Nazi Germany, yet the battle scene is accompanied by a backdrop of rural England. Why? The battle actually did take place in England. But so, originally, did the coronation! Mixed metaphors send mixed messages.

Why, since the production is set and costumed in the 1930s, does the battle take place in suits of armor with swords? At the height of the play and the production, the director has abandoned his entire concept. One can only presume, the change from the 1930s to medieval suits of armor is trying to point out that wars repeat themselves. But that's not the point of *Richard III*. Ultimately, the play isn't about the circularity of wars (which are fought through the ages for different reasons). As Jan Kott said, the play is more crucially about the enduring amorality of the universe. No, Mr. Eyre had to abandon his concept because it doesn't work. To carry the Nazi metaphor through to the famous battle scene, he would have had to make a most serious change in the text. "My tank, my tank! My kingdom for a . . ."

And Mr. McKellen's performance, caricature Duke of Windsor accent and all? All eyes are on him, of course, but I have never seen a weaker cast as the Royal National Theatre offers us. Almost everyone, with the exception of Charlotte Cornwell as Queen Elizabeth, is dead from the neck down. Here is a living murderous nightmare of butchered wives, husbands, fathers, and sons—all killed in the cause of one man's ambition. Give us some range and *feeling*. They give us instead the outer option of the refined "English Style," leaving Anglophiles too easily impressed. Mr. McKellen impresses naturally, with his renowned bravura and ease, and awesome command. But you would never accuse him of underacting here.

I prefer the younger, more internally energized McKellen of his riveting *Macbeth* to the highly theatrical nineteenth-century tragedian he's since become. As Richard III, he literally doesn't miss a trick. "He's semi-paralyzed," explained director Richard Eyre in an interview. "He only uses one arm, but he's doing his best to insure we don't notice it." The truth is, his star never lets us forget Richard's deformity for a second. Mr. McKellen is a showoff mix of old Adolf with discreet hump, along with Dr. Strangelove. Of course it's impressive to see him open his cigarette case and light a cigarette in one swift assured movement of one hand. It's amazing to see him take off his coat and put it back on again, with one hand. And when he held up that same hand so all could witness the astonishing feat of *the hand* putting a glove on itself, which is a near impossible thing to do, it wouldn't have surprised me in the least had he next balanced on his nose while revolving on a silver ball.

Oh, the hours! the days! the weeks! Sir Ian McKellen must have spent in front of the mirror perfecting that glove trick. Like the accent, the trick *is* the message. See through the mirror.

Country Matters

Now, in my romantic way, I shall be defending Ivan Turgenev, who's dead, and Helen Mirren, who's very much alive. But if, following the *New York Times'* impertinent review of her golden performance as Natalya in Turgenev's classic *A Month in the Country,* the most exciting actress in our midst had briefly contemplated jumping off the Brooklyn Bridge, it would have been understandable.

I've little doubt that her costars, F. Murray Abraham and Ron Rifkin, would have joined her on the bridge. Ms. Mirren would have said to them, "Hello, boys. Who's first?" To which the downcast director, Scott Ellis, would have replied, "Me."

The *Times* had clobbered the production as a miserable failure. It had crushed a butterfly. But then, as the suicidal troupe from *A Month in the Country* swelled in numbers, to be joined by the set designer Santo Loquasto and the entire hierarchy of the Roundabout Theater Company, a voice would have been heard telling them all, and Ms. Mirren in particular, not to do it.

"Don't do it," says the voice urgently, which belongs to Ivan Turgenev.

My feeling is that Turgenev would have been delighted by this production of *A Month in the Country,* whatever its faults (which are few). I believe he would have been pleased and relieved by the good humor of it all, the care and style and, above all, the lightness of this tragedy of love, which the playwright described as a comedy. Chekhov—whom Turgenev predates and anticipates—also described his plays as comedies. We think, how can those melancholic, "soulful" Russians possibly see life as a comedy? The achievement of Ms. Mirren's Natalya is that she shows us how funny romantic love and suffering can be, precisely as Turgenev intended.

Natalya is a woman stupid in love. And much more besides—passion-ate, farcical, confused, mad, absurd, ruinous in love. The beautiful married lady, living out a half-life of pampered lassitude on the estate—only Russ-ian playwrights can make a signature tune out of the word "bored"—finds herself falling wildly in love with her son's young tutor, Aleksei. By the play's end, she has ruined at least four lives, including her own, if we assume her life wasn't ruined before the play began.

It is the humanity of Turgenev that still appeals to us so much. His then-new "psychology" of character—*A Month in the Country* was written in 1850—has caught up with him. "A poet must be a psychologist, but a secret one," the playwright wrote, and it sounds like a discreet warning to pon-derous productions of his work. A stylized, psychological "Russianness" does in Turgenev, but the open, natural playing of Helen Mirren and com-pany and the pleasure they communicate in performing for us do the reverse and delight.

What do theatergoers want? Whatever happened to fun (as opposed to grunge and low camp)? And more to the point, what does the *Times* want? You see how discreet I am straining to be. I am not even mentioning Vincent Canby by name. But if the *Times* can say of Kathleen Turner in *Indiscretions* that her performance is "a triumph," a scale of values compels us to conclude that Ms. Mirren in *A Month in the Country* must be giving a performance of such God-given talent that it would have forced Sarah Bernhardt herself into premature retirement. But I read that even poor old Turgenev was right to feel pessimistic about his own play.

"Audiences will find it tedious, and they did," the *Times* quoted the great novelist as saying about the first production of *A Month in the Coun-try*, which took place twenty-two years after he wrote it. Seven years later, the play was well received in St. Petersburg. "Turgenev was grateful," the *Times* continued, "but, with some reason, still skeptical."

Not skeptical enough, incidentally, to stop Turgenev from falling in love with the young actress who played Verochka in the St. Petersburg troupe. But it wasn't until 1909—too late for Turgenev—that Stanislavsky at the Moscow Art Theater rescued the play for posterity. As the saying goes: Never trust what an artist says about his work, only what he creates. Turgenev famously dismissed his own plays. It was the temperament of the self-effacing man to do so. The treatment of his theater work—banned, censored, and never fully achieved in his lifetime—would be enough cause for his despair. What of the soul of the troubled artist, a Turgenev struggling in private doubt to create a new form of theater with *A Month in the Country?* "To hope, till hope creates from its own wreck, the thing it contemplates," Shelley wrote. Never seeing his one great play staged as he imagined, the despairing Turgenev looked into the wreckage and said, "To hell with it! Read it instead."

So the literal-minded *Times* advises us to read *A Month in the Country* "to find out what it's all about," before passing up the opportunity to see this rarely staged though "seriously flawed production." It's marginally better advice, I guess, than the paper's critic on Sunday advising us to read Tom Stoppard's *Arcadia* instead of actually troubling to see it. No playwright writes plays to be read. Don't they write them for the stage? The *Times* Play-Reading Society will be announced shortly, but I doubt its chances of success. Most of us find it difficult to read plays—unless, as happened in my case when I returned to the text of *A Month in the Country* after seeing it, you can still hear the actor's voice.

No, I have absolutely no doubt that you will "find out what it's all about" just by seeing the Roundabout production, and that you will see what Ms. Mirren is up to. I last saw her onstage at the Royal Shakespeare Company playing another lady consumed by love, Cleopatra. Her Natalya is a catalyst for disaster, and Ms. Mirren touches all the bases. She is circumspect, willful, dangerous, and laughably honest. Turgenev's heroine must see through herself and the farce of romantic hothouse love. She is saying, in effect: "My God! I'm in love!" and at the same time, "It's ridiculous!" And how Ms. Mirren manages to do this simultaneously is remarkable, like her flickering looks that suggest a tragic heroine in one moment and a self-deluding girlishness the next. Her Natalya, like Turgenev's, is an actress at heart: she transforms and pretends, as if watching herself play a part, until the game is over and the love that flared up "went out like a light."

I very much enjoyed that odd stage couple, F. Murray Abraham and Ron Rifkin, together "bringing up the rear" as their characters seem destined to do. Mr. Abraham as the secret class-hater and public court jester, Doctor Shpigelsky, is like his character's name. He "shpigels"—seizing the role with delight, overdoing it a bit with his hankie business, but exactly and charmingly right. So, too, Mr. Rifkin as Natalya's masochistic admirer and lapdog, Rakitin (Turgenev's alter ego), beaten by his one-way "sickly, consumptive affair." Everyone is good, but special mention ought to be made of Kathryn Erbe's seventeen-year-old Verochka, who must travel overnight—or over a month—from innocent child to adolescent with a crush, from Natalya's ward to womanhood and rivalry in love.

It's an awfully pretty production, though Santo Loquasto's single lapse is to rake the stage for the garden scenes at a perilously steep angle. Costume designer Jane Greenwood has done her very best work, with Brian Nason's refined lighting. We could claim that Mr. Ellis's production isn't dark or "tragic" enough in its picturesque lightness. Perhaps; but the passion and furies and foolishness of romantic love aren't always gloomy. Turgenev wasn't Chekhov, and Chekhov was never Chekhovian. It is enough to suggest the melancholic, which Ms. Mirren can do at a glance. Scott Ellis's fine production of *A Month in the Country* should be seen and enjoyed. Don't read the play.

Oscar Wilde's Brilliant Lunatics

There are very good reasons to see Oscar Wilde's *Ideal Husband* at the Ethel Barrymore Theater on Broadway, and one of them is Oscar Wilde. My astounding revelation will not, perhaps, make headline news around the world. It is, after all, quite well known that Wilde is witty, and no one appreciated his wit more than Wilde. At the same time, Peter Hall's confident London production of the 1895 comedy makes clear that Wilde isn't as seriously flippant as he may seem.

"Lord Goring, you are talking quite seriously," Lady Chiltern, a chider, pious, too good a lady, says to Goring, the dandy, the most indolent man in London. "I don't think I ever heard you talk seriously before."

"You must excuse me, Lady Chiltern," he replies, laughing. "It won't occur again, if I can help it."

"But I like you to be serious," she adds, unfortunately.

"Dear Gertrude, don't say such a dreadful thing to Lord Goring," comments Lady Chiltern's jolly (and witty) sister-in-law, Mabel, breezing into the drawing room. "Seriousness would be very unbecoming of him. Good afternoon, Lord Goring! Pray be as trivial as you can...."

That's more like it. Flippancy, particularly under fire, is the preferred calling card of the English gentleman. Style is all in the English game of appearances, and stylish is the least a dandy can be. The surprise of Mr. Hall's production is that it reveals an Oscar Wilde who might have been a Christian moralist in disguise. *An Ideal Husband* is an enjoyably creaky Victorian melodrama, a Georges Feydeau farce, and a Wildean comedy of unexpected substance and humanity, as if Wilde's mask of frivolity had slipped. The paradoxes of the dramatist's "beautiful idiots and brilliant lunatics" that decorate and despoil London society go to the moral center of his witty play.

The action takes place in aristocratic Belgravia. (Is there anywhere else?) Its subject is dirty secrets, public disgrace, and stifling virtue. In other words, it is about England—thoroughly decent, thoroughly hypocritical England. Wilde's definition of the typical Englishman—"always dull and usually violent"—is contradicted by the gentlemen in the play, who are rarely dull and usually above the fray. An Ideal Husband is more a comedy of English manners and class, Wilde's knowing take on gentlemanly codes of honor, on public and private morality, and double lives.

The play was first staged in London shortly before the disclosure of Wilde's homosexuality and his downfall. In that sense, An Ideal Husband is the encoded drama of Wilde's own life, in which his dramatic incarnation, the dandy Lord Goring, saves the golden politician Sir Robert Chiltern from public scandal and ruin.

Chilly Chiltern—wintry, austere, morally impeccable, and corrupt. In his youth, Sir Robert sold Cabinet secrets to a foreigner and made his fortune—a lapse in the form of Victorian insider trading, brought on by the tragedy of his being born an impoverished aristocrat. Mrs. Cheveley, a common femme fatale described by Wilde in his stage directions as "a work of Art, on the whole, but showing the influence of too many schools," arrives at the Chilterns' happy, complacent home to blackmail Sir Robert. She possesses a compromising letter that will expose him. But even the blackmailer is Wildean: "If one could only teach the English how to talk and the Irish how to listen," Mrs. Cheveley announces, "society here would be quite civilized!"

Wilde, the talkative Irishman, can't help himself—throwing his dizzying asides to whichever character catches them. "The Ten Commandments in every stroke of the pen!" is Mrs. Cheveley's memorable observation of a note written by the unyieldingly pious Lady Chiltern. "Nothing ages a woman so rapidly as having married the general rule," concludes elderly Lady Markby, prattling on over tea. "To love oneself is the beginning of a lifelong romance" is the priceless epigram that could only come from one source, however—Wilde's stand-in, Lord Goring.

Martin Shaw's padded-out embodiment of Wilde in the foppish form of Lord Goring is a treat. His star turn has been nominated for a Tony, and he would win it were people not so serious. His Wilde/Goring has a Noël Cow-ardesque accent and looks as if he's eaten too many chocolate truffles. We think, with pleasure: This is how he must have been. Mr. Shaw lolls, he lounges, he drapes, he decorates; he sulks only when a buttonhole isn't quite right, for artifice must keep the highest standards. He is spoiled and well liked, not only by himself. He is charmingly and democratically snob-bish about everyone. His hooded eyes hint at the debauched. He is self-mocking, never earnest. He enjoys life immensely.

And so we enjoy his company. Beneath the cultivated languid surface, this fine actor gives us the unexpected decency of the man. The frivolous, lordly hero—"the first well-dressed philosopher in the history of thought"—turns out to be the compassionate voice of good sense and charity, as Wilde wished for in his own wretched life. "All I know is that life cannot be under-stood without much charity, cannot be lived without much charity," Goring tells the unforgiving Lady Chiltern when she learns of her husband's decep-tion. "It is love…that is the true explanation of this world, whatever may be the explanation of the next."

English actors can perform the plays of Oscar Wilde in their sleep, and they frequently do, but this is a splendid cast. Penny Downie's Lady Chiltern, "pitiless in her perfection," succeeds in being uncompromisingly priggish, yet human; David Yelland is flawless as Chiltern, the ideal husband and fallen idol. Anna Carteret as Mrs. Cheveley, Victoria Hasted as Miss Mabel Chiltern, and Denis Holmes's Phipps, the perfect butler with the perfect mask of a sphinx, could scarcely be better.

It was a particular pleasure to see Michael Denison as the affectionate old duffer, the Earl of Caversham, and Dulcie Gray as Lady Markby. New Yorkers may not know them well, but Mr. Denison and his wife, Dulcie Gray, are stars in England, and favorites too. For a half-century or so they have been working actors. They do theater, and this production, proud.

A-Plotz
for David Ives

You have been hearing wonderful things about the dizzying plays and language of David Ives and what he calls "the weirdness of being alive." But as this unusual dramatist himself might put it: "Mock vots diss minsky?"

What does this mean? It means that David Ives delights and surprises us. Which leads to a certain giddiness. It is impossible to second-guess what Mr. Ives will come up with next during *All in the Timing,* his six one-act plays—or playlets—at the Primary Stages Company. Mr. Ives is an original, or an educated nutcase, and you really ought to see *All in the Timing* as soon as you can.

Not for Mr. Ives another doleful evening of the urban apocalypse. His *All in the Timing* offers us instead plays about a demented dating game; three monkeys trying to write *Hamlet;* a romance in a new language; Philip Glass buying a loaf of bread; a state of being known as stuck "in a Philadelphia"; and variations on the death of Trotsky, who appears with a pickax buried in the back of his head.

Who could begin to imagine such a collection of inspired oddities and ideas? All of the apparently wildly divergent plays are linked. They are about time and randomness, or the comedy of communication and language. Mr. Ives owes a debt to Tom Stoppard and to the higher lunacies of Monty Python. But the near-insane invented language of one of his plays, "Unamunda," can be understood by all—including the word "tonguestoppard" ("to stammer").

His curtain-raiser, *Sure Thing,* amounts to many variations of "Come here often?" A young man tries to pick up a young woman, or vice versa, in a café. Every time a conversational gambit fails, a bell rings and the characters start hopefully again where they left off, as if pressing a fast rewind button. I counted thirty-nine bells. Maybe I missed a bell or two. So *Sure Thing* amounts to thirty-nine variations on a theme of reinventing yourself, or a satire on stumbling toward a date.

He: "I believe that a man is what he is."

(Bell)

He (beginning again): "A person is what he is."

(Bell)

He (beginning again): "A person is what they are."

She: "I think so, too."

He: "So what if I admire Trotsky."

(Bell!)

Words, Words, Words follows with three monkeys named Swift, Kafka, and Milton typing into infinity. The hope of Professor Rosenbaum, an idiot of Columbia University, is that the three monkeys will sooner or later write *Hamlet*. "We're getting peanuts here, to be somebody's hack!" chimp Swift protests. "Writing is a mug's game, anyway, Swifty," says Milton. "Well," Swift replies, "it hath made me mad." The whole thing's a riot, and wonderfully silly. It's a sendup of the pretensions of academia, literary types, and certain intellectual sensibilities concerned with "expressive intensity and pungent lyricism." Anyway, the chimps get to write *Hamlet*.

My favorite, *The Universal Language*, is about a lonely lady with a stammer who finds love and happiness—and loses her stammer—by learning the new universal language of "Unamunda" from a fake professor. "Velcro! Bell jar, Froyling! Harvardyu?" ("Welcome. Good day, miss! How are you?") The prof only speaks "da linkwa Looniovershal" (the universal language). "Squeegie (Sorry). Alaska iago (Unfortunately I) parladoop (don't speak) johncleese (English)."

Normal English is John Cleese! Ives's *Universal Language* is mesmerizingly virtuoso, and romantically touching in its loony way. It isn't "a testicle" (a test). It intoxicates via a fever of invented words and ingenuity, fizzing with the musicality of words. It is flantastico flan (fantastic fun), and I give it an A-plotz (A-plus).

Philip Glass Buys a Loaf of Bread is something else again. It is just that: Philip Glass buying a loaf of bread. During which Mr. Glass appears to have mistaken a woman in a white dress on a jetty for a rowboat. But what Mr. Ives has pulled off in sustained fun is a satire of Philip Glass and a simultaneous tribute to him. His words sing in circularity, as if—and very exactly—directed by Robert Wilson. The dramatist with his repeat riffs and rhythmic pleasures is a Philip Glass wordsmith. He relishes the musician's kind of hypnoticism, and cleverly creates the verbal and visual equivalent to Philip Glass.

The Philadelphia is Mr. Ives's even more absurdist idea of communicating—this time in reverse. That is, his characters fall into a black hole of language in which it is only possible to get what you want by saying the opposite. So if you say to someone: "Get lost!" they'll reply: "I'm here!" Or: "I hate you" will compel the response "I love you madly." Such a twilight-zonish metaphysical condition is known as existing "in a Philadelphia." It could be worse. You could be "in a Cleveland," which is "like death, without the advantages."

Lastly, with *Variations on the Death of Trotsky,* David Ives delights us again with a farcical sketch concerning Mr. and Mrs. Trotsky and the 1992 *Encyclopedia Britannica* account of Leo's death via an ax in his head. "Funny," the fastidious Leo says. "I always thought it was an icepick." *"A mountain climber's ax!"* Mrs. Trotsky insists. "Can't I get that through your *skull?"*

Praise be for David Ives and *All in the Timing.* All, and Mr. Ives in particular, are well served and energized by the imaginative wit and fine-tuned ear of director James McConnell Buzas. Now, if only Mr. Ives would kindly come up with a full-length play. These post cards from the weirder edge are a pleasure that only makes one wish for more.

No. 1 Dance Hall Chicken
Inna New York City

Danny Hoch's solo *Some People* at the Public Theater is a fantastic break-through, and in many ways I'm still in shock. This twenty-three-year-old street kid, a raw, electric, fresh talent, an urban griot of New York City in tumult, is giving us a meeting place on stage that we've never really seen—or, more to the point—heard before.

He possesses a perfect ear for all the clashing, frightening divisions of race and attitude and argot in our troubled city. He has reignited the possibilities of the one-man show. He takes us to the outer limits—and more authentically beyond Eric Bogosian's safer, now almost too well known territory, beyond even the solo docudramas of Anna Deavere Smith or the showbizzy performance art of John Leguizamo. That's some praise, but Mr. Hoch is the voice of a new generation, seeming to owe little or nothing to what has gone before.

He doesn't "perform" (or preach) in any polished, theatrical sense. I was told that he's hip, and I can see why, but I found him to be refreshingly unhip: a spontaneous, unselfconscious natural who says to us, "Listen to these people you avoid."

He says it unthreateningly, but we are threatened a bit even so by his cast of urban characters named Caribbean Tiger, Madman, Toño, Al Capón, Flex, and César. "This hour strictly Soca music!" Caribbean Tiger announces. "We goin see if you can wind your waist one time. My phone lines are blinkin people! Wild fire inna studio! I'm going to the phones right now. Hello good morning you're on the air."

"Ere dat boss. Wha'appnin Mister Morris?"

"Who am I talkin with this morning?"

"Disya Daddy Sluggy, seen."

"Daddy Sluggy! O.K., Daddy Sluggy where you callin from?"

"Me inna Brooklyn, yeh."

"O.K. Daddy Sluggy from Brooklyn. You ever call before?"

"Na boss. Aeda check you show fe years, but si is a first me a pick up de phone an call you pon radio station, seen..."

Some People is actually about language—the English language as spoken by Jamaicans, Jews, Puerto Ricans, Cubans, African-Americans, in the fractured, ethnic real world according to Danny Hoch. But it cuts deeper into the paranoia and urban barricades of "foreign" language and "differences." "If I was President, you know what I'd do to solve all the problems this country has?" says a thirtysomething white boy, owner of a Jeep. "I'd teach everybody how to speak English. Because that's the problem. Nobody speaks English anymore. I mean, how are we supposed to communicate for, you know, peace?"

The same character, a bigot in self-ignorant disguise, is in a Baskin-Robbins. "I'm always taking advantage of these little small-talk opportunities. You get to know people really well. So I ask the guy his name, and the guy says Mohammed. The guy's Moroccan, he's Iraqi, Libyan, he's Hindu. They're all connected. They're all terrorists, all right? They're all in the same little boat there. Because why do you think they're all named Mohammed? You think it's a coincidence? Let me ask you something, do you watch Dan Rather? Oh, you gotta watch Dan Rather, you get the whole story *right there.*"

Danny Hoch himself appears to reveal no anger. This is how people are, he's saying. Can we hear them? His characters, black or white, might reveal rage or massive ignorance, like Flex, the rapper and self-deluded bum who's ordering Chinese takeout. "Napkins, all that shit kid. Lemme get extra I want *extra...*I said you a immigrant. You know what I'm sayin? You ain't from here. You ain't from here, I'm from here. This is *my* shit yo. Understand that. How I know? Nigga can't even talk English talkin bout how I know? What the fuck *you* know? You don't know shit! I'm an American son, you don't know me."

Mr. Hoch is a white boy from Queens. What is he doing, then, impersonating black guys (or, persons of color)? And what are we—a mostly white, middle-class audience, as far as I could tell—doing at the Public, watching him do it? Danny Hoch is far too talented and genuine to be patronizing, or an easy way into scary issues. This is what he sees and hears in the New York streets, this is what he does. But are "we" on a guilt trip, the *"we and dem"* of his message?

Put it this way: where I live on the West Side, I see Mr. Hoch's characters every day. I say to myself about strangers in the hood: "I am a tolerant person. *Keep away from me.* I don't want to be killed, okay?" So, at first, with Mr. Hoch's *dem,* I found myself thinking that I was on some roller-coaster cab ride with the "wrong" driver who's probably stoned, and doesn't know the way, and has the radio blasting the "wrong" station, and I just want to get the hell out of there. But as Mr. Hoch's Jewish mother character puts it to her son: "I am *not* a scared liberal complaining *reactionary!"*

No, siree. But I would say that I resist touristy guilt trips to the theater (Gee! So this is how Puerto Ricans really talk! Good. See ya!) But that isn't at all what Mr. Hoch is encouraging. In a divided, scared, group-stereotyped America, he's asking for a more generous response.

Sometimes he's plain funny, as in his portrait of the Jewish mother who's trying to persuade her rebellious, genuinely tolerant son to get health insurance: "Fine, 36 percent. You're *not* 36 percent, you're my son, David. So let the 36 percent sit for ten hours waiting in some dirty emergency room somewhere bleeding to death with flies and urine and five hundred sick people with tuberculosis…I know white people shoot people with guns, David. But not on the *train*…I just want you to be happy and not dead. David, don't hang up! I want to talk to you!"

At other times, Mr. Hoch's stories are modestly humane, like the Polish plumber struggling with English ("Halo, eh. You, something broke?") or the terrible sadness of the virtually unspoken in the final story of César, who lost his beloved son, probably in a shootout. Danny Hoch falters occasionally, with a looseness in storytelling or with one of *dem* that even *we* know, or feel we know, too well. He is young, and a fine artist in the making. Goodness knows where he's heading at twenty-three. But he's arrived, with love and squalor, and a unique voice in theater that compels us to listen, and maybe to hear. Who are *dem?* Who's Danny Hoch?

"I want you to know I am the No. 1 dance hall chicken inna New York City," he sings amiably in a mad calypso epilogue. But the ultimate message may be hard: Don't be chicken. *Dem* ain't so dumb, *dem* are human beings.

Lost in
Suburbia

Karen Finley—who has done more to close down the National Endowment for the Arts than Senator Jesse Helms could have wished for in his wildest dreams—is best known as the performance artist who smeared her naked body with chocolate. I'm sorry I missed it.

She has also been known to shove yams up her ass. I don't know how I feel about that. As a friend of mine asks: "Why yams?"

Then again, why not? It's obvious—all too obvious—there are no boundaries in the consciously shocking art of Karen Finley. Now forty-one, she is said to have mellowed a bit. The yams are behind her. Her so-called outrageousness isn't a particular concern of mine, however. Crudeness matters more, and whether she's as good as some claim matters the most.

Her new one-woman show, *The American Chestnut*, downtown at Performance Space 122, is my first experience of Ms. Finley's howl on behalf of oppressed womanhood and others. I didn't know exactly what to expect, and I enjoy the feeling. But Ms. Finley's new performance piece isn't so hot. *The American Chestnut* is named after the tree cursed with a disease that kills it before it can mature. The tree battles to overcome—just as Ms. Finley battles against the social ills of America. But her show began badly.

She entered through the audience vacuuming the aisles in a wedding dress—a comment, I guess, on newlywed domesticity, marital entrapment, or the house-proud. It was okay until the Dustbuster broke down. These were among the slightly embarrassing moments when the uninitiated earnestly ask, "Is it part of the show?" But a number of things were to go blithely wrong later, and they obviously weren't deliberate. For instance, Ms. Finley couldn't find a costume at one point. But it didn't seem to matter much. She stepped out of character and disappeared backstage to emerge after a while wearing nothing but an apron, which was more or less as good as anything else.

When something goes wrong during a Karen Finley performance, it is and it isn't part of the show. It doesn't bother her, but it bothers me. Obviously, this is because I'm a perfectionist. As I see theater, it's just a little sloppy, that's all, to forget your costumes, misplace a few props, knock over the video camera, and blow the opening of your show that's about the unacceptable face of American culture.

The haphazard, the accidental happening, can make a thrilling improvisation. But not so here. Ms. Finley stops and starts, stops and starts, as if not fully prepared. She reads a good deal of the show from a script. She isn't a good reader, but let it pass. Some of our best actors are poor readers. But is Ms. Finley's *American Chestnut* a reading? Partly a reading? A fitful work-in-progress? Or a real *performance?* It was first seen two years ago at the American Repertory Theater in Cambridge, Massachusetts. Are we entitled to wonder why she doesn't know her own script by now? We are entitled.

I couldn't always hear what she was saying. Nor could others. Performance Space 122 is an intimate one, yet there were long stretches—particularly when she was reading—when we couldn't hear her clearly. Stories and poems about misogynistic tyranny, homophobia, and the genteel pleasures of gardening were mostly lost on me. One catches—and ought to feel privileged to catch—what one can. Yet it's understandable to think, Speak up, dear! Project! In such irritating ways, Ms. Finley can turn a libertarian into a disapproving, half-deaf old fusspot.

On the other hand, she shrieks. Her basic style is neurotic stridency and rage, which leads to peculiar voice changes, ranging from her own flat midwestern to a kind of whinnying to a visceral uncontrolled scream to a deep neo-southern black imitation that has no logic. At one point, a loony in the street outside could be heard competing with the apparent loony inside (which was truly enjoyable).

Ms. Finley is the raw-edged shaman of the fringe—raging about Bosnia and AIDS, Hillary Clinton and Martha Stewart, censorship and female oppression, and where is God when we need Him or Her. And all of this is fine and worthy and important, no doubt. But the age-old battles grow weary, the parodies of male sexism familiar, the disjointed feminist manifesto labored. There's a surprising domesticity and whimsy—tales of problematic breast-feedings, a reevaluation of Winnie-the-Pooh. (Ms. Finley, the eighties hipster, now has a four-year-old daughter.) "In her free time," the *New York Times* was eager to point out recently, "she straps her daughter into a car seat and takes her for a drive in her Ford Explorer, like any other suburban mother."

Hey-ho. What with all the work to be done around the house, "scrubbing the tub, vacuuming, mowing the lawn," it's a wonder the Suburban Mom ever finds time to strip for her show. The *Times'* cloying normalization of Ms. Finley annoys us as much as her connivance in it. She's a limited performer whose remembered pain is real enough. She is sincere, but intellectually slack. Her use of video is self-consciously amateur. (She's telling us she isn't slick and superficial, but "real.") I could have lived without the video image of deformed feet; also, the home movie of her lactating onto a painterly canvas.

But if her outrageousness once shocked America, we've gotten used to it. Her language is explicit, but no cruder than the fuck-yous of our street life. Her use of the C-word is cathartic. It's her nakedness that palls. Ms. Finley deliberately neutralizes her sexuality by treating her own naked body on stage as matter-of-fact, like performing in a nudist colony. What a bore. Bodies *are* sexy, aren't they? So are real, live people, I assume.

Yet no performer flashes more than the desexed Ms. Finley. And what sort of feminism is that? At one point, she sat on a small stool with her ample bare bum displayed for all to view at their leisure. Why?

Why yams?

She was telling a story, seated with her back toward the audience at the time, which concluded with the ludicrous revelation, "She learned that humor and humiliation are very similar."

Now, you and I know they aren't. Humor and humiliation are very different, unless one happens to relish the performance art of Don Rickles. But if Karen Finley doesn't see the difference, there's nothing we can do, concerned though we are about the blight on American chestnut trees.

Voltaire-Shmoltaire

Success doesn't suit Jackie Mason. I'm not certain when the comedian lost his sense of humor, or most of it, but I suspect Oxford University has a lot to answer for.

Appearing triumphantly in England, Mr. Mason received an honorary degree from the Oxford University Debating Society—only the fourth such honoree in its long history. President Kennedy, President Carter, Mahatma Gandhi, and Jackie Mason.

You are doubtless thinking: What's President Carter doing in such distinguished company? But, obviously, the Oxford honor was the decisive moment for Jackie Mason. For one thing, Gandhi wasn't Jewish. Nor, I think, were the two presidents. If it's any of our business, this proves that the honor bestowed on Jackie Mason ranks even higher than theirs. He is the first Jew in a thousand years to receive the honorary degree from those *alter kakers* at Oxford. Even Einstein didn't get one (and we all know why). But times change, and so has the man who came down from the Catskill Mountains.

I regret that he has now become a political commentator onstage as well as off, a pompous pundit, a malcontent, and a kvetch. Though *Jackie Mason: Politically Incorrect,* his new one-man show, or diatribe, on Broadway, has a few typically Mason comic moments of happier memory, the know-all tone of this new version is shot through with self-importance and bile. He has become a self-proclaimed champion of free speech—along with, he reminds us, Voltaire.

"I have the decency to tell the *truth!*" he berates us at the end of his performance. "I took a chance." What chance, whose truth? It might be that Mr.

Mason genuinely perceives himself as going where no man has dared tread before. (Rush Limbaugh and Howard Stern make similar claims.) It might be that his sour and simpleminded missionary zeal concerning such tired topics as Tonya Harding ("vicious yenta"), the raked-over mendaciousness of President Clinton ("a fuckin' liar"), or the cultural differences between "us" and "the shvartzers" represent some kind of truth for some. (Oddly, he never refers to "goyim," only to "gentiles.") The hectoring and awfully smug Mr. Mason, encouraging a smug response from the faithful, has a right to say what he wishes, and to be as coarse and offensive as he pleases. But at center he reveals himself to be an ill-tempered and prejudiced man.

I didn't always find him so. Along with many others, I enjoyed his first Broadway show, *The World According to Me.* "For twenty years, I've been in the Borscht Belt wilderness," he said at the time. "And now with the same material I'm suddenly a great artist!" Only a killjoy would have deconstructed his underlying Jewish and gentile stereotypes; he was too funny for that, and pretty accurate, too. "Well," he said at the end of his performance then, "I'm a star!" And one felt pleased for him. "The *New York Times* says I'm a genius," he added. "Mind you, it took a few dollars...."

He was never a sweetheart, but he seemed of good humor. I was glad to meet him, interviewing him for a British paper on the eve of his appearance in London for a Royal Variety Performance for the Queen Mother. "So tell me," he immediately asked in kibbitzing preemptive strike mode. "Why did you change your accent?" I explained I was born in England and this is how we talk. We can't help it. He leaned forward. "You Jewish?" he asked conspiratorially. I said sure. "You *see!*" Jackie Mason exclaimed in triumph. "You changed your accent!"

His comic logic was the secret to his success, I think. Because for Jackie Mason all Jews—in fact, everyone on earth including the Chinese and British royalty—really talk and think like Jackie Mason. Was he nervous, I asked him, at the thought of appearing before the Queen Mother? "*Noivous?*" he replied. "Why should I be *noivous?* The queen's at the palace before the show. And she says to her servants, 'So? Who've we got in the show tonight?' And she's told we've got this act, we've got that act, and we've got a short Jew from New York she's never heard of. You're telling me *I* should be *noivous? She* should be *noivous!* The queen's the one who should be *noivous!*"

Well, he was a great success. And he still is with some. But his good-humored comic logic has deserted him for the pulpit. The cracks now show among the stereotypes, including his stereotypical self-satisfied Jews; sometimes a polemic has no punch line; other times, he comes alarmingly close to losing his temper on stage. He appears dated now, locked in a sharp suit and a time warp of low comedy and offensive observations. He concludes his *Politically Incorrect* evening with a routine about incompetent Indian taxi drivers during which he points out, to laughter, that they are ignorant; they talk in strange accents; they play foreign music; they have incomprehensible names; they smell; and they all look alike. Ring a bell? There is a difference between ribbing and bad-mouthing, between free speech and ignorance, between the politically incorrect and the socially intolerant. Mr. Mason has lost it.

The Asterisk Problem: Sho**ing and Fucking

Mark Ravenhill's *Shopping and Fucking* is the first play in the history of the-ater to become world famous because of its title. To be sure, there are those who will swear on the Bible that it's a great play, a barbarous, shocking morality tale of our amoral times, a unique stage portrait of a lost genera-tion of dehumanized youth rotted by callous social and economic abuse, yadda, yadda, yadda.

But we don't know that—not yet, anyway. What we know is the title (which has already been translated into ten languages). Mr. Ravenhill's *Shopping and Fucking,* his first play, comes to the New York Theater Work-shop—the original home of *Rent*—via notoriety and success in London. And everywhere it goes, its title is sure to precede.

As the *Times* of London put it shrewdly: "The F-word still strikes many people with the crack of a rifle shot. There is still no consensus about its printability. The *Times* favors the f*** formula."

On the other hand, the *New York Times* favors the "it doesn't exist" for-mula. It has prudishly renamed the play *Shopping and…* The paper of record doesn't even give it an asterisk or two. Three little dots must suffice. "How was it for you, darling?" "That was the greatest three little dots I ever had in my life."

It can lead to failures of the imagination. Suppose, for example, in all innocence, you don't know what the three little dots actually stand for. Sup-pose you think the play is entitled *Shopping and Saving.* If so, the chances are you wouldn't be rushing to see it. Who *saves* anymore? The *Times* helpfully filled in the dots for us in its review of the play to avoid any misunderstanding. Explaining "the gerund that completes its title, *Shopping and...*," the paper pointed out that it's "a form of a much-used but still widely unprintable Anglo-Saxon verb referring to carnal intercourse."

This new title, *Shopping and Carnal Intercourse,* doesn't quite do it for me, either. I prefer what the *Times* calls "the gerund that completes the title." Very suggestive word, *gerund.* No one knows what it means, but it sounds dirty. *Shopping and Gerund.* There, that works!

But we'll go with the more prosaic *Shopping and Fucking.* Mr. Ravenhill's so-called dark urban comedy might shock you, if you're a tourist. The play belongs to the voyeuristic British tradition of theatrical slumming. *Nostalgie de la boue* has always been a heady strain in English life. The gutter is currently the hip place to be in the theater. Two other successful London imports—Mike Leigh's sordid (or "dazzlingly sordid," depending on your point of view) celebration of ignorance, *Goose-Pimples,* and the cartoonesque working-class spivs and psychotics of Jez Butterworth's *Mojo*—are now joined by the dehumanized grossness of *Shopping and Fucking.*

Within seconds of its start, a junkie and former stockbroker called Mark has vomited all over the place. Exactly the same vomit scene takes place with the drunk Arab in *Goose-Pimples.* Throwing up is a metaphor for the state of England, you see. The actor secretly hides green and yellow stuff in his mouth. Then he goes "Bleeeeagh!" Thus, *Shopping and Fucking* is seen as a subversively shocking drama of the alienated unemployed of England and the corrupting power of money. It follows as sure as the sun also rises that there should be explicit sex scenes, in this case homosexual. Then again, the fourteen-year-old juvenile hustler, Gary, fantasizes about being sodomized with a knife, having been raped by his stepfather. The violent sex, Mr. Ravenhill is saying, symbolizes a rotten England corrupted by a corrupt consumer culture.

Right. But the play's fallen characters—the heroin junkie Mark, the sexually abused, masochistic male hooker Gary, the unemployed, dim Ecstasy pusher Robbie, and his punk friend, the wannabe actress Lulu—don't symbolize a culture, only a marginalized subculture. In that narrower sense, *Shopping and Fucking* is a minor play that has been mistaken for a major one.

"I mean, are there any feelings left, you know?" asks Mark forlornly. There aren't, really. There are needs. And the cause of all this sullen alienation? Money! Mr. Ravenhill's message about the corrupting power of the god of consumerism amounts to the unsurprising pronouncement that money is the root of all evil. Unlike Irvine Welsh of *Trainspotting*, Mr. Ravenhill is a moralist. He warns us repeatedly in almost every scene that everything is the art of the deal, like sex and shopping. There's even a pseudo-*misterioso* prince of darkness, named Brian, who's the drama's Faustian amoral conscience. He comes out with such stuff as, "At the final reckoning, behind beauty, behind God, behind paradise, peel them away and what is there?" (Answer: money.) He goes even further, asking his punk protégés in disaffection to repeat the lesson and the mantra that money is civilization and the transaction is all.

"Yes. Yes. I'm teaching. You're learning. Money is civilization. And civilization is...*say it*. Don't get frightened now. And civilization is. . ."

"Money," they all dutifully reply.

Poor babies. If only they didn't live in a consumer society, they could be *happy*. They could have relationships. Maybe get a job. Learn to love. Whatever...Mr. Ravenhill's slack, simpleminded message is as empty as the neon signs that illuminate the drama's anonymously slummy set. Yet several admiring articles I've read about the play compare it favorably to the social rage and newness of John Osborne's 1956 *Look Back in Anger*. How is it possible?

The Osborne landmark shocked an entire theatergoing generation into a new awareness of England precisely because nothing like it had been written before. Its antihero, Jimmy Porter, is characterized by passion, not Mr. Ravenhill's empty disenchantment. The play is about love. It's about love and class war and bad marriages and boring Sunday papers. It's also about a nostalgia for the civility of Edwardian England. Above all, it glories uncompromisingly in the power of unsullied language—the English language. In other words, *Look Back in Anger* is about everything that *Shopping and Fucking* isn't about.

Mr. Ravenhill's inarticulate antiheroes have nothing to say, nothing to tell us, nothing for us to hold burned in our memory and our conscience.

Shopping and Fucking is a commonplace drama with simulated anal sex for voyeurs. In the Clinton–Talk Show era, in which nothing is particularly private, it fails even to shock. To the contrary, a naughty soft-porn fantasy about Princess Di has been edited out since her death on grounds of taste. It has been replaced by another fantasy involving Fergie, Duchess of York, the perennial understudy. What a fate! But Fergie is safer ground, and easy, and no one in the audience will be offended.

Et In Arcadia Ego

I'm still very much enjoying *Arcadia*. Tom Stoppard's dazzling plays have often given me fun and headaches and too much homework. The twin spies and quantum physics of *Hapgood* sent me to the bottom of an overcrowded class. *Jumpers* and *Travesties* sent me quite happily and too guiltily home, feeling compelled to take a crash course in logical positivism, Dadaism, and God. "Ah! That's what it was all about! I *think*." Well, at least I'm foolish enough—or in Stoppardian terms, clever enough—to admit it.

The playwright of brilliant, showy ideas stands loftily alone, Wilde and Nabokov not having written much lately (and Mr. Stoppard's spiritual shadow, Vaclav Havel, too). But he isn't easy, except when he is—that is, just bright and witty for the sake of being bright and witty. But if the higher mathematics of *Arcadia* had me on the ropes, this play is so touchingly complete—and "touching" isn't a word usually pinned to Mr. Stoppard—that I look back on it in surprise.

I even felt at the curtain that I had grasped the metaphysical meaning of Fermat's Last Theorem. Not to worry! The *Playbill* for *Arcadia* contains three short, learned essays that are most helpful: on the Newtonian vision of the universe versus the modern mathematics of deterministic chaos, thank you very much; the mystery of Byron's sudden departure from England in the summer of 1809 (unsolved); and a potted history of English gardens from classical symmetry to the esthetic of irregularity and romantic wildness. The moral of *Arcadia*, therefore, is to get to Lincoln Center a little early and scan the scholarly guide with the aid of a flashlight, together with, of course, your private library on metaphysics. But not necessarily.

"In speaking of Classical and Romantic literature, painting, music, sculpture, architecture or even landscape gardening," notes the erudite J. F.

Shade (1898–1959), "we balance reason against imagination, logic against emotion, geometry against nature, formality against spontaneity, discretion against valor. But in so doing, we are drawing attention not so much to different esthetic principles as to different responses to the world, to different tempers."

Those "different tempers"—personified ideas in opposition and war within the Western mind—go to the heart of *Arcadia*'s high comedy, which proves irresistible. Mr. Stoppard is either seriously trivial or trivially serious. He is always mind-bogglingly entertaining. He's a clever sausage, pursuing un-English intellectual activities while being more English than the English. There are times when, if he were half as clever, he'd still be too clever by three-quarters:

"Oh, pooh to Hobbes!" exclaims Thomasina, the thirteen-year-old child prodigy of *Arcadia*. "Mountains are not pyramids and trees are not cones. God must love gunnery and architecture if Euclid is his only geometry."

What! What was that again? But such lapses into Stoppardian denseness are mercifully rare and the sheer exhilaration and wit of *Arcadia*'s game—an accessible detective game—keep the play from spinning dizzyingly out of our grasp in this superb production directed by Trevor Nunn. Not having seen Mr. Nunn's original National Theatre production, I have no problem comparing this one favorably to it. It's a beautiful production, too. Set in a grand country house in 1809 and the 1990s—two separate and uncannily simultaneous worlds—the design by Mark Thompson is among its many seductions. His room with a view is effortlessly inhabited by two centuries, two time zones, and one apple. There's pleasure and mystery in this elegant time-bending. The same apple exists in the different time zones, but whose apple is it, anyway? The nineteenth-century tutor's? The contemporary gardening expert's? Newton's? Or Adam's and Eve's?

"Septimus, what is carnal embrace?" Thomasina asks her twenty-two-year-old tutor (who might be a genius, too) in the play's startling opening line. "Carnal embrace is the practice of throwing one's arms around a side of beef," comes the tactful response. "Is that all?" "No. A shoulder of mutton, a haunch of venison well hugged, an embrace of grouse…caro, carnis: feminine; flesh." And Tom Stoppard's intellectual comedy—itself an apparent contradiction in terms—is off and gaily running. A great deal will happen in that one room, including a sex comedy, past and present; the fate of a bad, cuckolded poet who is bitten by a monkey; the fate of bad poetry; farcical challenges to duels; goings-on in gazebos; a costume drama; the scholarly hunt for a hermit; the computerization of historic grouse shoots; the fate of Byron and his brilliant, oafish historian; a tragedy; and for good measure, the unfolding of the secrets of an unknowable universe.

The story—or the nineteenth-century part of it—concerns the prodigy in mathematics, Thomasina, and her discovery that God's universe will end in cold and oblivion. (Without realizing it, she has solved the 350-year-old mystery of Fermat's Last Theorem). The romance—and romance of ideas— between Thomasina and her handsome tutor (and friend of Byron) are a particular pleasure. "You hate her?" the tutor asks of Cleopatra. "Why?"

"Everything is turned to love with her," she replies. "New love, absent love, lost love—I never knew a heroine that makes such noodles of our sex. It only needs a Roman general to drop anchor outside the window and away goes the empire like a christening mug into a pawn shop."

With wit as witty as that, Thomasina is a prodigy we'd care to have around. Her family and extended family are something else—among them Noakes, the master gardener transforming Sidley Park's grounds into romantic chaos, "the Gothic novel as landscape"; Chater, the bad court poet dishonored by his flighty wife. "You insulted my wife in the gazebo yesterday evening!" he accuses the handsome tutor. "You are mistaken," the tutor replies. "I made love to your wife in the gazebo." And there's the mistress of the house, Lady Croom, who also spends a great deal of her imperious time in the gazebo. "Do not dabble in paradox, Edward," she snaps at her brother. "It puts you in danger of fortuitous wit." Oscar Wilde would have been as pleased to have penned that line as Tom Stoppard surely was.

But the masterstroke of the drama, the narrative underpinning that keeps it aloft and our curiosity on the boil, is the present in the past. In a series of alternating scenes, the 1990s characters also inhabit the house, including its new aristocratic owner and Oxford student, the scientist Valentine Coverly; sister Chloe; historian and gardening expert Hannah, in search of the identity of the estate's hermit; and the comically absurd and over-ambitious academic Bernard Nightingale, trying to solve the mystery of Byron's disappearance from England.

It's like a dance with history, for each explores the past of the estate as we actually see the past unfolding. It's a nimble and very beguiling detective game. We know the truth, and we don't know it. Who will solve the puzzle? The answer is the playwright. It's the least he can do. The contemporary mathematician Valentine has the original notebooks of Thomasina, romantic historian Hannah has the knowledge of the entire estate, and professor Nightingale has the letters the tutor, Septimus, kept in the folio of Chater's awful poetry. But when Mr. Stoppard produces the rabbit out of the hat and has past and present merge on stage, the abstract and the humane beautifully coalesce and all is memorably complete.

When all is said and undone, when discoveries are joyfully (and sadly) made, two couples from past and present waltz in the room through time, through the looking glass. Why this final image should prove so touching is the ultimate mystery, though we know that Thomasina will die tragically young and only poets and the insane know the mysteries of the universe. It's a melancholic end: they waltz together in different centuries, in timeless space, or universal chaos, and the waltz goes on. "I had a dream which was not all a dream / The bright sun was extinguished, and the stars / Did wander darkling in the eternal space..." (Byron).

As I say, the *Arcadia* ensemble couldn't be better. We would expect Blair Brown as Hannah in her sensible shoes to be excellent; so too Victor Garber as seriocomic Nightingale in his peacock vest. They are what the English call "spot on." Robert Sean Leonard as Valentine and Billy Crudup in his Broadway debut as Septimus are very appealing. Everyone is. But special mention of Jennifer Dundas's Thomasina: For an adult actress to play a youngster, and a child prodigy at that, is an awesome challenge. Ms. Dundas is utterly enchanting in the right way, not cute, least of all lovable, but the near impossible—innocent, and innocent on the verge of knowing.

To say *Arcadia* is currently the best play on Broadway is to say less than I would wish. Let's settle, simply, for the best.

The America Play

Is there a more compelling, fresh talent on either side of the Atlantic than Suzan-Lori Parks? I sing her praises without apology, and gladly. There is no dramatist like her at work in theater today.

The America Play gives us great good cause to celebrate in the name of an important new drama, though its message causes us to grieve. In its poetic imagination and search for meaning in an America that has lost its moorings, the piece is arguably as much a breakthrough as the epic drama of our time, *Angels in America*. Ms. Parks, a minimalist in comparison to Tony Kushner, has dynamited all the traditional narrative forms. In that modernist sense, she's the heir to Beckett (though her voice remains uniquely her own). But as *The America Play* takes place in the surreal world of a black hole wasteland, comparisons with *Godot* are inevitable and similar questions are being asked. What does *The America Play* mean?

I can't tell whether the audience at this superb production, which comes to the Public Theater via Yale Repertory, was finally stunned into virtual silence from confusion, emotional turmoil, or having witnessed a remarkable event. But if we can avoid an overliteral response and permit *The America Play* to wash over us, as unforgettable echoes and memories and images can, its dark humor and tragedy of America are accessible and will leave us badly shaken.

On one appealing level, *The America Play* returns us naively to the roots of all theater: it tells a good story—and a bizarre one it is. Act 1 is the life story (rivetingly told and acted out by Reggie Montgomery) of a black gentleman known as the Foundling Father who bears, it's said, an amazing resemblance to Abraham Lincoln. He's a grave digger by trade—"digged them quick and they looked good, too." All his life, it turns out, this digger in search of posterity was utterly fascinated by the assassination of his look-alike, Lincoln. It took place, of course, during the performance of an awful play, *Our American Cousin*, at Ford's Theater. "Shoot, he couldn't get that story out of his head…"

So one day, the Foundling Father digs himself A Great Hole of History. Hall of Wonders! Minstrel Gallery! (Or American theme park.) There, he reenacts the shooting of Lincoln in the president's red theater box. Members of the public, some dressed as John Wilkes Booth, pay a penny to act out shooting him. "The South is avenged!" they cry, joining in the Lincoln story. Or, "Thus to the tyrants!" The Foundling Father becomes quite famous, in his way….

Act 2 takes place some years later. Our hero's widow Lucy (Gail Grate) and their son Brazil (a terrific performance by Michael Potts) return to the black hole to find his remains, the artifacts he left behind, and bury him.

Now that, I suggest, is some story. But within the dramatist's playfulness and punning and Joycean delight in language—between the spoken lines, in a startling fresh image or the ricocheting echo of a gunshot—is an entire, tragic universe. I don't see *The America Play* specifically as a "black drama," though Ms. Parks is a black American (and the dramatist of the 1990 lament *The Death of the Last Black Man in the Whole Entire World*). *The America Play*—which takes as its premise John Locke's "In the beginning all the world was America"—transcends all narrowly conventional narrative, not in anger but in unique focus. Ms. Parks speaks unsentimentally for us all, of historic lies and fakery, white icons and black despair, fathers and sons, truth and hearsay, theater and illusion, an America Lost.

Nor is it an America easily found again. If ever. The pretend Booths pretend to shoot the Lincoln look-alike. Therapy or fun? But this repeated, mesmerizing history-play or psychodrama is performed with a fake cap gun. A children's game then? And yet that single image sends chills down our spine. Ms. Parks taps into our collective unconscious and national nightmare. The black actors, portraying the deranged white assassin, Booth, are playing out a terrifying dream: they shoot the genial black man and faker who's pretending to be the nation's hero and white icon, Abraham Lincoln. "Note thuh hole thuh fatal bullet bored," he announces. "And how thuh nation mourned…"

The America Play is digging feverishly for life and meaning in the detritus of America's fabled history and its theme-park present. The restaged, surreal scenes from the nineteenth-century bourgeois entertainment *Our American Cousin*—"Haw! Haw! Haw!" the president laughs—are ghostly sideshows, a comic irony in the sure hands of Ms. Parks's brilliant director Liz Diamond and her design team. "Keep the story to scale!" advises Lucy, the mother-wife of the piece. Well, I'm trying.

There are stories within stories in this wonderful, haunting drama and dreamscape—and "stories too horrible to mention," as the dramatist puts it. There is the human being—it is said—in the Lincoln beard, with his respectful, dutiful nod and a wink to posterity, yearning for some recognition, some place, some lasting role to play. There is the shuffling mother-wife searching for a past that barely existed, or a present survival, a half-life in the American wasteland. And there is the young lost son and heir to history whose future will follow in the void, trapped in the footsteps of his Foundling Father, who worshiped the Father of Liberty.

Search for the true. Dig, weep, dig, weep, fake, *dig*. Spade, paw, pah, haw! haw! haw! Look on the bright side! Shoot, black hole, hole in the head. So much to live for! In this sweet land of liberty.

Suzan-Lori Parks's *The America Play* comes from nowhere and everywhere. She has written the most staggering American play imaginable.

How America Was Lost

"What-what!" as King George III likes to exclaim, when sane. What fun to see at last Alan Bennett's witty tragedy, or tragi-farcical-political-historical-medical-satirical-regal comedy, *The Madness of George III.* I don't quite go along with those who feel that Mr. Bennett has written a savage satire of English life and royalty (or politicians and other clowns and impostors). He can be lethal, but quacks and clergy and kings are in Mr. Bennett's British blood, and affection is his unmistakable tone, even for things he satirizes, even for England.

Look how fond he is of poor old George III, who lost America and his mind. And so, of course, is the audience—royalist Anglophiles or not, preferably not. Mr. Bennett rights a wrong in a sense: the wrong assessment of history. The mad Farmer King was not mentally ill, but more probably suffered from a hereditary metabolic disorder known as porphyria, which attacks the nervous system. The king was therefore mistreated and tortured by physicians who didn't know what they were doing in the first place. So we sympathize with genial George from the start. We are on his side all the way—and cannot fail to be—as appalled witnesses to his medieval medical treatment, and as delighted witnesses to a great performance by the actor to whom the role of the king will always belong, Nigel Hawthorne.

It's such a pleasure to see him at the height of his power, seizing the stage with such awesome command and relish to give the performance of a lifetime. The pace and depth and exactness of so moving a portrayal are uncanny. Mr. Hawthorne has hitherto kept my expatriate British self wallowing in a certain nostalgia with his dry, laconic portrait of the civil servant in the public television comedy series *Yes, Minister.*

His Tony Award–winning performance in *Shadowlands* was moving, but that was in a lesser play and seems a breeze now compared to the Lear-like heights he scales as George III. "I am not going out of my mind, " the king protests. "My mind is going out of me." Mr. Hawthorne achieves an acting miracle, which is that he seems to be watching himself as we watch him go mad.

He loses his body, too, and it's gruesome at times. He is bled, blistered, tortured, gagged, and straitjacketed, until at the end of act 1 he's manacled, howling, to a chair, his new throne of the insane. We do not think: Poor pitiful king, only, Poor man. Robbed of all dignity, of pomp and circumstance and divine privilege, the king becomes a human being. The fragility of power and outer appearances has long been a major theme of Alan Bennett's plays. "I have always been myself even when I was ill," the king says, when apparently recovered. "Only now I seem myself. That's the important thing. I have remembered how to seem."

The Madness of George III is a play for England, that travels nicely. But in the context of New York, the play unavoidably loses some of its English resonance and immediacy. "We have lost America" raises a laugh, but Mr. Bennett's intentions are more profound. "Soon we shall lose the Indies, Ireland even," the king continues in a fine speech, "our feathers plucked one by one, this island reduced to itself ere long, a great state mouldered into rottenness and decay."

"Awfully good stuff!" (as the king says later of Shakespeare's *King Lear*). Similarly, the portrait of the royal family as emblem of a sick England, or of thick pampered minds, would have had a particular, even shocking, urgency in London. "Wait! Wait!" cries the Prince of Wales in protest. "My life has been waiting....To be heir to the throne is not a position; it is a predicament. People laugh at me. What must I do to be taken seriously? I tell you, sir, to be Prince of Wales is not becoming to a gentleman."

To which the playwright has a peach of a response: "Yes. It takes character to withstand the rigors of indolence."

Mr. Bennett is an eccentric man perceived as odd, who has written a play about an eccentric king perceived as mad. "The matter is, sir, that it is morning," the king announced irritably. "That is the matter. Morning is the matter. Not being attended to is the matter. And don't mutter. Or mutter will be the matter...." How the playwright also manages to combine the central, disturbing tragedy of George III with knockabout potty jokes concerning the color of royal piss and the state of magisterial stools is a tribute to the dura- bility of English schoolboy humor and a jolly specialty of Mr. Bennett's. Would that Nicholas Hytner's spiffy Royal National Theatre production were in a more intimate theater than Brooklyn's cavernous Opera House, which adds legions to the hard of hearing. No matter! One catches what one can, and there is much to catch. A little too much on occasion, for the play is overstuffed with Affairs of State—the political canvas, the comings and goings of Prime Ministers Pitt, Fox, and Burke, the crackpot physicians, the foppish Prince of Wales and his circle, et al. We see a grand and pleasing pageant, as elegant as Thomas Rowlandson's caricatures. But the narrative flow flattens out, and the political panorama is sketchy. Mr. Bennett, with typical candor, says as much in his amusing introduction to the published play:

"As I struggled to mince these chunks into credible morsels of dialogue (the danger being that characters are telling each other what they know *in their bones*), I often felt it would have been simpler to call the audience a quarter of an hour early and give them a short curtain lecture on the nature of 18th-century politics before getting on with the play proper."

He's right. "But it is about the madness of George III, the rest amusing, intriguing, but incidental." Right again. However, he can't resist giving *The Madness of George III* a happy end. Wrong! In reality, the king was horribly doomed. But the play ends by resurrecting the pride of England and the royal status quo, celebrating the institutions it lampoons. No matter to that, either; we all have a fondness for things we see through, and there are great fun and games along the way. Nicholas Hytner has licked into shape an impeccable ensemble—far superior to the National Theatre troupe's last visit with *Richard III*, the tragedy about the king who merely lost his horse. *The Madness of George III* belongs triumphantly to the supreme performance of Nigel Hawthorne. If Alan Bennett hasn't quite written a great play, he has written a great role. And the evening is memorably made.

These Gentle Artists

The Three Lives of Lucie Cabrol goes to the heart of a theater of the imagination. It is the Théâtre de Complicité's playful, near naive delight in theater itself that we embrace as the drowning cling to a life raft in an awfully literal world. We badly need generous, epic stories like *Lucie Cabrol*. For what is the best theater but a good story well told?

The critic John Berger, who wrote the original story on which the drama is based, admiringly describes the London-based troupe as "these gentle artists." They are gentle and gifted, conjuring up worlds from next to nothing. In *Lucie Cabrol,* with a little help from a few wooden planks, a kitchen table, or a bathtub, they can bring to life the land, animals, villagers, children, and the dead. The Théâtre de Complicité, one of the most admired alternative theater ensembles in Europe, could even transcend the civic formality of the vastly anonymous Alice Tully Hall, where apparently they had no choice but to play. It's a concert hall, not a theater, scarcely the ideal intimate space in which to act out the life and afterlife of a dwarfish child of the earth born in France in 1900.

The power of imagination is the complicit point of the proceedings, as if we are all jointly engaged in an illicit act. Théâtre de Complicité liberates the theater and returns it to the actor as creator. *The Three Lives of Lucie Cabrol* is devised by the company itself. Simon McBurney, one of its founders, is the innovative director of the play, which he coadapted with Mark Wheatley; Mr. McBurney, an Englishman born in Cambridge, also began life as an actor and plays Jean, the drama's narrator and Lucie's one love.

Like other members of Complicité, he trained over a decade ago in Paris with the visionary mime teacher Jacques Lecoq. (The only comparable troupe in America also possesses a French name—the Théâtre de la Jeune Lune in Minneapolis—and their formative influence was also the Lecoq theater school in Paris.) The total creativity of the Complicité performers—in mime, speech, sound, song, and movement—accounts for their exhilarating pleasure in play. In their assured hands, a wooden plank becomes a mountain path, an upheld hand a nettle, and an old bathtub a coffin, a river, a slaughterhouse. And in that imaginative sense, they are also heirs to Peter Brook's international troupe.

At the beginning of the play, Lucie is born as quickly as it takes to scatter a bucket of potatoes across the stage, which is built of earth. In essence, the staging is almost childlike. "It's a girl!" goes the cry as the potatoes roll and Lucie appears like a tiny ferret, red and burning, and another actor playing a pig is dragged squealing to a swift slaughter.

The Complicité actor—rather than the writer or director—is the king and ruler of the stage. The ensemble of just seven international actors makes it seem as if the stage is teeming with life. Working with everyday objects, they are unpretentious, physical, and full of good humor. They can convey the simmering sensuality of the French countryside by simply suggesting the sound of cicadas, or capture the tumult of the big city by a change in body language. Sometimes they slip briefly in and out of various languages—French, German, or gobbledygook—like jazz musicians quoting another melody in the midst of a solo. Yet we still understand the play that transcends language.

The story of Lucie Cabrol (played by the amazing Swiss actress Lilo Baur), who was born in a dung heap and could kill things at a glance, is both a fable and an extraordinary tale of what John Berger says "is habitually marginalized, dismissed, belittled, made voiceless." *The Three Lives of Lucie Cabrol*, on the one hand, is about the backbreaking life and poverty of its voiceless heroine; on the other, it is a fabulous affirmation of her life and tenacity and spirit. It is about love.

I saw the production twice and still feel haunted by its heroine. Perhaps she's a French Mother Courage or a witch. Her first life consists of her years of hard labor on the family farm, where she's derisively nicknamed "the *co-cadrille*" (a freak, something that's born from a cock's egg). She is abandoned by her one lover, Jean, and banished by her family. Her second life tells of her exile and a survival as a peddler and smuggler. "America, America," she says to Jean, whose two boys are both working in the United States. "Money can change everything. Money can eat and dance. Money can make the dirty clean. Money can make the dwarf big. I have two million!"

"I hope you keep it in a bank!" says Jean.

"Fuck off! Fuck off and get away !" she replies, and strides away.

She has waited forty years for Jean to return to her. And when he returns to the village, she asks him to marry her. "Before I could give her my considered answer, she was dead." Jean tells us. Lucie Cabrol had been murdered and robbed. The blade of an ax had split her skull.

Mr. McBurney as Jean gave us the information without milking it for a second. It was a fact of life, like Lucie's belittled life. Yet an audible gasp of shock and sorrow came from the audience just the same.

And Lucie Cabrol's third life follows, which is the afterlife where injustice is impossible. "I have land now," she tells Jean happily. "Land but no season."

At the play's end, a fantastic end, a house is built in the forest. The troupe raise three big beams, like three crosses. The back wall of the stage is shingled like the roof of a house. And sometimes the vast wall becomes a mountain that Lucie climbs, or a forest, or heaven. But when in the last moments of the play, Lucie disappears, everything collapses.

The tile shingles and the wall fall, and Jean falls, coming back to earth—back to reality and his memories of Lucie Cabrol. The wall falls forward and comes to rest on the beams. And the house is a skeleton, an abandoned shell.

"But there are moments when I see something different," Jean tells us quietly. "Moments when a blue sky reminds me of Lucie Cabrol. Then I see again the roof which we raised, built from the trees. And then I am convinced that when I leave the forest I will leave it with the love of the Cocadrille."

Lucie's life was never small. Her life was big and true, as her love was true. She was dismissed as a nobody, yet she changed life. She was abandoned, yet Jean, who left her, says that her life makes his life seem like a failure. She was uncompromised and very real, as her spirit is real. This is such a beautiful production. In the ruin of the world, Lucie Cabrol is hope.

The Jerry Stiller
Three Sisters

With Anton Chekhov, with this generous, realistic man, everything changes. He is the only dramatist whose success or failure I take personally. If his plays are badly produced, I find that I actually take it personally, wishing to protect him as if he were one of the family. His great dramas, balanced precariously between melancholy and yearning, are easily misunderstood, easily wrecked. We want to shield this most humane of dramatists from a careless world.

"My holy of holies," Chekhov wrote, "are the human body, health, intelligence, talent, inspiration, love and the most absolute freedom—freedom from despotism and lies."

We feel more honestly whole in his company, knowing that he affirmed the possibilities of life even in the despair of lives stifled like weeds. "I think that in Anton Chekhov's presence everyone involuntarily felt himself a need to be simpler, more truthful, more oneself," wrote Maxim Gorky. We romanticize him, but Chekhov is our wise father. He understood better than anyone the frailty of everyday life.

But what if you are careless with him? What if you fail to respect this man—while protesting, no doubt, that no one could respect him more? You will end up with a production like *Three Sisters* at the Roundabout Theater and you will be sunk.

Displayed in the foyer of the Roundabout is Konstantin Stanislavsky's comment on Chekhov's plays, and it tells us everything. Stanislavsky was, of course, his director, and in a sense he was also his savior. "Read him in the kitchen of life, and you will find nothing in him but simple plot, mosquitoes, crickets, boredom, gray little people. But take him where art soars, and you will feel in the everyday plots of his plays the eternal longings of man for happiness, his strivings upwards, the true aroma of Russian poetry....."

The Roundabout production has given us only the kitchen—only the inert, tedious surface of life. There is no poetry in it, no Russia. There is simply no evidence of the drama's emotional nuances and delicate balance. The Roundabout has done good work in the past with its classic revivals, though they are too much in the middle of the road. Scott Elliott, the director of *Three Sisters* (whose gay version of Noël Coward's *Present Laughter* is currently and blatantly on Broadway), reveals no understanding of Chekhov. Nor, sad to say, do leading members of the cast, who appear to think that the mere sight of movie stars gracing the stage with their presence is enough.

Look at Mr. Elliott's mistaken—or plain silly—casting of just one of the minor roles (though in Chekhov, no role is minor). We know from the Moscow Art Theater that even a supporting role would be played by a leading actor. Every care ought to be taken, even in miniature. The elderly army doctor, Chebutykin—drunk, corrupt, irredeemably disillusioned Chebutykin—is one such key role in *Three Sisters*. He is the only character in the entire play who has completely given up on life. He no longer even comprehends reality. It is a role that would have challenged an actor as great and otherworldly as Ralph Richardson. The director has cast Jerry Stiller, the borscht belt comic, in the part.

Mr. Stiller would be perfect if only Chebutykin lived in the Catskills. Unfortunately, Chebutykin is living and wasting away in provincial Russia at the turn of the century. The director obviously sees the old army doctor as merely a comic buffoon, and what we receive is the first Yiddish comic buffoon in the history of Chekhov productions. Mr. Stiller, if truth be told, is actually playing Jackie Mason. As it were: "Do I exist? Do you? Who knows!" When he slumps—*shlumps*—in an armchair with an almost audible "Oy," his lassitude seems less the outcome of a Chekhovian mourning for life than a case of dyspepsia brought on by eating too many pastramis on rye at the Carnegie Deli.

The production shall henceforth be known as "The Jerry Stiller *Three Sisters*." At any rate, the symptom of Mr. Elliott's waywardness—sometimes described as bold casting against type—is there in his cartoon Chebutykin.

The production has been miscast and underrehearsed. There is no sense of time or place or period. There is nothing evocatively Russian about the chic, gray set (gray as a symbol of provincial life, you know). These desperately unhappy sisters yearning for their cultivated Moscow and spiritual home have never lived and wept in such a place. Their brand-new clothes—costumes—have never been worn before. Those perfect polished boots have never seen mud (or snow). Nothing in the production is truly lived, or lived in.

We are Nowhere, nowhere real or authentic. Naturalism on stage—a form, at its best, of artlessness—was central to Chekhov. The everyday rhythms and texture of life are to be captured. To be merely "Chekhovian"—actorish, overrefined, stylishly atmospheric—only produces an artificial replica of Chekhov. That's essentially what has gone wrong here. To act boredom is hard. (The actor risks boring us.) But the despair of Chekhov's characters is stirred by the joyful wish to *live.*

The aliveness is fatally absent. Lili Taylor's Irina is beaten from the start; Jeanne Tripplehorn's Masha is sulky rather than tragic; Amy Irving's spinster Olga is merely monotonous. (They are, incidentally, the wrong ages.) Crucial to Chekhov, there's no sense at all of ensemble acting. Ms. Taylor's accent is solidly Bronx; Ms. Tripplehorn's seems to come at first from the South of Tennessee Williams. We can scarcely believe that the three sisters are, in fact, sisters.

Then again, Calista Flockhart's Natalya shouldn't just be a pretty little foot-stamping upstart. She's poison—the most dangerous woman Chekhov created. (The unfaithful Natalya ruins her husband's life, and chucks the sisters out of their own home. No cutie-pie, she.) Paul Giamatti fares better as her husband, Andrei, capturing his slow-drip descent from happiness to waste and defeat. But even Mr. Giamatti is allowed to drift into melodrama. David Strathairn's unhappily married Vershinin, who sweeps poor Masha off her feet, is solid but unexciting. "Happiness is something we never have, but only long for," Vershinin says in a famous line, but Mr. Strathairn makes the yearning matter of fact. His passion has a dull edge. Eric Stoltz "does a turn" as the timid Baron, and one could see him acting gauche from the tip of his false mustache down to his shiny new army boots. The usually reliable

David Marshall Grant oversimpers as the cuckolded, foolish Kulygin; the dashing Billy Crudup's neurotic Captain Solyony is a presence, though a nervy bag of tics.

This is a starry, poor production, another lost opportunity for a decent Chekhov in town. In apparent indifference to the patience or fortitude of the audience, the evening limps to an end, with the predictable three sisters posed tableaux, at 11:15 P.M. The overlong running time alone should have been a clue to the director of a serious mistake—but no. If the troupe had spoken at a normal pace—spoken naturally, as Chekhov intended—at least half an hour could have easily been shaved off. The pace is too slow and ponderous. But even on that self-evident score, the director, in his carelessness, cannot sense what the tired, dispirited audience is telling him.

Needles
and Opium

Though I have reservations about the surrealistic brilliance of Robert Lepage's *Needles and Opium*, the thirty-five-year-old Mr. Lepage has it within his grasp to shake theater to its foundations.

Needles and Opium is his performance debut in New York, the first chance I've had to catch the work of the wunderkind director, writer, solo performer, and designer. And what a designer! His stage pictures and dreamscapes can blow your mind. He quite literally appears to walk through walls—to expand the frontiers of theater while creating images of great beauty.

Mr. Lepage is celebrated in Canada (his home country) and in Europe where his innovatory work is rooted in the experimental techniques of Jerzy Grotowski, Jacques Lecoq, and Alain Knapp. His recent *Midsummer Dream* at Britain's National Theatre sounds like a wonderfully wayward mess. He staged it in a sea of mud. But the gossip about his *Dream* didn't prepare me for the exquisite precision of *Needles and Opium* at the Brooklyn Academy. The performance piece itself is an homage to surrealism and coincidence, a theatrical oddity in its daring way. In 1949, the French surrealist Jean Cocteau visited America when Miles Davis visited Paris for the first time. Their paths crossed. Both Cocteau and Davis were at the barricades of the modern, and both were addicts (opium for the poet; heroin for the jazzman).

The action takes place in a Left Bank hotel room once inhabited—Mr. Lepage wittily informs us—by Jean-Paul Sartre and Miles Davis's lover and flame of existential angst, Juliette Greco. At one point, the phone rings in the middle of the night and Mr. Lepage, as himself, answers the call in the hotel room, hoping it is his lover calling from New York. The caller wants to speak to Jean-Paul Sartre. Mr. Lepage, a mild-mannered stage presence, patiently explains that Sartre is dead. But the caller insists on leaving a message. "I took the message," he tells us.

So the piece is also slightly mad, beguiling, surreal. Cocteau and Davis are conjured up for us brilliantly by Mr. Lepage, who plays all the roles. The action dissolves seamlessly into the surreal, as if in a film. Mr. Lepage consciously uses film technique—the most innovative use of it I've ever seen onstage. But my reservations—and how I wish I didn't have them—concern the intermingling story of the Quebecois in the Paris hotel room, Robert Lepage as the lonely character called "Robert." I see the point: the lovesick Robert is as much addicted to his estranged lover in New York as the ghosts of Cocteau and Davis were to dope and ideas. For myself, this slender narrative of solitude dissolves only into self-pity, clashing in its forlorn realism— "the hell of rejection," Mr. Lepage describes it—with the airborne surrealism of the piece.

Yet, from the staggering opening image, I felt that I was witnessing theater of a different order. Mr. Lepage is literally airborne as Cocteau. A fan in the hotel room turns into a propeller, a screen turns—and there he is! Mr. Lepage in midair as Cocteau the flying machine. It's a wonderful *coup de théâtre*, and utterly and unpretentiously natural. This is the extraordinary thing about Mr. Lepage: he creates his own conventions. He works with sound, jazz, language (sometimes French), shadow play, and film. So do other experimenters. But Mr. Lepage is so good that he can use a mere screen, in all ease and fluency, as the sky, a floor, an expanding universe, a moving graphic, or a wall to be walked through. At one point, we see him looking over the screen at an image of Miles Davis swimming *underwater* back to America. Then, in a split second, he seems to plunge into the screen, becoming Miles Davis.

Shades of Cocteau's *Blood of a Poet*. Shades elsewhere of Buñuel's *Chien Andalou*. It's only right, and appropriated. In *Needles and Opium*, Mr. Lepage is in the instinctive free fall of the surrealists. But there's danger involved if *Needles and Opium* is his aesthetic credo. The surrealist movement of Cocteau, Breton, and Duchamp reached a dead end, like the school of automatic writing. They produced arresting images (and an enduring ballet, the Picasso *Parade*); they shook up the bourgeois status quo; they freed the unconscious. But in the end, the surrealists weren't free; they were stylized. Where was their content but lost in pretty stream-of-consciousness words, or jokiness and arty trances? Robert Lepage's new theater of image and feeling is an extraordinary contribution. He is an original. But where is he going? He will be returning to BAM with two more pieces: Bartók's only opera, *Bluebeard's Castle*, and Schoenberg's first opera, *Erwartung*. What Mr. Lepage will do with them is anyone's guess. One thing is certain: they won't be boring.

The Three Ages
of Woman

Three Tall Women, the New York City premiere of Edward Albee's full-length 1991 drama at the adventurous Vineyard Theater downtown, is said to mark the return from virtual oblivion, or critical disfavor, of a once-renowned dramatist. But that's an awfully New York judgment. *Three Tall Women* was first produced in Vienna, and Vienna does exist; so do all the other theaters in Europe and America that have been glad to produce Albee plays over the last twenty years or so. Yet New York, letting its provincialism and short memory show, has discarded the playwright who wrote *Zoo Story* (1960), *Who's Afraid of Virginia Woolf?* (1962), *A Delicate Balance* (1966), and *Seascape* (1975)—as if to say, "All well and good. But what have you done for us lately?"

A lot—as the season of Albee plays at the Kampo Cultural Center in NoHo is boldly proving in tandem with *Three Tall Women* at the Vineyard. The touching and darkly funny chamber piece *Three Tall Women* is Edward Albee at his more accessible. He has written the kind of memorable drama that used to be presented automatically on Broadway—though the playwright, now in his late sixties, wouldn't take Broadway today as an accolade.

Act 1 *seems* conventional: A wealthy, ninety-something dowager named "A" lies in bed dying the farce of death. She is Mr. Albee's rambling, imperious, childish, squabbling portrait of a privileged old woman's life. (She is also based on the playwright's own mother, who rejected him.) The near senile "A" is in the company of a character called "B," a capable, stooping, middle-aged stick of a nurse and companion, and "C," a fastidious family lawyer in her twenties who's trying to keep the old woman's finances in order.

The first half of *Three Tall Women* belongs almost entirely to the riveting Myra Carter as the old woman in the twilight between the salvation of forgetting and the pleasure of remembering.

"Harry died!" she announces suddenly, and bursts into tears.

"That was thirty years ago," her companion reminds her.

"I knew that!"

This frail creation is a force of life even so, with her reminiscences of days long gone, a gilded age, an illicit affair, her wealthy husband with the glass eye ("Which eye?"), her own mother ("She hated me! She stank. She hated me because I was strong. I had to be—"). There are hints of betrayal, the abandonment of a son. But at the close of the first act, with a Beckettian exhalation of breath, the old woman has a stroke.

Where was Mr. Albee heading?

His act 2 throws down an unexpected ace that changes everything, including our own memory of what has gone before. Characters "A" (the ninety-year-old), "B" (the middle-aged woman), and "C" (the twenty-six-year-old) are the living embodiment of the three ages of woman as well as of the elderly heroine's life. *Three Tall Women* is about the mutation of aging—from an optimistic, brashly blind beginning to a pragmatic, sour middle, to an exhilarated end.

"That's the happiest time! When we come to an end," says the old lady.

"*This* is the happiest time!" protests the middle-aged spirit, with a silly youth behind her, the knowledge of vistas of decline and obsolescence ahead.

"I will not become you!" insists the twenty-six-year-old in disbelief.

But this is what they all become, over time, in a single life of youthful giddiness turning into bitterness, of sexual memories and family intrigue—the husband's whores, the hated bisexual son—in a lifetime spent in fading grandeur.

So these three tall ladies gather round the deathbed—but there is nothing maudlin about it, not wistful, not melancholic, just true. It is as true as memory can be. What made this woman who she is? What does she even know of herself? It is like looking at faded photographs of one's own family. They contain a mystery. Do we know who that mother figure really is, or was?

At one point the abandoned son, who in turn has cut loose from the mother, enters the scene to grieve and remember silently at the deathbed. He has no need to say a word. His other self, the playwright, has his three muses speak for him. In this delicate balance, there are no easy showdown scenes, no slam-bang emotional confrontations. It is too authentic a play for that. In its modest, thoroughly absorbing way, *Three Tall Woman* restores, or confirms, Edward Albee as one of America's leading playwrights.

Three Tall Women *was awarded the 1994 Pulitzer Prize in Drama—Albee's third Pulitzer.*

The God of Lies

We love Spooky Ricky Jay. His card tricks—though "tricks" is too lowly a description—bring the audience at the tiny Second State Theater to a state of befuddled wonder. He fools us, and we are happily fooled. How does he do it?

He's such an easeful master illusionist that if he explained the secret, he would still deceive us. During *Ricky Jay and His 52 Assistants*—which has been directed by a fan, David Mamet—he shows us how to deal an ace from the bottom of the deck. "That's cheating," he announces somberly. Then, at lightning speed, he produces the ace astonishingly from the middle of the deck—as if telling us, "Now, that's not cheating. That's miraculous." Which it surely is. As con artists go, he's the best. He does not belong to the magic glitzoramas of David Copperfield or the usual suspects. He does not work with pigeons. Not for the purist Ricky Jay the mundane of special-effect illusions or mirrors and smoke and fake mystification. Nothing is hidden. His fifty-two assistants are his deck of cards, pure and simple.

His stage set is a kind of Edwardian playroom, which might belong to a child or an eccentric. Ricky Jay himself seems odd, as if he has emerged in public from seclusion. He is big and bearded and soft-spoken and almost courtly. There is a melancholy behind his eyes. Once or twice, no more, his eyes darkened scarily. He wasn't acting then; he cannot act. To the contrary, he appears to be utterly natural. But the first thing we notice about him is his most seductive statement: the sleeves of his rumpled jacket are rolled up.

The magician is showing us that he has nothing—absolutely nothing—up his sleeve. In that naked sense, he's the most unlikely disciple of Peter Brook I've come across. His artistry is naked, and his illusions are therefore the purest form of theater. Ricky Jay, the illusionist with nothing up his sleeve, makes it look easy. He's a teacher, in his beguiling way. Explaining to *Time* magazine how one man with a deck of cards can create an evening of theater brimming with so much surprise, he said, "The trend toward overelaborate theater led me to this. The kind of thing where people think more about helicopters than actors. The idea of walking on stage with a deck of cards and entertaining for an evening seemed a lovely way to go against the trend."

It is a lovely way. He doesn't "perform," strictly speaking. He is himself, whoever that may be. What kind of man would practice in solitude for hours and hours, or for years, the near secret art of the card shark? Or, for that matter, trouble to master the decapitation of a rubber duck by a card thrown at a distance with deadly, Zen precision? Such a man would have to be a lonely, whimsical obsessive, a quiet fanatic.

Watching Mr. Jay's wizardry—watching his hands until I gave up trying to spot how he does it—he seems to control reality, like an alchemist. He made a mistake the night I saw him. It wasn't the stumble that high-wire artists make deliberately to remind us of the danger. If the performer makes the remarkable seem too easy, it is no longer remarkable. So Ricky Jay makes his deliberate mistakes, too. He deals a volunteer from the audience three aces, saying "Oops!" Then he throws down a royal flush that had no right to be there in the first place. His genuine mistake was very surprising. Shuffling and cutting the cards, he failed to produce the expected ace. He looked surprised, too, and even offended, as if saying to himself, "This could not possibly happen." For Mr. Jay, the shaman, the split-second reversal was itself an illusion, for nothing in his performance could possibly just *happen,* not even a mistake.

Ricky Jay is a vanishing breed, a direct link with the fairground sideshows and the card sharps, hustlers, freaks, and illusionists of the nineteenth century. He talks darkly of the four queens in the pack as "these women, with tact and discretion, who can easily elude suitors." He is an erudite scholar telling us, among many delights, of a famous eighteenth-century illusionist who produced his wife from under a tin cup. He offers us, charmingly, bursts of ornate poetry and gambler's doggerel. He's a keeper of the flame, a fanciful linguist, a loving historian, a carnival barker, a trickster.

In his entertaining company we are returned to the roots of popular theater. Now you see it, now you don't. We urban skeptics lose our cynicism, yet he compels our disbelief. It's his perversely great achievement. In theater, we willingly suspend disbelief. The actor performing Lear confides to us in effect: "I'm only pretending. But meet me halfway. Pretend with me." Ricky Jay, performing some unbelievable feat of three-card monte, is saying: "You know I'm going to deceive you. Be on your guard." His unflamboyant daring and sorcery are unique. He asks us not to believe him in an honest way. Ricky Jay is the archetypal trickster who plays by the best rules of theater and breaks them at the same time. He is saying to us: "I am the God of Lies, and that's the truth."

Mametspeak

One day, Alexander Woollcott was attending a new play that irritated him beyond measure. Suddenly, as the action drifted on, a telephone rang onstage. "It's for me!" Woollcott cried, and swept regally out of the theater.

Well, that wasn't very nice of him. But I'm afraid I was overcome by similarly disrespectful feelings during David Mamet's new play, *The Cryptogram*, which has opened at the Westside Theater via its world premiere in London. I was waiting for the telephone to ring—anything to relieve the frustration caused by Mr. Mamet's cryptogram, the dark code to be deciphered.

As with the occasional hand-to-hand combat that broke out among warring factions in the audience following his drama of sexual harassment, *Oleanna*, provocation seems to be the name of the game in *The Cryptogram*, which concerns child abuse. Mr. Mamet infuriates us knowingly. His psychological power plays, the repressed undercurrents of anxiety and simmering violence, the oblique, disjointed Mametspeak that has become his signature style, are meant to dislocate and disturb us. His blood-sport dramas are emotional games and wars by stealth in which the deceptions of language itself can turn brutal. In perverse ways, he brings out the worst in us.

Perhaps, as I did, some of you found yourselves wishing to kill the sexually harassed victim in *Oleanna*. "There you are!" Mr. Mamet's admirers said at the time. "You're no better than the average male chauvinist pig." The playwright had therefore made his subversive dramatic point: if you sided with the male hero—the professor who happened to be innocent—you were no better than an abuser (or were smugly indifferent about important issues). But Mr. Mamet had so loaded the dice against the vicious—and deranged—victim of *Oleanna* that nausea was the only response to her, and to the playwright's heavy-handed manipulation. Some disagreed with that assessment, violently. And some will no doubt object to my "callousness" about the ten-year-old child in *The Cryptogram*, whom I found myself wishing to kick upstairs to bed, and worse.

"Why aren't you asleep?" is the weary entrance line of the child's mother Donny (Felicity Huffman). In three short, perilously underwritten scenes, Mr. Mamet's eighty-minute drama unfolds with deliberate nondrama. Directed by the playwright—I assume at a consciously flat pace, a form of innocuous hyperrealism until the explosion in the third scene—virtually everything that is spoken appears to be banal. It *is* humdrum—in Mr. Mamet's arch, stylized fashion.

"Well, there you go," says Del, the family friend (Ed Begley Jr.), when the mother drops a symbolic teapot offstage. He is talking to her young son who can't sleep, apparently in anticipation of a camping trip with his absent father.

"Well, there you go."

"What?" the boy answers.

"...a human *being*..."

"Yes?"

"...cannot conceal himself."

"That, that's an example?"

"Well, hell, look at it: anything, when it is changed...any, um um, 'upheaval,' do you see? All of a sudden..."

Well, hell, look at it: um um, Mametspeak. I mean, it's, it's...there to, to—what's the word? To reveal...*conceal* the...um...What?...meaning.

The mystique of Mametspeak creates its own barriers of self-consciously circumspect style. Harold Pinter's parodiable nervous ticks and linguistic concealments are close to it. (Mr. Pinter directed *Oleanna* in London.)

"Is it wool? Is it wool?" asks the *Cryptogram* child.

"What?"

"Is it wool the blanket?"

When Del (who might be the mother's lover, until it becomes leadenly clear that he's gay) toasts their friendship, she searches for the right word:

"May we always be..." she says.

"Yes?"

"As…"

Here you would expect him to reply, "Close."

"Unified," he replies.

"Well, let's pick something more moving than that," she suggests.

"Alright….be, be, be, be, be-*nighted*? No, that's not the word I want to use….be-*trothed*…? No."

"Close…"

"Yes."

Irr…irr, irr, irr, irritating, isn't it? Very few people—except stammering Mamet characters—would mystify a simple toast by reaching out to relish the word "benighted" (implying darkness), mistaking it, in turn, for the more suggestive "betrothed," which in its turn is a deliberate confusion. "May we always be *be-trothed?*"

Who talks this way?

The self-conscious surface style, the convolutions and cadences, are only part of the problem. *The Cryptogram* is David Mamet's "child within," and perhaps it's a personal exorcism. He has written of his own traumatic upbringing in a Chicago suburb, and the emotional terrors of John, the boy played by Shelton Dane with the close-cropped hair of the adult playwright, relate to Mr. Mamet's own troubled childhood. The play is a tale of adult betrayal, of a gradual, apparently ordinary descent into parental abandonment. But the drama within *The Cryptogram* is surprisingly and dangerously slight, though the message is clear enough—so clear, in fact, there's very little to decode.

What actually happens in the three short scenes? The play takes place in 1959 in a family living room where, judging by John Lee Beatty's sparse design, the shabby, lifeless setting with its token furniture and staircase up to the attic is either a bleak reality or a symbol. There are two adults and one child, but no evidence that a child lives here, no toys, no sign of anything but alienation. The child should be asleep upstairs, on the eve of a promised camping trip to the woods with his father.

But young John can't sleep; he can't find his slippers. Del talks to him, offering stilted cold comfort. Mom asks: "Why aren't you asleep?" "Why isn't

Dad home?" replies the boy. The truth is being concealed; the teapot has crashed—ominous moment. The child brings in a torn blanket—a comfort blanket—from the attic. "Because we *think* a thing is one way does not mean that this is the way that this thing must be," Del advises the boy, who is sullenly, understandably confused.

What was that again? "Because we *think* a thing is one way does not mean that this is the way that this thing must be."

From the outset, the child's needs are evident. The child can't sleep—it couldn't be clearer—because he's unloved, a nuisance, a pest, an obnoxious intruder giving his uncomprehending mother the withering stare of a dead albatross, and who could blame him? "I need a rest," she complains forlornly. Or: "The older I get the less I know." And before too long, the audience begins to feel the kind of agitation that Mr. Mamet provokes in us. "For God's sake," we might think, shifting impatiently in our seats. "*Hold* the child. Give him a hug, give him some attention." Or mutter to ourselves when the child has reappeared from upstairs, nagging and sleepless for the umpteenth time: "Kick the little darling back to bed. Tell him in no uncertain terms: 'No sleep, no camping trip.' " Mr. Mamet at least makes loving parents or disciplinarians of us all.

At the blackout of scene 1, a note is found on the staircase from the absent father, informing his wife that he's left her. "He's leaving you," says Del. "Why would he want to do that?"

We know. Either these two dreary adults are dim or they're lying to themselves and each other. But the cryptogram "mystery" doesn't ring true. In a complicated explanation that follows in scene 2, the supposed friend Del is tripped up by a lie about a knife. He explains that Robert, the husband and ex-pilot, had given him the knife, a "war memento," during a camping trip the previous week. But it wasn't a war memento, and the knife had been seen more recently in the attic. It now turns out there never was a camping trip and Del, colluding in betrayal, had lent his room that day to the unfaithful Robert. The knife might have been used—we learn, should we care to—for cutting the tangled lines of parachutes. Or, it is implied, the knife is a symbol for cutting ties with tangled relationships. (Oh, dear.) Anyway, Del's "reward" was the knife, a gift from the husband for helping him in his betrayal. Now, why an adult should be content to receive an old army knife as some kind of reward is another Mamet mystery. But the slenderness of the dramatic cryptogram is apparent.

The staircase, the attic, the torn blanket, the woods, the knife, the child's voices in his nightmare abandonment are heavy-handed signposts and symbols. The child's very real needs are underpinned by thin air made "meaningful" and ponderous. The emotional explosion in scene 3 is merely a melodramatic projection by the abandoned mother onto the son. "Do you have no *feelings?*" she cries at him. "Can't you see that I need *comfort?* Are you *blind?* That you treat me like an *animal?*"

We, in turn, are meant to project our fears for the child—and perhaps our own childhood problems—onto the play, as we might a fearful message onto a blank canvas. "Do you ever wish that you could die?" asks the child. By the end of *The Cryptogram,* he is climbing the stairs, the blade of the knife flicked open in his hand. He will have his revenge. "Things occur in life," his mother said. "And the meaning is not clear." But the meaning of *The Cryptogram* is all too obviously clear, and my frustration is with Mr. Mamet's portentous play, rather than with his abandoned child.

How Good Is David Mamet, Anyway?

I'm beginning to see David Mamet as the Andy Warhol of theater. They are, of course, outwardly as different as a crew cut is from a lopsided wig, but they link in the superficial essentials. Both, for example, claim that their art reflects the culture, or America, in this convenient way: if you find nothing there, so much the better. Mr. Mamet explained to the *New Yorker* recently, "As Bettelheim says in *The Uses of Enchantment,* the more you leave out, the more we see ourselves in the picture, the more we project our own thoughts onto it."

It's a trick that works (and Mr. Mamet is known to be fond of illusionists). Warhol said about himself that there's nothing there. He said it to anyone who cared to listen. Mr. Mamet says the same, only different: Everything's there, you just can't see it. It's all hidden in the coded subtext! You may wonder what's hidden there, exactly. And the answer is, a projection of yourself.

Where, then, is the drama? It's up to you. I didn't find much drama in Mr. Mamet's *Old Neighborhood* at the Booth Theater on Broadway, but lots of other people have. Some people have even found a masterpiece. I didn't even find a *play.* I saw three separate and inconsequential sketches that had been strung together for ninety intermissionless minutes. The last act lasts only fifteen minutes. It has its fifteen minutes of fame. But the more you leave out, the more we are meant to see ourselves in the picture.

We are told that *The Old Neighborhood* is a fine play—or, say, a tone poem, a Mametian version of Bach, a Cubist mystery—and therefore it must be a fine play. We've always been told that Warhol's nonart is great art because it's an artful comment on the state of art. Thus the *New York Times* can describe Mr. Mamet as "this most private of writers" while conducting a major interview with him. He rarely gives interviews, as he also explained in a *New Yorker* interview. He's said to be a mystery. Yet we know all about his difficult upbringing, his divorced parents, his writer sister, and his renewed sense of Judaism from his own autobiographical essays. I even know all about his new kitchen—having come across a picture spread of it in *Elle Décor* during a dental appointment. It looks very nice.

Mr. Mamet is a famous private man in the sense that Woody Allen is famously a recluse. It's the game he plays, like his pretense of being a neo-Brechtian intellectual in disguise. In *True and False,* his latest book of ideas, his advice to actors would dehumanize them ridiculously, but it *sounds* challenging: "If you learn the words by rote, as if they were a phone book, and let them come out of your mouth without your interpretation, the audience will be well served."

The audience won't. And no actor deliberately sleepwalks through a role. But if you're irritated by Mr. Mamet's absurdity, you will be told by his disciples that that's the point. "You see! You're having a dramatic *reaction!*" If you found yourself nauseated by the character of the sexually harassed student in *Oleanna,* your intolerance was showing. If you were provoked into protest by the faux mystery and traditionally oblique Mametspeak of *The Cryptogram,* you were being callous about the fate of its abused ten-year-old child.

The dramatist of earlier, superior plays, such as *American Buffalo* and *Glengarry Glen Ross,* has long since settled for dramatically less. Mr. Mamet now prefers merely to provoke. Here he is, in one of his "rare" public moments, discussing a production of *Hamlet* he's been working on for two years: "I want to see people clawing each other to death outside the theater," he says. I expect they will be. Mr. Mamet's old friend William H. Macy is the unlikely Hamlet. We trust Mr. Macy is playing the prince as if he were a phone book. The cast has also included Whoopi Goldberg as the Player King—yeah, sure—the diminutive Michael J. Fox as Laertes—it's a new interpretation!—and the dramatist is hoping to persuade Steve Martin to play Claudius.

Memo to Steve Martin—don't do it. Mr. Mamet's forthcoming Holly-woodized *Hamlet* is already antagonizing us into a reaction because it will be no *Hamlet* at all.

The two-character opener of *The Old Neighborhood*, "The Disappearance of the Jews," promises much from its bold title. But it just turns out to be a doodle about two middle-aged guys kibitzing about the good old days. Bobby (Peter Riegert), Mr. Mamet's somewhat droopy alter ego, links the three acts; Joey (Vincent Guastaferro) is his inarticulate childhood friend. "Fuck that shit, fuck that shit," says Joey. "She's got a point in my ass, what the fuck did they ever do?"

The laughter comes easily from many in the audience, as if attending a ritual. "I should never have married a shiksa," Bobby confesses, and the word "shiksa" brings smug laughter, too. What's going on? The guys talk about girls they knew. "And so which broad was mine?" "Rosen...I don't know...Rubovitch." "Some Jew broad...Some folk dancer. I don't know. Some Jap. Some Eskimo...How's Laurie?" "Fine."

They don't seem too bright. They seem tired. They shoot the breeze about the past, imagining a sentimentalized version of shtetl life. "They'd say, 'There goes Rob Lewis, he's the strongest man in Lódz.' I'd nod. 'He once picked up an ox.' Or some fucking thing. I don't know if you can pick up an ox, Bob, but I tell you, I feel in my heart I was meant to work out in the winter all day. To be strong."

Joey, the caterer, would rather be a rabbi tilling the fields in a shtetl, it seems. But neither of them believes it. Nor do we. It's just small talk. The subtext—ah, that mysterious subtext!—is meant to convey the disappearance of the assimilated Jews and a desperate search for meaning and roots. Big and important issues—reduced to a shrug, a comedy turn, a vague, slack nostalgia.

Act 2, entitled "Jolly," is the most autobiographical of the evening's trio. The not so jolly character of Jolly (Patti LuPone) is based—we've read widely—on Mr. Mamet's sister, who's a writer living in southern California. It's about a middle-aged brother and sister maimed by uncaring parents. But it could just as well be entitled, "Why I'm Still Bitter Because Mom Didn't Give Me Skis for Christmas."

"Jolly" is little more than a loud, prolonged whine from unforgiving, self-hating, foul-mouthed sis. Poor thing. She wanted skis for Christmas, cocksucker! And she's a Jew! You think that makes it sleazy? *Easy.* That makes it fucking easy? Uh-uh. Fuck them. It's not the *skis.* It's what *they stand for.* They gave her a fucking *book bag* instead. What are you gonna do? It ruined her life. Schlepping the fucking *book bag* around all day long, for years, you know, fucking years, because, because she was never…fucking *loved.*

Get over it. (We think.) It's time. On the other hand, if you wish to project your own childhood resentments onto the aggressive little piece, this is the perfect opportunity. There's much universal material—need for parental love, understanding, Shabbos candles, *haimish* food, skis for Christmas.

"Suffice it to say, we are not the victims of a happy childhood," Mr. Mamet's sister said in an interview about the upbringing of them both. "It was emotional terrorism. In my estimation, we are survivors of a travel route that included a 1950s version of Dachau and Bergen-Belsen, and we both still bear the numbers on our arms."

Ms. Mamet—think what you're saying, for God's sake. And count your blessings.

As for the slender fifteen-minute last act of *The Old Neighborhood* that brings down the curtain, it's about lackluster Bobby saying good-bye to his wan wife, Deeny (Rebecca Pidgeon, Mr. Mamet's real-life wife), who comes out with stuff like: "I was thinking of tribes who mutilate themselves…."

Enough!

Beckettscape

Another heavenly day. And so, these notes from the Beckett wilderness:

There could have been no grander way of passing the time during the Lincoln Center Summer Festival—though the time would have passed anyway—than attending the nineteen Samuel Beckett plays produced and performed by Dublin's Gate Theatre. It was like a marathon wake for humanity. Or as the famously upbeat line goes in *Endgame:* "Nothing is funnier than unhappiness, I grant you that."

Misery loves company, you see. But still, all nineteen Beckett plays would have put me away for good. I saw six of them, which left me contentedly crawling around in darkest depression just the same.

When Michael Colgan, the artistic director of the Gate Theatre, first told Beckett a few years ago that he would love to stage all his plays over a short period of time, the great man replied simply and typically: "You can't be serious."

His stock in trade was light irony, gallows humor. In the best-known story about him, he was walking through a London park with a friend on a glorious day and seemed, most uncharacteristically, happy. The friend said it was the kind of sunny day that made one glad to be alive. "I wouldn't go that far," replied Beckett.

To meet him where he lived in Paris (he died there in 1989) was like a pilgrimage for the lucky ones. He wasn't a recluse, as is often imagined, but he guarded his privacy and—uniquely for so famous a man—refused to give even a single interview. I never met him, but our paths literally crossed. One day, I was coming out of the National Theatre in London and was walking across the nearby Waterloo Bridge when I saw him. He was walking alone across the bridge toward the theater. It was unmistakably him, for no one looks like him. That day, he looked like an elegant elderly tramp, with his shock of white hair, a knapsack on his back. He was a beautiful man, like an eagle.

"My goodness," I thought as our paths crossed. "It's Samuel Beckett!"" He was peering at that great, anonymous stone monolith, the National Theatre, shaking his head in bemused disbelief. It was as if he couldn't imagine what the colossal civic *thing*—at the time the National was nicknamed "Alcatraz"—could possibly be *for*.

During the Lincoln Center Beckett festival, I saw his 1952 *Waiting for Godot*—the play that changed everything in theater—as if seeing old, affectionate ghostly friends again. Beckett's two tramps in the wasteland, Vladimir (known as Didi) and Estragon (known as Gogo), are a perfect bickering dark comedy team, as are all happy couples in overlong marriages. As Pozzo, the bully, puts it: "That's how it is on this bitch of an earth!" Is there hope at hand? Rescue? Salvation? Is there a more renowned line in the whole of modern drama than "Mr. Godot told me to tell you he won't come this evening but surely tomorrow"?

Beckett himself hated waiting. In every other aspect, it seems, he was considerate, modest and patient. But if you kept him waiting at the small café inside the Hotel PLM, his hangout in Montparnasse, it was a mistake. Dustin Hoffman, who toyed with the notion of playing Gogo in a Mike Nichols production—he would have made a fine Gogo—committed the fatal blunder. According to the critic Mel Gussow, who knew Beckett and did a great deal to support his plays in America, Beckett was dubious about Mike Nichols's projected production of *Godot*. "Every other line a laugh?" he asked, when advised of Mr. Nichols's gift for comedy. But the nub of dissatisfaction was Dustin Hoffman. A meeting had been arranged in Paris, but the star unforgivably didn't even turn up. "He had something better to do," Beckett said. He was waiting for Hoffman—not worth the candle compared to waiting for Godot.

Much—too much—has been written about Beckett's fondness for vaudeville and slapstick, and how Laurel and Hardy would have been ideal as Vladimir and Estragon. *Godot* with the red nose of a clown has become one of the clichés of Beckett production. The fatal flaw of Mike Nichols's starry 1988 Lincoln Center Theater Group production of *Godot*, with Robin

Williams, Steve Martin, and Bill Irwin, was that Mr. Nichols assumed it to be a knockabout comedy (every other line a laugh). But it is a tragedy, or tragicomedy, not just a vehicle for comedians. The memorable achievement of the Gate Theater's production of *Godot* is that its great actors—Barry McGovern, now the leading Beckett actor anywhere, with Johnny Murphy and the rest—proceed from a pure tragic center that only makes the comedy farcically worse, or better.

The Irish, via the Gate Theatre festival, have at last proudly reclaimed Beckett, the Irishman, as their own. He lived mostly in France and wrote most of his plays first in French. He was yet another of Ireland's great writers who lived in self-imposed exile, like James Joyce (for whom Beckett worked). He was seen as a citizen of the world, but his language and humor and soul remained Irish. Beckett consciously avoided Irish lyricism and sentimentality, distilling drama to an essence, the marrow of bones. You don't have to be Irish to perform Beckett well—Billie Whitelaw of the north of England is one of his most celebrated interpreters—but these Irish actors are on intimate terms with him in their blood.

I question only the tree in the *Godot* production. The director, Walter Asmus, is a prominent German theater director who worked with Beckett on many occasions and was his friend. But one of us has the tree wrong. That tree is no tree at all. It's a mingy little thing, more a symbol. It is not a tree on which to hang yourself, should you so desire. It is more a tree on which to hang your coat. "Everything's dead but the tree," goes the line. But this tree is not alive with any possibility.

Nevertheless, I run against the prevailing view that Beckett was essentially about the triumph of the human spirit within the darkness. Gallows humor camouflages anguish, and Godot is not coming and never will come. Beckett was an unapologetic realist about the absurd tragedy of the human condition, and we should not sentimentalize him. To be sure, his characters—enslaved or lost or dying, or miraculously jaunty and heroic—endure. They can't go on; they must. They are playing a role, playing at being alive, in remorseless unhappiness.

"We'll always find something, eh Didi, to give us the impression we exist," says Gogo. The play's opening line is not too optimistic: "Nothing to be done." The two tramps, like everyone, were born "astride of a grave and a difficult birth. Down in the hole, lingeringly, the gravedigger puts on the forceps. We have time to grow old. The air is full of our cries...."

Beckett is the greatest poet of despair who ever half-lived. Suicide is a hovering option in *Happy Days*, during which the middle-aged heroine, Winnie, is famously buried up to her waist in act 1 and up to her neck in act 2. She must therefore keep up appearances. It's a wonderfully alive performance that Rosaleen Linehan gives as Winnie, who battles and prattles in her genteel, superior way. "The sadness after a song. Have you run across that, Willie?" she calls to her husband, who lives in a nearby hole. "In the course of your experience. No? Sadness after intimate sexual intercourse one is familiar with, of course. You would concur with Aristotle there, Willie, I fancy."

Winnie's opening words are, "Another heavenly day." And some of us can mouth a number of lines, like a mantra of ironic discontent, from the big Beckett plays on which we were reared. Yet the dark humor of the plays no longer had me laughing, though many members of the audience laughed uproariously. Perhaps unfairly, I found their response too knowing, and their easy laughter grated on me. I wanted to call out to them like the character in Eugène Ionesco's *Bald Prima Donna:* "Stop grinding my teeth!"

I could no longer laugh with Beckett, and it troubled me. Terrible thing, to take tragedy so seriously. But the answer was in *Endgame*, the harshest of Beckett's big plays. Nell says the famous line: "Nothing is funnier than unhappiness, I grant you that." Then she adds: "Yes, yes, it's the most comical thing in the world. But it's always the same thing. Yes, it's like a funny story we have heard too often, we still find it funny, but we don't laugh any more. *(Pause)* Have you anything else to say to me?"

Robert Brustein's Unfortunate Dance Lesson

There are times when performers are so extraordinary at what they do that you just shake your head in disbelief and laugh. They're too good; they're laughably good. Because what they're doing is, quite simply, out of this world. That's the great pleasure of Savion Glover and the entire company of the Public Theater's *Bring in da Noise, Bring in da Funk,* now successfully transferred to the Ambassador Theater on Broadway. I originally wrote of George C. Wolfe's production, "Welcome at last to the 21st century." The show cooks and boils and hits us up with such emotional force and originality that it points the way to the future.

Telling the story through tap of black history from slavery to the present, *Noise/Funk* isn't preachy. It's a revelation. "Tap" as we know it doesn't convey what's going on. Mr. Glover—a virtuoso genius at twenty-two—is doing things onstage that have never been witnessed before. He has taken dance into another realm.

Playing across the street is *Grease.* (I know where I'd rather be.) These are still safe, revivalist times, in spite of Savion Glover. *Rent* is too downtown cozy, a nineties *Hair* for tourists. But the emergence of anything young and contemporary in the Broadway musical is itself phenomenal, and *Noise/Funk*—with Tony Award winner Jeffrey Wright joining the show as its silky narrator in rap—is a thrilling achievement. The one thing I don't think it is, or could conceivably be, is racist. Yet it is said that the "victimized" black cast are angry racists. We take a deep breath. But that is the astonishing view of the distinguished drama critic of the *New Republic,* Robert

Brustein, who is also artistic director of the American Repertory Theater at Harvard University.

Mr. Brustein referred in his theater column to "four frenetic tappers" who are "pounding the stage floor to splinters." (Hardly.) He described "two galvanized drummers whacking away as if possessed." (Whacking away: possession. Hmmm...) And "a powerful jazz singer screeching at high-decibel level." (He's referring to the show's immensely gifted narrator in song, Ann Duquesnay.) But let the professor's pounding and screeching and whacking away pass. And say only this, for the moment: If an artist as supreme and generous as Gregory Hines can say of Savion Glover that he is "possibly the best tap dancer that ever lived," who is Mr. Brustein to disagree?

He goes on to wildly state that "the evening is less an exhibition of black talent than a chronicle of black oppression"; that "blacks are consistently paraded before us as victims of racial prejudice" in a "marathon display of victimology"; that the beat "is angry, staccato and percussive, as if the dancers were stomping on the faces of their oppressors." And this: "But the major effect of the evening is to reinforce the old stereotype that black people have a great sense of rhythm. As for whites, they are left with a great and lonely sense of apartness...."

Well, Mr. Brustein and I obviously haven't seen the same show. For one thing, I didn't feel "a great and lonely sense of apartness," but the reverse. We would expect a story of black history to show oppression and injustice, wouldn't we? Let's rise above Mr. Brustein's observation concerning black people having a great sense of rhythm. Not for a single second, beat, or heartbeat throughout the entire show is there any "victimology"—"paraded" before us or "stomped" into our faces or otherwise. If that were the case, the show could not soar and it would not succeed. No, there is so much inherent love in what these artists are doing, and so much intoxicating skill in their performance, that any notion of victimization is absurd.

Then again, Mr. Brustein feels it necessary to point out that tap "was also the domain of many inspired white performers"—among them Fred Astaire and Gene Kelly. And why are they excluded? But Mr. Glover is not telling us the story of the whole of dance, or of Fred Astaire. He is telling the story of black Americans through the symbolic dance of tap. One of the major

highlights of the show is Mr. Glover's mesmerizing solo before three mirrors—a tribute to his four mentors, Lon Chaney, Chuck Green, Jimmy
Slyde, and Buster Brown. He's telling the story of their proud heritage and
his own story, that's all. Of course there are white tap dancers, as Mr.
Brustein points out. But the show isn't about them, is it? If a show were about
the birth of the blues, would it be obligated to include a tribute to Joe
Cocker?

Mr. Brustein wishes to see things in *Noise/Funk* that should not be
there, such as a dramatization of affirmative action or a mini-lecture on middle-class black advancement in the universities, the media, and professions.
(Boy! What a thrilling show that would be.) And he sees things in the show
that aren't there, such as black racism, separatism, and of all hallucinatory
things, the finger. He writes that there's "one character representing Colin
Powell (and carrying his new book) who comes onstage to dance with
street kids. But even he ends up giving the audience the finger."

Oh, dear. Either the director, George Wolfe, has gone insane, or Mr.
Brustein has got it all wrong again. This is what actually takes place: in the
sketch entitled "Taxi," four black men are all trying to hail a taxi in New York.
A detail: they're not "street kids." One is a student; another middle-class;
another is the General Powell type. No cab will stop and pick them up. I
wrote in my original review, "Amusing and lightly performed, it's a near
throwaway interlude. But those same black performers who bring audiences
to their feet will have a problem getting a cab to take them home after the
show." The sketch doesn't end—as Mr. Brustein imagines—with the Colin
Powell character giving the audience the finger. It ends with all four characters giving the finger to the cabdrivers who won't stop for them. That's the
point.

Mr. Brustein, hello! Or rather, good-bye. Let's skip the other strange and
offensive points he makes in his case against the show. He even mocks the
personal histories of the performers when they quietly describe the influence
of their families and their debt to dance. "Tap sort of like saved me," he
quotes one of the cast as saying, and his superior, mocking tone is insultingly
clear. Mr. Brustein, a word in your ear: more likely than not, tap did save that
dancer. Half of all African American children still live in poverty; the lead-

ing cause of death among young black men is gunshot wounds. Without the support of their families and love of dance, the cast of *Noise/Funk* might have self-destructed, or be dead, by now.

That is just one of the reasons why George Wolfe can honorably say that Mr. Brustein didn't "see" the show, though he attended a performance. Because it is an extraordinarily joyful and defiant and gifted "affirmation of the human spirit and the power of art to transcend." And because Mr. Brustein can affirm only his own joyless, noisy muddle, which is an awesomely polite way of putting it.

Everything
Is Beautiful

Whenever the English catch a whiff of the sewer, they're in heaven. The excitingly revisionist, flawed, and appropriately sordid production of *Cabaret*, which comes to us via acclaim in London, is a case of *nostalgie de la boue* run riot. Its hot English director, Sam Mendes, takes no prisoners; his style here is Weimar Berlin in your face. And there are times when what's in your face is quite surprising.

Put it this way: if there have been hairier showgirls in the history of Broadway, I don't want to know about it. The Kit Kat Girls (of the show's notoriously seedy Kit Kat Club) are real, almost too real, with their heroin eyes and plump, insolent thighs, with their body scars and bruises and stinky armpits. I adored them, actually. They make a change. Also, they play in the band. They're different. They are not the traditionally honed hookers of John Kander and Fred Ebb's other hit revival across town, *Chicago*. The Kit Kat Girls are loose and sexy, depending on your taste. But they look as if Mr. Mendes and his codirector, the American choreographer Rob Marshall, dragged them *out of* the sewer, which is as it should be.

In re-creating the sinister Berlin nightlife of the 1930s, the production is dirtier and more uncompromisingly decadent than anything in Hal Prince's memorable original 1966 production. Mr. Mendes is in the top league of British directors who reinvent the classics, including vintage Broadway musicals, and his hands are all over his new production. He has thrown down two bold aces in Natasha Richardson as Sally Bowles and Alan Cumming as the MC, for both of them are brilliant actors rather than natural musical performers. Ms. Richardson's last Broadway role was an acclaimed Anna in Eugene O'Neill's *Anna Christie*; Mr. Cumming's last role was Hamlet in London. This *Cabaret* is defiantly and blatantly antishowbiz, and certain seductive powers have been lost in the process. Yet the two stars triumph remarkably over the enduring memory of the two showbiz legends, Liza Minnelli and Joel Grey, who owned the roles before them.

Mr. Cumming has achieved some kind of demonic miracle by utterly reinventing the nameless host and MC played by the great Mr. Grey as a sex-less Satan in whiteface, a seductively vaudevillian *thing*, a malevolent, evil sprite that in a different life might have been an avenging angel. I still remember Mr. Grey shocking and repulsing me—suckering us all with show-biz charm—in his song and dance routine with a gorilla, "If You Could See Her Through My Eyes" ("She wouldn't look Jewish at all"). Mr. Cumming, on the other hand, makes no pretense of even ironic charm. His "Willkommen" isn't an invitation to mere naughty pleasures; his crooked finger beckoning us inside the club "where everything is beautiful" makes us hesitate. He's saying, Enter at your own risk.

Mr. Cumming is a creepily androgynous host with glitter nipples, a swastika tattoo on his bum, and low-cut leather jock strap hung, it seems, from some postmodern medieval contraption involving garters (costumes by William Ivey Long). He could be an S&M pervert's wet dream. He is not a pretty sight, but he's a startling invention.

I wouldn't go near him on a Saturday night. Yet after the intermission, he invites coyly obliging audience members to do a little dance with him onstage like a cheap entertainer ingratiating himself with giggling tourists. Who are they dancing with—the actor, or the character he's playing? It's a peculiar moment that doesn't belong in the show, as if the foul MC of Mr. Cumming no longer catered to the wormy subworld of 1930s Berlin but had become the jolly host of a cruise on *The Love Boat*. His performance, nevertheless, is an awesome achievement—alive and menacing, grotesque, icily clever, uncompromising, and unafraid.

Natasha Richardson's coked-up, cut-price Holly Golightly from Chelsea, England, is another excitingly dangerous creation. The actress walks the high wire without a safety net, and has reinvented Liza Minnelli's iconic version of Sally Bowles. Ms. Minnelli didn't play Sally on the stage, incidentally; Bob Fosse's 1972 film of *Cabaret* made her legend. Ms. Richardson doesn't pretend to be able to belt out a Kander and Ebb showstopper as Ms. Minnelli sure can. Her Sally is a loser, for one; a willful hedonist, a naive second-rater. We would expect this actress to mine the unglitzy depths of a role that has been, till now, Ms. Minnelli's tremulous hymn to hope and a devil-may-care future. But she gutsily reverses the showbiz cliché and makes the traditionally glamorous Sally Bowles frighteningly real. Her "Maybe This Time" is the cry of someone who isn't going to make it. Her blistering version of "Cabaret"—as in "Life is a cabaret, old chum"—is a raw emotional embrace, not of survival in a life of easy pleasure, but of oblivion. Ms. Richardson's achievement makes us aware, for the first time, that Sally will die young.

Kander and Ebb's memorable score (and tribute to Kurt Weill) is always a pleasure, though "Tomorrow Belongs to Me" remains a rousing hymn to the wrong cause. (You catch yourself humming it along with the Nazis.) The book by Joe Masteroff, based on Christopher Isherwood's *Berlin Stories* and John Van Druten's stage adaptation of them, *I Am a Camera*, suffices, but it can seem underwritten. The writer-hero, Clifford Bradshaw, aka the young Christopher Isherwood in search of Berlin boys, is a colorless fellow, and the dullish John Benjamin Hickey can do little with him. The accomplished Mary Louise Wilson is surprisingly uncomfortable in the role of Fräulein Schneider, the landlady turned Nazi collaborator. (The legendary Brechtian, Lotte Lenya, originated the role and gave it its biting edge.) Ron Rifkin's Herr Schultz, the Jewish grocer who melts Fräulein Schneider's heart with—of all sweet things—a pineapple, sings like a wounded bear howling in the forest, but it doesn't matter. Everyone loves him. He brings honest, dignified sentiment to the piece. Mr. Rifkin is genuine in everything he does.

After the sensational opening scene, I wasn't always happy with the Bob Fosse–inspired choreography of Rob Marshall. Once you've seen a hundred crotch shots, you've seen them all. I thought the idea of performing the show in a specially designed cabaret room with little tables and faux Thonet chairs replacing the orchestra seats gimmicky. It's meant to simulate decadent Weimar Berlin. But we're not in decadent Weimar Berlin. We're in a dump on Forty-third Street. "You're part of the show," I was told earnestly. Sure! Me and Mike Nichols at the table next door.

Director Sam Mendes believes the cabaret room breaks through conventional theater barriers. But it doesn't. It just creates another convention of a theme park in miniature. At the same time, as soon as the show begins, everyone seated at the tables quickly rearranges their chairs to face the stage, exactly like a conventional theater. And best wishes to *you*, Mr. Mendes.

Still, whatever the flaws of this uncompromising *Cabaret*, pause a moment and look around you. Among the Broadway musicals this season, we have a pious fairy tale *(The Sound of Music)*, a superior cartoon *(The Lion King)*, a historical American pageant *(Ragtime)*, an American history lesson *(1776)*, and a romantic adventure *(The Scarlet Pimpernel)*. *Cabaret* may be in your face, but there's more vital rough humanity in it than in any of the others. It's essential to Broadway. *Cabaret* isn't corporate culture, Disney, or safe revivalism. It isn't for children.

Pimp Fop Flop

Some musicals are so bad, they're truly enjoyable. It's why I enjoyed the camp of *Jekyll & Hyde*, in which the star, Robert Cuccioli, performs both Jekyll and Hyde with his hair.

When he transforms into Jekyll, he tosses his hair one way, and when he transforms into Hyde, he tosses it the other. Sometimes he alternates his hair tossing with such dazzling élan that you can't be certain whether he's Jekyll or whether he's Hyde. Or whether he's just having a bad hair day. But it's riveting whichever way you look at it.

Alas, *The Scarlet Pimpernel* is bad in the wrong way. It's too bad. Frank ("This Is the Moment") Wildhorn, the composer of both *Pimpernel* and *Jekyll and Hyde*, is really bad. He's a specialist in skating music who writes big, bland emotional ballads to triple-toe loop to in sequined leotards. He numbs us with his limited repertoire of Loud, Surge, and Throb while reprising his theme of double identities—the monster within the Hyde, the fop within the Pimp. If only he had thought of the phantom within the opera.

Baroness Emmuska Orczy's 1905 novel has been through several reincarnations, including a cartoon entitled *The Scarlet Pumpernickel,* starring Daffy Duck. The novel was more of an exotic romance in the tradition of Danielle Steel than the swashbuckling classic 1935 movie with Leslie Howard suggests. Until the current musical version, however, I hadn't appreciated that the piece might be a parody of gay fashion freaks.

The languid aristocrat, Sir Percy Blakeney, better known as the daredevil Scarlet Pimpernel who secretly rescues victims of the French Revolution, pretends to be a fop mincing about the place to avoid suspicion. His beloved wife, Marguerite, a pert Frenchwoman with a past, is surprised. As she puts it in the musical: "Ee eezn't ooh I zought 'ee waz." And as camped up by the pleasant Douglas Sills in his Broadway debut, 'ee certainly eezn't.

The Frenchies in the show are performed with accents that are a tribute to Peter Sellers's Inspector Clouseau. Zey spick like zees, except when they forget. When they forget to spick like zees, or can't be bothered, we have a problem deciding who's French or who's English, unless they're American. The breezily muddled opening number, saucily entitled "Madame Guillotine," I took to be French. Some poor soul was being guillotined by either Inspector Clouseau or Maurice Chevalier. The usual suspects—overmiked angry peasants left behind by a touring company of *Les Misérables*—were screaming and shouting to searing skating music: "I know the gutter, and I know the stink of the streets!"

Do they, indeed? I doubt it. "God, can you feel the terror, like a fire in the air!" goes another inspiring lyric. The book and lyrics by the fiery Nan Knighton give us hope of many secret pleasures. The Harvard-educated Ms. Knighton even takes almost three hours to set up a terrible joke about Madame Tussaud, which would take another three hours to tell you. That's my girl! And so is this: "Where's the girl who could turn on the edge of a knife / Where's the girl who was burning for life?"

I can tell you. She's writing the lyrics for *The Scarlet Pimpernel.* "This fragile world of ours / Spins us off into the storm / Hold onto me / And I'll be warm." The lyrics for "Vivez," the giddy bridal-night duet between Sir Percy and the ex-slut Marguerite, are almost as good. "You have one life /let it be gay!" It sort of rhymes with *vivez,* you see—as does have a nice day, every which way, bouquet, and oy vey.

Such pleasures, however, are regrettably fewer than we had hoped. Terrence Mann, who was the original evil police inspector Javert in *Les Misérables,* as well as the original Beast in *Beauty and the Beast,* is evil Chauvelin, the Beast of the Guillotine in *The Scarlet Pimpernel.* Do we sense typecasting? Mr. Mann, who is rumored to be half alive, is a little wooden. Christine Andreas's Marguerite is a little Edith Piaf. Douglas Sills's Pimpernel is a little overeager, his Sir Percy over the fop. There are other perversely pleasant distractions. In the fleeing horse-and-carriage scene, I could see a stagehand behind the curtain frantically shaking the carriage to create the impression it was bouncing over the cobblestones of Paris.

Nice try. Zee rest eez strictly for zee birds.

Hakuna Matata!

As you may have heard, the stage version of *The Lion King* has opened at Disney's New Amsterdam Theater on Broadway, and to that I say two little words: "Hakuna matata."

"Hakuna matata" is, of course, Swahili for "no worries." It's the Elton John–Tim Rice version of "Don't worry, be happy." Simba, you will recall, is the young lion who blames himself for the death of his heroic dad, King Mufasa. During his rite of passage, he flees his homeland into the forest, where he pals around with the happy-go-lucky Pumbaa, the warthog, and Timon, the meerkat. Simba, the prodigal son, adopts their philosophy of "hakuna matata."

It also happens to be the philosophy of the Walt Disney Company. Perhaps that's why the song has always irritated me. It doesn't leave you alone. Once you've heard "Hakuna Matata," you can't get rid of it. I've a sneaking suspicion that Julie Taymor, the high priestess of the avant-garde who's the director of *The Lion King*, might feel the same way. She achieves many lovely things in the production, but the big "Hakuna Matata" number is surprisingly lackluster. It's as if she couldn't quite face the unquenchable Disney optimism of it, as if she secretly whispered to herself, "Not 'Hakuna Matata'! I've got enough problems with 'Can You Feel the Love Tonight.'"

The admired director of such experimental, highly visual pieces as *The Green Bird* and *Juan Darien* doesn't solve those problems, either. The sentimental junk of "Can You Feel the Love Tonight"—the only other hit song from the original movie—also jars Ms. Taymor's cultivated seriousness. She's more at home with the hypnotically earthy African music and songs and chants that the South African composer Lebo M has adapted from the album *Rhythm of the Pride Lands*. The stage pictures they inspire are simply beautiful.

When it comes to the popular "Can You Feel the Love Tonight," inspiration deserts her, as if the big number were in a different show. She dresses it up with—of all things—an arty pas de deux that might have been costumed in Las Vegas. Along with another uncharacteristic lapse—the aerial ballet of, I assume, sprightly woodland nymphs—the additional business is meant to distract us from the cartoon mawkishness of the song. She won't let it speak for its sentimental self.

According to the parable of *The Lion King*, in spite of the pleasures Simba finds in his alternative way of life, he must abandon "hakuna matata" and assume his adult responsibilities. Then let us be adult about this musical for children, and for adults who would like to be children. I would like to say that Ms. Taymor's production is utterly enchanting (it would be easier). But for all its spectacular achievements, it amounts to a gigantic culture clash (which will make everyone a zillion smackeroos just the same).

Disney—intending to marry commerce to art, or cartoon culture to high culture—was shrewd to offer Ms. Taymor its Faustian bargain. They could either reproduce an animated film on stage (as they did with *Beauty and the Beast*), or try something new. Newish! What, after all, is Ms. Taymor's specialty but puppets?

Exceedingly cultivated puppets. Ms. Taymor, who also designed the costumes for *The Lion King* and codesigned the puppets and masks (and wrote the lyrics to an undistinguished new song, "Endless Night"), is strongly influenced by the theater traditions of Asia and Africa. They include Japanese Noh and Bunraku, the rod puppets of Java, African mask work, and shadow plays that have been performed over centuries—all of which are on display in one form or another in *The Lion King*. Her work is an exotic synthesis of the ritual cultures of other countries—here adapted, packaged, and appropriated by Disney on Broadway.

We are all tourists now. Cultural "borrowings," or "tributes," or "homages" are nothing new, of course, even on Broadway. Jerome Robbins borrowed from classical Balinese dance in *The King and I*'s Uncle Tom's Cabin sequence. Art makes Disney feel good about itself. Strictly speaking, Disney isn't getting art from Ms. Taymor, however. Her cultural influences are as popular in their own countries as animated cartoons are here. A carved

African mask isn't seen as art in Africa. The African language of Hausa has no word for "art." There is no word for "theater," either. There's only life.

Is there life flowing in all its fullness and creativity through this production? The show begins astonishingly well with the procession of the animal kingdom through the audience to the enchanted African plains on stage. As in the animated movie version—whose opening sequence is among the most beautiful Disney has created—a giant sun rises meltingly on Ms. Taymor's unique Disney parade. With her scenic and lighting designers, Richard Hudson and Donald Holder, the director embraces the playful imaginative heights in the opening scene, never to reach them again. There are other exquisite images—the grasslands swaying, a stampede, a pack of lions on the move, a weird antelope bicycle moving across the stage like some stately constructivist sculpture. Human giraffes lope on stage, too; a shaman baboon laughs manically; an evil masked lion kills a rat to announce laconically that life isn't fair.

In such vignettes, all is well (and fun). We are way above the usual Broadway fare. Our eyes are dazzled by the ingenuity of these human animals that, against the Disney grain, are rarely cute. Lapses aside, if appearances were all, Ms. Taymor's *The Lion King* would be magnificent. But if this is the first Disney show to avoid cuteness, it's the first to shy away from another Disney stock in trade: sentiment. Only this oversolemn director would discuss *The Lion King* in terms of a near-sacred death and rebirth ritual. It's a cartoon! For kids. And it ought to touch us a bit. In a particularly self-conscious moment following the beloved Mufasa's death, the grieving lions cry ribbons. Ribbons unfold artily from their eyes. Tears would have sufficed.

Emotion is made remote and symbolic here. Mufasa's death scene is turned into a secular ceremony and is not dwelled upon. Parents complained that the scene in the film upset their young children too much, but that isn't why Ms. Taymor couldn't quite face it, any more than she could deal with the hokey "Hakuna Matata." Easy Disney sentiment is avoided like a sugar attack. But how about good old-fashioned honest sentiment? Would Dickens have thrown away a death scene?

So the busy spectacle becomes its own special effect, overcrowding the narrative while trying to disguise its flaws. The film of *The Lion King* runs for

88 minutes, the stage version for 2 hours 40 minutes. It's too long, too weighty. All the elements of the successful film have been staged or developed. Tsidii Le Loka's shaman Rafiki is an electric leap forward; the three screaming hyena stooges of Stanley Wayne Mathis, Kevin Cahoon, and Tracy Nicole Chapman are another improvement on the original. John Vickery's evil Scar ought to be less campy, more slippery; the king's clown Zazu, played by Geoff Hoyle, is a daunting achievement; the oddest couple, Tom Alan Robbins's Pumbaa and Max Casella's Timon, are a delight and the closest Ms. Taymor comes to pure cartoon.

The preachy story was always slender, the Elton John–Tim Rice score by no means their best. Ms. Taymor has kept it all afloat in a sea of hype and art and record-breaking advance bookings. She would sooner be making a bigger statement and directing another show—call it "The Lion King Meets the Rhythm of the Pride Lands." She has! But one is Disney, and one isn't. Not that it matters too much. Try getting a ticket. Hakuna matata! as the philosophers say.

Don't Shoot the Composer

The new production of Irving Berlin's vintage *Annie Get Your Gun* is a key event in the history of the American musical: it is the first politically correct musical of our time. Permit me, then, to reach for *my* gun.

Skip, for the moment, that Graciela Daniele's production is as woeful, I'm afraid, as some road company that we'd caught one miserable night in Idaho, or that its miscast star, Bernadette Peters, appears to be playing that mythic Mack truck of musical comedy, Annie Oakley, like Dolly Parton. I'll come to the production and its one saving grace—the ease and stage charm of Tom Wopat's confident performance as Frank Butler, the misogynistic sharpshooter whose defenses are down.

No, what disturbs me more than anything is the farcical belief that the original 1946 version of *Annie Get Your Gun* must be rewritten lest it offend anyone. Here we have a romantic *musical comedy* whose timeless central message is no more, or less, than "Have fun!" And for a half-century, fun is exactly what it has achieved, in company with Irving Berlin's masterly, sunny score. There are at least a half-dozen Berlin standards in the show, including "There's No Business Like Show Business," "You Can't Get a Man with a Gun" and "I Got the Sun in the Morning." Berlin wasn't a sophisticate like Cole Porter or a dark ironic wit in the manner of Lorenz Hart. His genius was that he unfailingly plugged into the heartbeat of purely American vernacular and sentiment, its confident, elegant zest and patriotism. In strict PC terms, his "God Bless America" is still okay; his "White Christmas" possibly questionable.

But what's causing such offense in the original *Annie Get Your Gun*—a nice, dopey story about two rival sharpshooters who fall in love—that contemporary audiences must be protected from at all costs? Cowboy gets cowgirl; they sing; they dance; they shoot; we go home happy. What is it about Irving Berlin's harmless, evergreen musical comedy that threatens the very social fabric of the nation?

It offends feminists and American Indians, apparently. In other lunatic PC words, *Annie Get Your Gun* is now considered racist and antiwomen. Speaking on behalf of American Indians and women, the veteran librettist Peter Stone *(Titanic),* an expert on American Indians and women, has drastically reshaped and revised the musical, whose book was originally written by Herbert and Dorothy Fields. For example, "I'm an Indian Too," Berlin's flip homage to a showbiz Wild West, has been cut from the new version.

"Just like Battle Axe, Hatchet Face, Eagle Nose / Like those Indians, I'm an Indian too / A Sioux," sings Annie Oakley in the original, having been made an honorary member of the Sioux nation. Now, forgive me, but I don't know a Sioux—do you? So I cannot speak for Native Americans. Naturally, I would be sorry if Irving Berlin's lyric offended anyone, and would ask only if they could possibly see a way to live with it.

Nevertheless, Mr. Stone is quoted, with approval, in the *New Yorker* for wondering how Broadway purists would react if somebody on stage sang: "I'm a Hebrew too / A Jew—ooo-ooo."

Fair enough. But that only proves that when it comes to the songwriting game, Peter Stone is no Irving Berlin. Does he remember, I wonder, the Yiddisher Indian chief in Mel Brooks's *Blazing Saddles*? A Jewish Native American! Now there's a happy compromise! Wasn't there a black sheriff, too? We trust that Mr. Stone, the politically correct censor, didn't run screaming from the movie theater.

But his imaginary lyric—"I'm a Hebrew too / A Jew"—doesn't offend me, for one, and least of all to the point of censorship. The only thing that offends me is bad writing. Of course, social values have changed in the fifty years since *Annie Get Your Gun* was created. But does this mean that everything that might conceivably cause offense in our cultural heritage should be rewritten? Where do we draw the line? Which self-appointed nanny has a right to rule on what is now "correct" and "acceptable," and good for us?

The outcome of Mr. Stone's revisionism—or airbrushing—is a double whammy of dubious taste. In his craven need to please, he ends up patronizing both the American Indian *and* the audience. Now all the Indians are good and *smart* Indians. And a character named Dolly has been introduced to the show. She's a white racist, for heaven's sake. She represents the baddies. That's why—we assume—desperate Dolly can't get her man. She's a stereo-typically prejudiced, ugly old cow. But isn't this meant to be a profeminist musical? Isn't it all meant to be fun?

Frank Butler, the sharpshooting stud, no longer sings "I'm a Bad, Bad Man." It's a song about loving women, you see. Apparently, it's a high crime for a guy to fancy so many women he wants them all. Even so, Mr. Stone goes in for boob jokes (and old jokes). In fact, his politically correct script still remains antifeminist! Pistol-packin' Annie famously sings "You Can't Get a Man with a Gun." It's why, of course, she ultimately throws the sharpshoot-ing competition against handsome Frank. She must make herself seem *infe-rior* to get him. Oops!

If the holier-than-thou political conscience of the show is a wee bit mud-dled, its artistic mediocrity is another story. Mr. Stone has introduced a new concept: *Annie Get Your Gun* is now the "concept musical" of a play-within-a-play. The tired idea, which is never sustained in any case, would have us believe that we're watching Buffalo Bill's circus tent production of *Annie Get Your Gun*. If so, Buffalo Bill isn't my kind of producer.

But why this "new" concept? Mr. Stone believes it's a distancing device that makes the show's innocence acceptable to a nineties audience. Spoken like a true cynic. The dispiriting presumption is that we are no longer capa-ble of open hearts.

I'd sooner shoot myself than believe it. Greater artists than Mr. Stone have struggled for generations with this question of theater's innocence. "Theater is a long-promised, long hoped-for child," said Konstantin Stanislavsky in lifelong search of an open naturalness. Shortly before Bertolt Brecht died, he said, "Do you know what my theater of the future would be called? 'Theater of Naïveté.'" And today, many artists hold up a mirror to innocence in a cynical age in the hope of an imaginative sharing, a naive trusting theater, born out of a child's necessity to play.

That is why the popular City Center Revivals of Great American Musi-cals in Concert are so infectiously enjoyable. They convey the pleasure of the past—and, yes, the politically incorrect, innocuously silly past—and they invariably leave us exiting the theater singing. Those musical productions trust the intelligence of the audience.

And that's why Tom Wopat's performance in this wayward *Annie Get Your Gun* stands alone so pleasurably. *He sings the songs*—freshly minted, unaffected, unjaded, with utter belief, doing what comes naturally. He conveys what it's like to enjoy a great score. Bernadette Peters isn't doing that. She's struggling uphill, playing cute. Her hokey southern accent is incomprehensible at times, an exaggerated cartoon. Her milked fragility is inappropriate for Annie, whose tomboy toughness must be seen to melt. "I got lost," goes the memorable lyric. "But look what I found." Ms. Peters—the star and near icon—performs mostly alone, as if appearing in her own cabaret act along with ho-hum choreography borrowed from other shows.

Perhaps the role of Annie still belongs ghostlike to the one and only Ethel Merman, who famously triumphed in the original '46 production and the 1966 revival. I was listening to the old sandblaster, as she was affectionately called, on the cast recording of the '66 revival. To hear Merman sing "There's no business like show business" is to believe her. You better believe her. As was her indomitable style, she cuts to the chase and rockets into orbit. She sings, "They say that falling in love is wonderful," belting it out as *"waaan-der-full!"* Love makes the lady ecstatic, and her sense of wonder overflows in its fullness.

So it was; so it should be.

A Great Electra

A performance of unarguable greatness is taking place under our noses. Let me not hesitate. Zoë Wanamaker's Electra is a magnificent achievement. Ms. Wanamaker, in David Leveaux's remarkable production of Sophocles's *Electra* at the Ethel Barrymore Theater, has the audience spellbound. Who would have imagined that a 2,400-year-old story of matricide would prove so popular—and on Disneyfied Broadway? There's a thought! Neither Sophocles nor Ms. Wanamaker are star names in New York. Which is why the usual bottom-line producers wouldn't invest in the production—though it had already played to acclaim in England and at the McCarter Theater at Princeton University. If only the ruling elites of Broadway would have a little more faith. This production shows the way, and its extended run is sweet justice.

Ms. Wanamaker's Electra is an original creation—an elemental, furious *creature*, both savage and childlike, a gaping wound, a broken image of obsessed eternal grief. She is a physically small actress giving a performance of staggering size. I had known her only in lighter roles—her gamine looks imply the impish rather than the tragic. Yet from her first riveting appearance, it's clear that she will compel us to meet her on a different, higher plane.

She first appears wearing the white mask of tragedy. She stands on a ladder, peering into the palace of her murdered father. She's dwarfed by the frayed old overcoat that she wears. Of course! It must be her beloved father's coat—worn as a living memory, a talisman, a shroud.

She descends in the white mask (which seems strangely natural to us). She is like a Beckett tramp. But her spiked hair reveals a bloody scalp. This is an Electra who tears her hair out with inconsolable grief. Then she removes the tragic mask, and reveals her own face of terrible tragic destiny.

Her plaintive rasping voice can frighten and touch us deeply. She is uncluttered and unfettered—an essence. She not only conveys pain but is its personification. Her first words are delivered to the gods as a calm ritual of primal furious need, like a fervent unanswered prayer: "Divine light, sweet air, again hear my pain." In her father's death is her death.

Sophocles's *Electra*—the spare ninety-minute adaptation is by Frank McGuinness—is a story of obsessive vengeance in a society that has lost its moral bearings. Clytemnestra, the hated mother of Electra, lives with her lover, Aegisthus. They murdered Agamemnon—Electra's father and Clytemnestra's husband—on his victorious return from Troy. The unforgiving Electra—"The world has turned bad and so have I"—awaits the return of her brother, Orestes, and longed-for retribution.

There are fascinating similarities with *Hamlet:* the murdered king in both plays is replaced by the queen's lover; the heir's fate is vengeance and a descent into further chaos. There's the Freudian interpretation of incestuous love: Electra and the father, Hamlet and the mother. Greek drama, after all, is an ancient form of public psychology. At center, *Electra* is a moral debate and argument about fierce opposites: betrayal and forgiveness; vengeance and compromise; memory and forgetting; blood or peace. How, the drama asks, and will not stop asking, do we live when crimes have been done to us?

These are universal issues, which should need no justification today in modern terms. Greek drama *is* modern (though it's obviously not bourgeois tragedy in search of "closure"). The truth and relentless grief of *Electra* is as contemporary as the ashes in Cambodia or Sarajevo; its fractured moral landscape is all around us; its family divided by a form of psychic madness and unresolved hatreds isn't unknown in our own families. It's why Mr. Leveaux, the director of *Electra,* points out that the play cannot be made "more convenient by making it more conversational." It cannot be made more convenient; a question of matricide is most *inconvenient.* These perpetual dilemmas of making timeless and already popular dramas somehow easier, more accessible, more "relevant" to modern times, grow wearisome. They cannot be easier—as pitiless fate and profound grief cannot be trivialized.

It's a question of balance between the present and the past, and Mr. Leveaux has got most of it splendidly right. The expressionist wreck of a set, designed by Johan Engels, evokes the ruinous wars of a blighted landscape literally rooted in the earth. I was less happy with the intended *coup de théâtre* when the inside of the palace is stagily revealed. Mr. Leveaux has no need of such theatricality when his production is characterized by its essential simplicity and stillness.

Then again, though there are some weaknesses in the ensemble, Claire Bloom is a beautiful, formidably reasonable Clytemnestra in perfect steely counterpoint to Ms. Wanamaker in their key scenes together. "I am not a cruel woman," she says (and has us believing her). "But I do abuse you because you abuse me so often...."

The secret to Ms. Wanamaker's superb performance is that she is uncannily both an adult and a child. What was murderously done to her as a child has never been resolved in her adulthood. In an elemental sense, she remains dangerously unformed. Electra is an unbalanced child of grief whose tragedy is that she cannot be anything else.

Nicole Kidman,
Live Naked Movie Star

Returning to New York after a trip to London, I see that Nicole Kidman has followed me. It's normal. Whither I go, London theater is sure to follow. And whither *you* go, too.

The Great White Way, or as it's more popularly known nowadays, David Hare Way, will have six major British productions this season—excluding the usual 222 Irish imports. Mr. Hare alone will soon have three of his plays on Broadway: *Via Dolorosa,* his fine monologue about Israel, written to be performed by the author himself; *Amy's View,* which is about the essential mystery of theater and stars Judi Dench; and, of course, *The Blue Room,* which is about Nicole Kidman, starring Nicole Kidman.

Do you by any chance detect a slight cynicism? Ah, but I have seen the now famous production in London. I have seen Nicole Kidman *naked!* Well, not *quite* naked. Something! There! In the discreetly lit, coy shadows. A glimpse! I don't know. It was dark. I can't be *sure.* My seat was in the wrong position. It was all over *so soon.* No! I saw her. They *promised* I would. "Roll up! Roll up! See the naked movie star! Live on stage!" And I did. Yes, definitely. I remember now....

I was there when all the hysteria began. Were the drooling, dribbling drama critics of London expressing a profound esthetic judgment when they swooned before the delicate little tootsies of Ms. Kidman—or would we concur with Aristotle that they're just a bunch of *alter kakers*? I couldn't possibly say.

The English have always been confused about sex. They prefer it in overheated doses, like porridge. But it is the furtive promise of sex, rather than the disgusting act itself, that goes to their voyeuristic heart. *The Blue*

Room is about Ms. Kidman's willowy charms on discreet silhouetted display in a peep show for the middle classes who don't go to the theater, but attend Events. Her nakedness, such as it is, is *necessary for the role*—a courageous act, therefore, of artistic integrity in our unprivate, celebrity-obsessed times. What the play itself is about is of no importance whatsoever, except to David Hare, his director, and their loving families.

"Even those who have seen the play have written about something that isn't really on stage," complained Sam Mendes, *Blue Room*'s director. "They wrote about the wrong things. They didn't write about the play."

Oh, I don't know. In interview after interview, Mr. Mendes has talked about little else other than the decisive moment during rehearsal when Ms. Kidman and her costar Iain Glen finally decided to take off their clothes. (It was tense at first. Awkward—but a necessary step in the creative process.) Mr. Glen's dick is on display throughout the proceedings. But let's not go into that now.

We have eyes only for Nicole Kidman. There's the rub! Mr. Glen is literally doing cartwheels bollock-naked on stage, and Ms. Kidman gets all the attention. Life can be so unfair sometimes. A prominent London newspaper even sent a reporter (female) to review Ms. Kidman's body.

"We knew she wasn't fat, we knew she'd look pretty good, but this!" wrote a breathless Shane Watson in the *Evening Standard*. "A figure (narrow hips, bosoms at armpit level, long rangy legs, no—repeat, no—cellulite or any interruptions to the all-over moonstone skin) that not only matches up to the best but would be exceptional on a 20-year-old. Whereas Nicole is 31."

Note the first-name terms. Nicole has no—repeat, no—cellulite! And Nicole is thirty-one! It was Charles Spencer, the likable, middle-aged, happily married drama critic of the conservative *Daily Telegraph,* who fell unashamedly head over heels in love with her. Mr. Spencer famously described what isn't actually onstage as "pure theatrical Viagra."

Viagra is for old geezers who have a problem. Not, of course, that Mr. Spencer does. "Everyone's reaction to this show is going to be conditioned by their own sexual preference," he wrote evenhandedly. Message: Gays shouldn't feel excluded from the rumored rampant heterosexual carnality on stage. "Even I found time to notice that Iain Glen is a very handsome hunk with fine cheekbones," he continued. "Most of the time, though, I had eyes only for Nicole Kidman. Eyes on stalks, in fact…The vision of her wafting around the stage with a fag in one hand and her knickers in the other as a delicious French au pair will haunt my fantasies for months."

It is believed that the smitten Mr. Spencer had to be calmed down with tranquilizer darts fired by crack marksmen from the theater balcony. Or so noted Mr. Spencer's own newspaper in an anonymous profile the following week, which revealed British journalism at its most enjoyably mischievous. Mr. Spencer's reference to Ms. Kidman "holding a fag in one hand," the profile explained, "is Brit-speak [for a cigarette] and not an allusion to her diminutive husband. Tom Cruise is not gay, nor is he sterile, nor is he *that* short. What he *is* is harder to say, since, thanks to their diligence, he is now defined almost entirely by negatives, with a bigger collection of 'nots' than a badge-winning Boy Scout. But he does have Nicole Kidman, and that puts him well ahead of most red-blooded males on the planet."

It certainly puts him well ahead of blue-blooded Charles Spencer, the drama critic, poor soul, who began it all—all the fun and games, the hype and *fuss.* A rumor that Ms. Kidman would be wearing a translucent body stocking on Broadway has been vigorously denied; there were no—repeat, no—rumors that Mr. Glen would be wearing one.

It was the anonymous profile writer of the *Sunday Telegraph,* however, who alone questioned Ms. Kidman's megastar status, which isn't playing the game at all. For all celebs are born equal—suffering equally at the unholy intrusions of the media. To suggest that Ms. Kidman *isn't* a megastar is therefore extremely rude.

The babe Nicole was born in Hawaii, though raised in Australia. She's an Aussie redhead transmuted into a Hollywood blond. Tom Cruise and Nicole Kidman are Scientology's First Celeb Couple, sharing top billing with Mr. and Mrs. John Travolta. She trained and acted at the Australian Theatre for Young People in Sydney and the Philip Street Theatre. It may not mean much to you, but she was nominated Best Newcomer by the Sydney Theatre Critics. Her London debut in *The Blue Room* was her first stage appearance in eleven years.

Ms. Kidman has been known, until now, more for her film work. She has appeared in turkeys opposite Mr. Cruise *(Days of Thunder, Far and Away).* She played a neurosurgeon in *Thunder,* a psychiatrist in *Batman Forever,* and a nuclear scientist in *The Peacemaker.* She has been living in London for the past eighteen months, filming Stanley Kubrick's forthcoming *Eyes Wide Shut* with Mr. Cruise. She was memorably amusing as the cute, homicidally ambitious weather girl in Gus Van Sant's black comedy, *To Die For.*

Let's not quibble about her precise film star status. The whole world loves *any* film star. Look what fame has done for Paul Sorvino—actor, singer, chef, New Yorker, seat-belt user. We should all be deeply grateful that a star of Ms. Kidman's magnitude has agreed to grace theater with her golden presence. It's why London's prestigious Evening Standard Theatre Awards have just given her *a special prize* for her role in *Blue Room.* Seeing a film star on stage, the judges said, "focuses the attention of an audience who might otherwise never give a thought to theater from one year to the next."

Welcome to Celeb Theater! It condescends to both theater and the public simultaneously. Movie stars sell theater tickets, it cannot be denied. Last season, Alec Baldwin wished to play Macbeth at the Public Theater, and play him he did. He was a big-name Thane. (His Mrs. Macbeth was played by none other than Angela Bassett.) The house was packed, but the production wasn't a success, nor were its uncomfortable new Shakespearean stars. Then again, *Macbeth,* a powerful commercial brew of blood, sex, and ambition, has somehow survived, and even triumphed, for centuries—without film stars.

Nicole Kidman is part of the transatlantic celeb trend. Recent guest appearances in London theater—apart from soap opera stars—include the Ralph Fiennes *Hamlet,* Kevin Spacey in *The Iceman Cometh,* Juliette Binoche in Luigi Pirandello's *Naked,* and Liam Neeson's Oscar Wilde in Mr. Hare's *Judas Kiss.*

But Mr. Neeson's Wilde failed to ignite; Mr. Fiennes's Hamlet was sometimes incoherent; and Mr. Spacey is more of a fine character actor than a heavyweight Eugene O'Neill tragic hero. Still, it's decent of them all to help out the theater (and the poor, ignorant public, too). Celeb Theater makes movie stars feel good, like cosmetic surgery. "We are working for peanuts," they like to say, "especially for you."

The Blue Room has catapulted Ms. Kidman into the kind of stardom she hasn't enjoyed till now in movies (she just made the cover of *Newsweek*). How come? Her acting isn't the point. The play itself is a perfect vehicle for celebrity voyeurism. The play is *about* voyeurism. David Hare has freely adapted Arthur Schnitzler's notorious 1900 drama *Reigen*, which became better known as *La Ronde* in Max Ophuls's 1950 film version. The film, a minor classic, seems wistfully and stagily predictable today, though it stars the young Simone Signoret, Gérard Philipe, and Jean-Louis Barrault. Schnitzler's plot famously consists of a game of serial seductions—a sexual merry-go-round in which five men and five women change partners until the action comes full circle.

Mr. Hare has updated the play to the present. Ms. Kidman plays all the women—a Cockney hooker, a French au pair, the wife of a smug politician, a coked-up model, an actress. Mr. Glen, the more experienced of the two (*Martin Guerre, Henry V,* various psychotics), plays a cabdriver, an insecure student, the politician, a narcissistic playwright, a repressed aristocrat.

Easy types, all; easy pickings. The confident, limited Ms. Kidman, a fantasy Barbie doll, is unconvincing as a middle-aged actress, just as Mr. Glen is too mature to play a student. He does well as the aristocrat looking for love in all the wrong places; she shines more as the fashion model—*the* celebrity job of our day, along with celeb chefs. But it is all pretty shallow stuff—undangerous, not erotic, modish, not carnal. During the sex scenes, the stage goes dark and a buzzer sounds, indicating the time that the sex lasts. What could be more coy? By the third, fourth, or fifth time, *we get the joke.*

That buzzer only emphasizes the potentially fatal flaw in Schnitzler's clever dramatic idea. As David Hare has noted, "In the theater, its circularity can easily come across as repetitiveness." The problem isn't solved here. Nor is the piece shocking or disturbing, as Schnitzler intended. God forbid! Instead, it is slightly suggestive; it is "entertaining"; a light sex comedy of manners, it is tamely, *acceptably* voyeuristic. It put me in mind of the old lady who had never seen the sea. One day, she was taken to see it. She watched it and said: "Is that all it does?"

In Schnitzler's turn-of-the-century Vienna, society paid a steep price for sex, and the crossing of class barriers led to social disgrace. Schnitzler's play is a metaphor for syphilis and disease. (He was also a doctor, as Anton Chekhov was.) Today, the metaphor would be AIDS. Mr. Hare has chosen a different route. He has placed the action in a neutral, faux poetic place. Why a blue room? (Blue moon? Blue movie?) All is explained when the playwright character in *Blue Room* sits at the piano to sing a song he's composed:

Blue, like blue like blue is how I'm feeling
Blew like how the wind blew all night long
And blew aside your cotton dress, revealing
This, the opening of the opening of a song…

There will be better nights in the company of David Hare, I'm sure. He has also claimed that the play is about projection and identity. (Schnitzler was a contemporary of Freud.) As *The Blue Room* song goes on to ask: "Are people ever truly what they seem?"

Oh, let's hope not. But, by accident, the distinguished Mr. Hare has gone to the core of our thriving celeb culture. Is Nicole Kidman truly what she seems? Roll up, roll up! Live on stage!

Judi! Judi! Judi!

Judi Dench, you may have heard a whisper, is starring in David Hare's *Amy's View,* and nothing could give us greater pleasure than the sight of the Dame herself returning to the New York stage for the first time in forty years. Forgive the brevity of this love letter to her, but a thousand more words wouldn't be enough to express what this lovely, great actress means to us.

If you're British (as I am), you grew up with Judi Dench. The English love their actors, but Ms. Dench is regarded as one of the family. In a sense, she's everyone's thoroughly middle-class sister or favorite aunt—the one who became famous, to everyone's surprise, including her own. She's unpretentious and *very* English. "Are you usually so reserved?" a dope of a TV interviewer asked her after the Academy Awards. "No, I'm not," she replied, a little crossly. "And we've only just met."

She's likeable and warm, an easy laugher (as many theater people are). You would trust her with your secrets. She's an excellent listener, as she is onstage, like a priest in a confessional. The Academy Award for her witty virtual guest appearance as Queen Elizabeth in *Shakespeare in Love* was a nice bonus in a long stage career. (Film acting invariably makes her uncomfortable.) She's a born stage actress, who can do absolutely anything—but nobody knows exactly how. She gets the terrors, yet everything she does appears effortless. She convinces us that great acting is a great mystery.

She plays an actress, Esme, in *Amy's View.* "Mummy is brilliant playing at comedy," says Esme's daughter to her boyfriend. "I'm usually best at playing genteel," Esme replies in amused, ironic form. "With something interesting happening underneath." Which reminds us of Tom Stoppard accepting *his* Academy Award: "I feel like Roberto Benigni underneath." The English specialize in layers.

At heart, *Amy's View* is about theater and acting, in noble defense of imagination versus literalism (and theater versus film). Esme defends her calling in her own idealistic fashion: "People say, 'Oh, everyone should go to the theater.' Why should they?" We don't want an audience being brought in by force. And for us, there's nothing more disheartening than playing to people who are there because they've been told it's doing them good."

"Quite," says Dominic, who finds theater irrelevant, like some fossil in a museum. He's her future son-in-law and nemesis who goes from fledgling film critic to media star to Quentin Tarantino-esque movie director in four acts.

"Let's play to people who actually like it," Esme continues, defending the theater. "And if there aren't many, so be it. But don't come because you've been told to. No, that won't do at all."

We immediately think: Quite right! It certainly *won't* do. Ms. Dench's reading of the line encourages no argument. Besides, her acting is characterized by its fierce commitment and honesty. There are other clues to the mysterious art of Judi Dench in the play, which David Hare wrote for her. "You say one thing but you're thinking of another. If you can't do that, then truly you shouldn't be doing the job," Esme goes on to explain. Ambiguity, like irony, is another English specialty in a nation of actors.

Esme's rival, a showy, craven actress named Deirdre, "practically goes down on the critics." But Esme doesn't. Her secret is "to please without seeming to try." Later, in the final—and best—act in the play, an apprentice actor in his early twenties asks Esme how she magically draws in the audience so that *they* somehow make the effort, not her.

"It comes with the passage of time..."

She shrugs slightly. "There it is."

We embrace Ms. Dench from her first shrewdly delayed entrance, though she isn't playing a particularly "lovable" role. As mums go, Esme can be a selfish old cow, certainly overpossessive, actressy, spoiled, living in some artificial dream world in life and onstage. Her daughter asks her to "take control" of her life, which is greeted with the contempt of an individualist who would reject fashionably easy concepts such as "closure." "What a meaningless cliché," Esme angrily protests. "If you ask me why men always make such fools of themselves, it's because they're in love with the ludicrous notion that there's such a thing as to be in control....Who's in control? Finally? I ask you. The answer is no one. No one! If you don't know that, you know nothing."

Yet Ms. Dench's Esme will ultimately take control of her life—going from apparently carefree, nicely self-indulgent middle age to bewildered penury to a sublime act of purest theatrical benediction sixteen years later. Even in this quite light, near-Shavian drama of love, death, and the theater, Ms. Dench achieves a radiance and transforming alchemy that might convince us that *Amy's View* is really a Chekhovian family tragedy. (Some say it is, with a nod to *The Seagull.*) But the notes she hits are phenomenal.

Her boisterous comic gift can spontaneously change in a second into the explosively feral, like a cultivated English rose with a mouth on her. She can make us laugh at ridiculous things, or stop an entire scene with a glance, or reveal the elemental essence of acting in absolute stillness as she makes up her immobile face in a bleak dressing room, as if painting on a mask. A mask upon a mask—of what? Grief, rectitude, resilience perhaps.

But then, this is an actress, height five feet nothing, who can somehow convince us she's tall. Everything about her seems to fly in the face of all boring logic. She was said not to be right for Cleopatra, but her 1987 Cleopatra with Anthony Hopkins triumphed in its impulsive emotional magnetism. (She decked the messenger with a right hook.) Believed to be too cozy, too "nice" to play Lady Macbeth opposite Ian McKellen a generation ago, she was the most coldly terrifying Lady Macbeth I've ever seen. For good measure, in younger days she played Sally Bowles in *Cabaret,* though she can't sing. She knows how to, which is another story.

Her Esme in *Amy's View* seems like a breeze for her. It's meant to, of course. There are other actors in the play, too—Samantha Bond as Amy uncannily resembles Ms. Dench, making the mother-daughter blood feuds all the more poignant; the American actor Tate Donovan not only plays Dominic with a perfect English accent, he's exactly, nauseatingly right as the media ignoramus on the make who's patronized by Esme's "permanent leer of good taste." The veteran Ronald Pickup is delightful as the pickled old lush and well-meaning neighbor, Frank, an epitome of English decency; Anne

Pitoniak and Maduka Steady complete the fine ensemble in Richard Eyre's first-rate production.

Amy's View itself is about many diverse themes—too many! It's about family life, of course, and bad marriages; high culture versus low culture; art versus money; England as theme park and boorish New Labor mediocrity; the role that chance, or fate, plays in our lives; and how we fail to make amends; and above all, the value of theater, believed in like a declaration of faith or foolishness.

There are times when Mr. Hare is deftly skating on thin ice. The theme park metaphor was tired before even Julian Barnes used it in his latest novel, *England, England;* as an apostle of antitheater and "low" culture, they don't come much more blatant than Dominic. I also found the unexplained death of Amy too convenient, and evil journalists (and critics) are, by now, a David Hare vaudevillian turn from way back when, which won't do at all.

But that final act and *coup de théâtre* are worth everything. Here Esme has at last found her reality—the Spartan backstage reality of theater, which is now her only home and her vocation. She is alone. "Fair enough, then. So we're alone," go her last words. It is a beautiful moment we witness, a blessing and form of baptism, which speaks to us of such a profound belief in theater that it amounts to a religion, a mysterious renewal, a way of life. There's no debate any longer about "Is Theater Dead?" or "Why Bother?" To the contrary, theater in that glorious moment is the only thing that makes sense of life to Esme, to the audience, and one suspects, to the incomparable Judi Dench.

Harv the Marv

At the end of the recent, nicely named "The Harvey Gala," Harvey Lichtenstein—who was being honored for his glorious thirty-two years as head of the Brooklyn Academy of Music—*danced* onstage. It was wonderful! The audience rose to him, and he kept dancing, and never wanted to stop.

Harvey, or "Harv the Marv"—as everyone calls him, including people who don't know him, like me—is seventy now, and retiring from the leadership of BAM and the Next Wave Festival, which have transformed the performing arts of New York to an astonishing, unequaled degree. He began his professional life as a dancer. The joyful, liberated spirit of the dancer within him accounts for a lot. We cannot let this week pass without paying tribute, then, to this Diaghilev of Brooklyn, who's also been described as "the last samurai," and even a "Prospero."

I can remember the bleaker times of the late 1970s when no one went to Brooklyn. Not even Bianca Jagger went. The trendy, all-black East Village image came later (and seems to have calmed down now). There's another remarkable achievement! It was as if we awesomely sophisticated Manhattanites were crossing into the dark, unknown territory of a foreign country until Harv the Marv somehow made it hip to go to Brooklyn.

How did he do it? When he took charge of the Academy in 1967, it had a great history—Enrico Caruso, Sarah Bernhardt, and Jascha Heifetz had performed there. But its future was perilous. Before he got there, the Academy was offering dramatic readings and leasing space to a karate class. He had nothing to lose! At the same time, he set out to attract a Manhattan audience by offering a radical alternative to the mainstream fare of Broadway and to the big culture houses like Lincoln Center. (That alternative—call it choice, or urgently needed lifeblood—is just as relevant today.) To be sure, he raided the existing downtown arts scene. He followed his own gut instinct and taste, giving the avant-garde a showcase, a home.

In his first, dangerous days, for example, he gave the revolutionary work of Merce Cunningham its first major New York season, and staged the New York premiere of Alban Berg's atonal *Lulu*. There quickly followed Twyla Tharp; Robert Wilson's *Life and Times of Sigmund Freud;* and the return from exile in Europe of the subversive Living Theater, a troupe I'd seen in London when a naked Julian Beck sat on my knee and announced, "You are not allowed to travel without a passport." Harvey Lichtenstein doesn't believe in passports, either—not in cultural ones, anyway. (The Brooklyn Bridge has always been open.) But look at some of the innovative American artists he has steadfastly supported—Philip Glass and Robert Wilson, Trisha Brown, Merce Cunningham, Bill T. Jones and Arnie Zane, Laurie Anderson and that favorite BAM dumpling, Mark Morris. I got to know them through BAM. We all did.

In one of the several loving tributes during "The Harvey Gala," the writer and director Jonathan Miller wittily referred to BAM's unique contribution in the context of a New York that's "the most spectacularly provincial city in the world." The audience laughed, seeing the truth in it. Not to worry, though. Mr. Miller sees his own hometown, London, as unspectacularly worse. It's why he joined the international opera scene, and directs straight theater only in Dublin. He's disillusioned with the pervasively bourgeois, seeing both the West End and Broadway as basically conformist and provincial, like Finland in the fifties.

What is undeniable is that the world-renowned artists who have also been produced at BAM expanded all horizons. Harvey Lichtenstein made the world accessible. It has been as vital a contribution to the cultural life of New York as Joseph Papp's principled campaign for free Shakespeare in the park. His greatest legacy has been the open, wholly enthusiastic embrace of the international.

The unstoppable impresario within him got the crumbling old Majestic, an abandoned movie house round the corner from BAM, reopened at a cost of $5 million to house Peter Brook's nine-hour epic, *The Mahabharata.* The new venue was modeled after Mr. Brook's own Paris theater, the Bouffes du Nord. The Majestic has now been proudly renamed the Harvey Lichtenstein Theater (and will doubtless be known as the Harvey). But look, too, at some of the Next Wave Festival's international names that were new to New York once upon a time. Apart from Peter Brook, there are the productions of Ingmar Bergman. (*The Image Makers,* directed by the eighty-year-old legend, has just played BAM via the Royal Dramatic Theater of Sweden.) The seminal experimental work of Jerzy Grotowski was first produced in Brooklyn; the great Giorgio Strehler's *Tempest* was the finest I've ever seen. On balance, I could have lived without the cutting edge of hip horsemanship, Zingaro. But where would the New York performing arts scene have been without the supreme work of William Christie, or of Robert Lepage, Pina Bausch, Peter Sellars, and Ariane Mnouchkine?

Until the 1970s in London, there used to be the invaluable annual World Theater Season—the equivalent, on an international level, of BAM today. The World Theater Season virtually educated an entire generation in England—first introducing London to the work of Brecht and the Berlin Ensemble, the Moscow Art Theater, and Noh theater. Today, the finances—and even the will—just aren't there to support it. But in "spectacularly provincial" New York, BAM holds the fort, and miraculously so, it seems.

Do I have any criticisms of Harvey Lichtenstein's tenure? Do the lights go down before a performance? There are bound to be niggles. A new, younger generation of European innovators has tended to be dominated by the older icons. He strangely seemed to undervalue the brilliant new work of the London-based Théâtre de Complicité (which became the hit of the Lincoln Center Summer Festival, even though the troupe has had to play in inadequate theater spaces). He boldly introduced—thank goodness!—the Cheek by Jowl troupe to New York, and the unforgettable all-male *As You Like It,* in particular. But none of Deborah Warner's London productions with Fiona Shaw have made BAM yet.

To an extent, BAM's favorites are now aging a little. So yesterday's avant-garde becomes today's cultural establishment. It's inevitable. But great producers stand by their artists, as Harvey Lichtenstein always has. And his contribution over thirty-two years has been, quite simply, magnificent. He didn't put just Brooklyn on the map, but the world.

There were many loving tributes during "The Harvey Gala," as I say. Philip Glass played *Études for Piano*, Paul Simon and the band played a set, Trisha Brown danced a scherzo she'd specially choreographed, and among much else, Erland Josephson—one of Ingmar Bergman's greatest actors— read a scene beautifully from Chekhov. And then Harv the Marv danced! And in its joyful freedom, the dance was his credo and heartfelt thanks.

Amazing Grace

Wit, the first play by Margaret Edson, has transferred to the Union Square Theater downtown, and long may it triumph there. When I say this is Ms. Edson's "first" play, don't be put off by that: *Wit* might be her twentieth, so remarkable is her achievement.

Who *is* the mysterious Ms. Edson? Her moving—and yes!—*witty* drama is uncompromising in its spare, rigorous discipline. It is about nothing less than love and knowledge (and love of knowledge). Or facing death without the usual cheap sentiment. "It is not my intention to give away the plot," Ms. Edson's acerbic heroine tells the audience, "but I think I die in the end."

An amusing play about death (and seventeenth-century metaphysics) is…unusual. We might resist an evening out in death's company, however literary. Half a century ago, the coproducer of *Death of a Salesman* desperately tried to persuade Arthur Miller to change the title. How to sell death when, as the poets say, death is a downer?

Unless, of course, it's an uplifting Hollywood weepy. Meryl Streep–Susan Sarandon–Shirley MacLaine *shining through.* Every week, our TV culture is propped up by dramas about near-dead people shining through. Broadway has had its share of mortal mush (*Who's Life Is It, Anyway? The Shadowbox).* Why, in *Life Is Beautiful,* humor even brings us shining through the death camps. Call it "Holocaust Italian Style"; the indominable human spirit can overcome *anything.* Can it?

Wit is of a different order. Its dying heroine, Vivian Bearing, a fifty-year-old professor and an expert on the poetry of John Donne, isn't particularly likable. Asked whether she's tough enough to take the vile battering of still-experimental chemotherapy, the question is redundant. She's a tough old bird, friendless and alone—without anyone in her life, it seems. Not that this bright, difficult, steely, *amused* spinster-professor could give a hoot.

One of the major achievements of the play is how we come to care for this stranger in our midst whom we scarcely know. It's as if the friendless heroine makes hundreds of friends with each performance whether she likes it or not. And for that, we must thank a wonderful actress, Kathleen Chalfant, as Vivian. You may remember her as the Mormon matriarch of *Angels in America.* She's giving the performance of her career here. She first greets us jauntily in a hospital robe and red baseball cap. Vivian is in Stage 4 of ovarian cancer. (There is no Stage 5.) The cap covers her baldness—the outcome of the course of chemotherapy. But what strikes us immediately is Ms. Chalfant's beady *aliveness.* Her Vivian is a fearsome teacher, not one to suffer fools gladly, if at all. "Shakespeare," she reminds us patronizingly. "I trust the name is familiar!"

Ms. Chalfant inhabits the role completely. When, at first, several audience members at the performance I attended laughed too hard, too knowingly, at Vivian's ironic asides, the actress raised a surprised, mildly disapproving eyebrow, as if to say in character: "Wit is *not* uproarious. Wit is dry and as sharp as a surgeon's knife. Settle down, if you please!" Which everyone surely did.

Vivian Bearing is a coldly brilliant academic for whom textual analysis and philosophical speculation are everything. For her, the study of Donne's sonnets—"Death be not proud"—is made for its own intellectual sake and pleasure. Mental acuity and learning are prized at the cost of "feeling," of feeling a simple, vulnerable emotional response. What happens, then, when Vivian herself is dying?

In a tender memory scene between the young Vivian and her elderly college teacher (Helen Stenborg giving a quiet, very appealing performance), an intense academic dispute about a semicolon in a Donne text takes on the professorial perspective of life or death. In that cloistered, donnish sense, *Wit* sometimes resembles the more arcane disputes of Tom Stoppard's play about the poet A. E. Housman, *The Invention of Love.*

But *Wit's* dramatist, Ms. Edson, is onto something else: the point where art and science meet (and where, in the mortal end, neither can help us). In a schematic move—which nevertheless doesn't weaken the play significantly—Vivian's clumsy young doctor in the oncology unit is as impersonally obsessed with medical research as she is with academic scholarship. Her pleasure is Donne; his, the fatal mystery of replicating cancer cells. It is called, he explains, "immortality in culture."

Their bond, if it exists at all, is in pure knowledge, the sensual pleasure of words, medical language, poetry. "It's just like a graduate seminar," she announces dryly. "Once I did the teaching; now I am taught." She is literally learning how to suffer and die. The dramatist doesn't build anything remotely sentimental between Vivian and the doctor. A lesser dramatist might have been tempted. *Wit,* the tear-jerker? Hardly. Yet we will be moved enough, in time.

It is the dawning of Vivian's own emotional needs that touch us so in their dignity and humor. "I can't believe my life has become so *corny!*" she protests, sucking on a popsicle like a contented child. She does not come *shining through.* She learns of kindness and simple things, like the tender compassionate embrace of a nurse who doesn't know the meaning of the word "soporific," or the warm nostalgic comfort of a morphine-induced dream about a bedtime story from childhood.

The ferocious penultimate scene is a fight for life, the afterlife. The nurse (Paula Pizzi, another fine actor in the cast) defends Vivian's wish to die against the doctor's compulsive efforts to keep her half-alive for research. "And death shall be no more, Death thou shalt die," goes the Donne sonnet. The struggle is over Vivian's soul—a state of grace—life everlasting.

Wit isn't just impeccably performed by Ms. Chalfant and the ensemble. The production is a model of excellence in every department. The director is Derek Anson Jones, a talent—new to me—to watch. And the dramatist Margaret Edson? We know only that she was born in Washington, D.C., in 1961. She has degrees in history and literature and worked on the cancer in-patient unit of a research hospital. She teaches kindergarten at Centennial Place School in Atlanta. And *Wit* is her first play. Some debut! I'm glad she prefers anonymity to celebrity. We've got quite enough *celebrities.* But not enough dramatists of Ms. Edson's gifted intelligence. *Wit* is the best new play I've seen for many a season.

Margaret Edson was awarded the 1999 Pulitzer Prize for Drama.

The Anglophile
New York Times

It always staggers me when New Yorkers—and New York theater critics, to boot—prostrate themselves before the altar of British theater, howling: "Thank you! Thank you! We are so inferior! Show us the way! Oh, thank you, thank you, thank you."

To which the English, hurrying home with sacks full of awards and cash, reply: "No, thank *you*."

I don't think I've ever quite experienced such a shocking display of Anglophilia as the conversation among the three theater critics of the *New York Times*—Ben Brantley, Vincent Canby, and Peter Marks—in the recent Arts and Leisure section. I'm sorry, attention must be paid. Messrs. Brantley, Canby, and Marks, a vaudevillian act, were part of a special theater section on British theater ("Why London Now Dominates New York," "A Parade of British Imports," and so on). The *Times* celebration is part of the problem. If I were an American artist working and struggling in American theater, I'd be inclined to jump off Brooklyn Bridge with the farewell words: "Give us a break!"

When was there ever a celebration of the enormous achievements and creativity of American theater? Messrs. Brantley, Canby, and Marks—Anglophiles to a man—see *only* the superiority of London over New York as if they're still colonized subjects. "Part of our embrace of the English is that in some ways we haven't got over England," said Mr. Marks, and no one disagreed.

Gentlemen, the War of Independence was won some time ago. And all is by no means so rosy in England, or as dire here. Let me comment on just a few of their points.

Compared to the "energy" and "buzz" among English audiences, Broadway audiences "go anesthetized" and "they leave anesthetized." Oh, really?

Are the shaken New Yorkers coming out of, say, *Electra* or *Death of a Salesman* suffering from anesthesia? Hardly. In fact, the reverse is the truer picture: The dominantly middle-class audience in England is by no means as animated as its American counterpart. Every British director and actor I know share this in common: They all pay tribute to the vibrant, un-English *enthusiasm* of New York audiences.

Jonathan Kent, who runs the Almeida Theatre in North London, is the director who brought the Ralph Fiennes *Hamlet* to Broadway. Here's what he told me about American audiences: "We English too readily want to believe that Americans are less sophisticated than us. It's *nonsense*. It's just possible they're less jaded than we are. English audiences have a certain knowledge, a heritage. We're not as demonstrative as Americans, but then we're not a demonstrative nation. But New Yorkers *want* to be there. They want to be part of the event. It's not their twenty-fifth *Hamlet* this year. And it gives the play an exciting *immediacy.*"

Then again, is American theater "conservative," and English theater "fresher" and "younger"? Well, I wouldn't say that the work of Tony Kushner, or the Wooster Group, Susan Lori Parks, Danny Hoch, Ellen Stewart's La Mama, Margaret Edson, Savion Glover, Richard Foreman's Ontological-Hysteric Theater, or the staging of *Hedwig and the Angry Inch*—to name a few—is conservative. Let it pass. The last thing English theater adds up to is "younger."

Would Messrs. Brantley, Canby, and Marks say that *The Prime of Miss Jean Brodie* and *Oklahoma!* currently in repertory in the two main houses of the Royal National Theater, are *young?* To be sure, the Royal Court import *Shopping and Fucking* was young. But was it fresh? Was it any good?

We tend to see the best of English theater in New York. Is it all great—as great as we are led to believe? This season alone, more than a few of us have found David Hare's *Blue Room* no masterpiece; Martin Crimp's modern version of *The Misanthrope* makes one wonder how they get away with such silliness in England; *Beautiful Thing*, Jonathan Harvey's slice of London working-class life and adolescent gaydom, is little more than a cozy TV sitcom compared to Diana Son's *Stop Kiss;* and the pseudochic prestige import of *Phèdre* with Diana Rigg disappointed us in its nineteenth-century acting histrionics.

Of course we get to see the work of terrific English artists. But why this craven need to overcelebrate them at the cost of American theater? One hundred and fifty years ago, New Yorkers caused an anti-British riot about theater. (I am encouraging another today.) The notorious 1849 Astor Place riots concerned a xenophobic rivalry over two productions of *Macbeth*. One starred the leading English thespian of his day, William Charles Macready; the other starred the American idol Edwin Forrest. Whether the riot was purely anti-English or opposed to English hams on tour I leave to scholars. Either way, there were thirty-four deaths and one hundred injuries. You see, New Yorkers felt American theater *counted* in them days.

The riots were the subject of a wonderfully funny Richard Nelson play, *Two Shakespearean Actors*. Mr. Nelson, an American, has had some half-dozen of his plays commissioned and subsidized by the Royal Shakespeare Company. The British system of Arts Council subsidy went unmentioned by Messrs. Brantley, Canby, and Marks—yet it accounts for the most crucial difference in our two systems. Virtually every British import on Broadway has originated in London's subsidized theater—from all of Tom Stoppard's plays to David Hare's, to Patrick Marber's *Closer*, to every Irish play recently on Broadway, too.

Tony Kushner's seminal *Angels in America* was produced at the National Theater before New York producers brought it home to Broadway. That says as much—if not more—about the unimaginative, Anglophile ruling elites of Broadway. They go for prepackaged "product." They shop—buying anything stamped with the English Good Housekeeping Seal of Approval. Broadway producers should invest in American talent, risk far more, and trust the intelligence of American audiences.

But look a little closer at the British scene: its Arts Council is under serious attack from the antielite populist Cromwellians of the Blair government. Cutbacks in subsidy have meant the decimation of the once-thriving English regional theater. The American regional powerhouses of Chicago, Washington, Seattle, and the West Coast axis are, in fact, producing more and far better theater than their English counterparts.

To which one might also add that the proud Royal Shakespeare Company is currently in financial and artistic crisis; that a new generation of English actors and directors is in revolt against the rhetorical acting style of its peers; and that no major theater in London reflects multiethnic England in the dynamic way that the Public Theater truly reflects New York.

They have a theater culture, *we* don't! I don't think so. They say tomah-toe, we say tamay-ter. Let's call the whole thing off. Meanwhile, may I ask Messrs. Brantley, Canby, and Marks to raise their right hands and kindly repeat after me:

"We do solemnly swear never to genuflect before British theater again. We'll cool it. We agree Anglophilia is blind. Thank you, John, for reminding us. We have seen the error of our ways. We faithfully promise to celebrate American theater. Because it is worthy of celebration, too. Because it is the right thing to do."

Iceman Cometh

A kind of miracle is happening on Broadway. It is home again to Eugene O'Neill, Arthur Miller, and Tennessee Williams. All three are playing simultaneously—as they used to a generation and more ago, before the Great White Way became a tourist mecca for family entertainment, before Disney. So all isn't lost?

I happen to believe that if you produce a great dramatist in a desert, people will find him somehow. There has always been an audience for serious drama on Broadway, like a starving man invited to a rare banquet. But to see the three Founding Fathers of American drama lighting up the marquees on Broadway again is an astonishing moment in modern theater history. And all three of their plays are about a tragedy of the American Dream.

The savage prison life of Tennessee Williams's newly discovered 1938 *Not About Nightingales* is as much drama of lost souls as the self-deluding barflies are in O'Neill's 1939 *The Iceman Cometh*. And *Iceman*'s con-man evangelist Hickey, arguably the ultimate salesman in American theater, is surely a blood relative of Willy Loman, mythic failed salesman of the American Dream.

God protect me from *Iceman*! The play scares me to death. I do not care for it—in the sense that one wouldn't care to have terrible suffocating nightmares. (But we have them, anyway.) *Iceman* stifles and exhausts. It flattens us, as if crushed by some unstoppable boulder rolling over us, again and again, without mercy, save for minor compensation in the clamor of a drunken song.

It is said that one doesn't attend O'Neill's sagas; one enlists for them. At four hours and fifteen minutes, Howard Davies's production of *The Iceman Cometh* is testing enough. Worse! Here we have one of the masterworks of the century, which at the same time is messily repetitive—well over twenty nagging references to its pipe-dream theme, lest we miss the point. Its structure can be clumsy, dramatically telegraphed, ponderous. "Get over it, you long-winded bastard!" Harry Hope, the good-natured bar owner, shouts at Hickey telling his relentless story of his marriage, and we laugh to ourselves because we share his impatient protest.

The long evening (with its two intermissions) has its inevitable tedium—as would the company of desperate flophouse drunks in any hellhole of a saloon. Yet for all its blatant rough edges that we sense O'Neill hammered obsessively into shape and imperfect form, *Iceman* is an overwhelming tragedy of self-delusion, as if God had gone missing along with salvation.

"What is it?" says Larry Slade sardonically, defining the lower depths they have all come to. "It's the No Chance Saloon. It's Bedrock Bar, the End of the Line Café, the Bottom of the Sea Rathskeller! Don't you notice the beautiful calm in the atmosphere? That's because it's the last harbor. No one here has to worry about where they're going next, because there is no farther they can go. It's a great comfort to them. Although even here they keep up the appearances of life with a few harmless pipe dreams about their yesterdays and tomorrows…"

Larry, the former romantic anarchist, has a nice line in bitter irony: "It's a great game, the pursuit of happiness." *Iceman* owes a debt to Gorky and Ibsen, but its bitter humor of despair anticipates Beckett. After all, the habitués of "The Palace of Pipe Dreams" are waiting for Hickey, their unexpected Godot, or savior.

To their utter disbelief, Hickey arrives newly sober and reborn, an evangelist of temperance. He has seen the light! Hickey, the hardware salesman, sets out to sell salvation by persuading his old drinking buddies to face a boozeless reality without the illusions and pipe dreams of a better tomorrow. But Hickey himself, we will learn, is living a terrible lie—he killed his wife—and the truth he's selling is death. The revivalist Hickey is an Angel of Death. The drunks of the "No Chance Saloon" choose the half-life of comforting booze and self-delusion to the oblivion of sober reality. "All we want is to pass out in peace, bejees!" cries Harry Hope. But if that were all there is to *Iceman*, it wouldn't affect us so deeply in its hopelessness.

It is an awesomely dark play. O'Neill, via Hickey and his rock-bottom characters, is actually telling us that self-knowledge kills. It does not free us: it disgusts us. He is saying that even the emptiest illusions are preferable to facing the truth about ourselves. Life itself cannot be redeemed. Because life is unlivable.

Was ever a bleaker message delivered from the stage? It's why, with regrets, I can't regard the new *Iceman* production and Kevin Spacey's central performance as enthusiastically as others have. My regret is over the good intentions of everyone concerned. But I believe that Mr. Davies, the director, is mistaken in his view that *Iceman* is essentially "funny." It is extraordinarily humane, but does it really flow from "a rich vein of humor," as he claims?

I'd say its vein was of the blackest blood. Of course, there's humor in it, and the spiky camaraderie of washed-up drunks is a form of beleaguered brotherhood. But the source of *Iceman* is in its pain. Mr. Davies, on the other hand, has said, "I knew from the start that what I wanted was a bunch of happy bums. I've always felt the play is very funny, and I cast it looking for actors with real comic skills."

It is as if the production has its own pipe dream—the illusion of an easier-to-digest tragedy. Was that why one or two of my colleagues were glad to note admiringly that the evening "flew by" (despite its length, of course)? Or why the audience found *Iceman*'s pathetic characters frequently amusing? Yet this young character at the bar, a betrayer, wants permission to kill himself; that aging lush hasn't set foot outside since his wife died; he's a near mad mystic hoping to drink himself to death; and that deluded one believes he can begin life all over again.

The key to *Iceman* isn't in its humor, but in the Heinrich Heine poem to morphine that Larry Slade quotes:

> Lo, sleep is good; better is death, in sooth,
> The best of all were never to be born.

The new production is compromised by its lightness—just as the entire ensemble uncannily looks the part of O'Neill's derelicts and Bowery bums, but the bar itself is too clean. Some of the performers play too broad. (The shrill stage hookers; Tony Danza's "typical" bartender, Rocky; Michael Emerson, the Oscar Wilde of *Gross Indecency,* too much of an actorly turn as the fallen Harvard lawyer.) Others in the nineteen-member cast are magnificent—Clarke Peters's scarily authentic black gambler, Tim Pigott-Smith's Larry Slade en route to schizophrenia, and James Hazeldine's tremendously sympathetic Harry Hope are three standouts in the committed cast.

I never saw Jason Robards's legendary Hickey, and there are those who claim the role that belongs to him has now passed to Kevin Spacey. But for me, Mr. Spacey's performance is all on the slick surface of things. Perhaps this is the way with salesmen, and Mr. Spacey's tricksy fast talk has surely broken some world speed record. He understands Hickey's fake warmth and his coldness, possessing the eyes of an assassin. He is a slight, coiled figure—a dangerous glad-hander on the move. But there is no variation in him, and no terror. In Hickey's ultimate collapse and confession, Mr. Spacey's tears are too easy, not hard-won. It is as if he's still selling himself to the end. And Hickey's marathon final scene of overwhelming elemental emotion fails to touch us as it should in O'Neill's compassionate search for absolution.

Act of Love

Tennessee Williams's unproduced 1938 play, *Not About Nightingales,* at Circle in the Square Theater, shouldn't be treated for one second as a minor curiosity, a virtuous excavation of the master's juvenile work. Trevor Nunn's remarkable production of the savage prison drama, together with the committed work of the British and American ensemble led by Corin Redgrave, have, firstly, done great honor to this forgotten play.

It is a fantastic act of love that we are witnessing, for enormous care and skill have been lavished on this ambitious apprentice work of conscience that would set Williams free. It is the first play that Thomas Lanier Williams signed "Tennessee." In finding himself, he began to find his own distinctive voice as a dramatist.

Tennessee Williams was a twenty-seven-year-old unknown when he wrote *Not About Nightingales,* his fourth full-length drama. Six years later, his 1944 play *The Glass Menagerie* would be the breakthrough that made him famous. The socially conscious Group Theater rejected *Not About Nightingales* (though subsequently awarded him $100 for his one-act plays). Cut to a half-century later when Vanessa Redgrave, then starring in Williams's *Orpheus Descending,* rediscovered the lost play. How she came to find *Not About Nightingales* was simple! She read the foreword Tennessee Williams wrote to *Orpheus Descending,* where he wrote:

"And so I drifted back to St. Louis, again, and wrote my fourth long play, which was the best of the lot. It was called *Not About Nightingales* and it concerned prison life, and I have never written anything since then that could compete with it in violence and horror, for it was based on something that actually occurred along about that time, the literal roasting alive of a group of intransigent convicts sent for correction to a hot room called 'The Klondike.'"

Vanessa Redgrave tracked down the "lost" manuscript via the eccentric Lady Maria St. Just, a close friend of Williams and executor of his estate. "There you are, Tall Girl!" Lady St. just exclaimed, handing over the script (which she had never read).

Seeing the electrifying production in New York, it struck me that it's a blessing it exists at all. The Alley Theater in Houston is one of its coproducers, and a number of its actors are in the cast. But the poor record of staging Williams's great plays in New York—let alone an unknown one of his—amounts to criminal negligence. Until quite recently, the same was true of the plays of Arthur Miller. Perhaps there's hope for Tennessee Williams yet. "Truly," wrote Trevor Nunn, explaining his admiration for Williams, "our respect for his work grows with every passing year, as his genius is increasingly revealed with each new visitation to his canon."

Harold Clurman of the Group Theater, which first rejected *Not About Nightingales,* would become an enthusiastic advocate of Williams's mature work. "Williams is a dramatist of lost souls," Clurman wrote. "His work describes a long laceration." So the early, compassionate *Not About Nightingales* is about society's misfits and a brutalizing imprisonment of the spirit, as well as an expressionist docudrama about inhuman prison life. Williams dedicated the play to Clarence Darrow, the champion of lost causes. And Williams, the lyrical poet of despair and tenderness, is there in the making.

The piece is a "living newspaper" based on fact—four prisoners in a Pennsylvania prison had been roasted alive in the boiler room. In that authentic sense, it's a public play rather than a personal one, more a social conscience drama in the tradition of Clifford Odets. It's also clearly influenced by 1930s prison movies and film noir (which the young Williams frequently escaped to). There are stock figures from prison movies: the brutish, corrupt prison warden, Boss Whelan (Corin Redgrave, playing bigger and freer, and therefore more dangerously than I've ever seen him); the thug named Butch (James Black) who leads the fatal prison riot; and the outcast homosexual, none too subtly known as "the Queen" (Jude Akuwudike). There's also a touchingly melodramatic romance between the naive prison secretary Eva (Sherri Parker Lee) and "Canary Jim" (Finbar Lynch), the stool pigeon who's as trapped as the twenty-seven-year-old Williams felt in his own gray existence.

"Every man living is walking around in a cage," says Jim, the play's hero, who will risk everything in desperate flight. As Williams later wrote about the fallen hero of *The Night of the Iguana*, he's "another beleaguered human being, someone who is in exile from the place and time of his heart's fulfillment."

Williams defensively denied that *Not About Nightingales* is mere melodrama. Very well; it's superior melodrama. The nascent dramatist was going beyond the conventional: his fluidly cinematic twenty-two episodes anticipate Brecht; he mercilessly satirized a hypocritical, callous clergy; he created a sympathetic black character; he argued for the poet as activist.

Real life, a caged life, is not about an elegiac "Ode to a Nightingale" by Keats. The younger, idealistic Williams believed it was about social reform, protest, justice. But even then the romantic idealist within him also believed in an escape to beauty. "He was like you," Eva says to Jim about Keats. "He had a lot of things he wanted to say but no chance to say them. He got out of his prison by looking at the stars. He wrote about beauty as a form of escape."

The seeds of the lyrical Williams are in the play, and compassion for fallible suffering humanity never left him. Within the sympathetic character of Eva we find all of Williams's women. What is Eva's dark sexual attraction to the abusive prison warden but Blanche Du Bois's ambiguity of refined manners in her desire for Stanley Kowalski?

Williams's future is in his past. At the end of *Not About Nightingales*, the play's hero makes his desperate escape. It is such a moving moment because we are also hearing—for the first time—the exultant liberation and hope of Williams himself in Jim's words: "Now is the time for unexpected things, for miracles, for wild adventures like the story books."

He'll take the gamble of being shot down, but there's just a chance he might make it and go on to miraculous, unexpected things. "Almost a chance! I've heard of people winning on a long shot."

The awesome, brutal reality of Trevor Nunn's production—its colorless, claustrophobic hell—is created by set designer Richard Hoover; the lighting design is by Chris Parry. Everyone, as I say, has done great honor to Tennessee Williams. Yes, we should make the pilgrimage and give them all our thanks.

Arthur Miller
Comes Home

Arthur Miller's *Death of a Salesman* is the American play that defines our theater, making it great and profoundly humane. If I had to choose between the major work of Tennessee Williams, Eugene O'Neill, or Mr. Miller, I would put *Death of a Salesman* highest. No play ever changed the world, but some have changed the way we see the world, and the way we see ourselves. More than any other American classic I know, *Death of a Salesman* quite simply breaks our hearts.

Mr. Miller has written eloquently about the theater, pointing out his admiration of Ibsen and epic Greek drama, but he is not a complicated man. He writes from experience—the family in *Salesman* is based on Mr. Miller's despairing, suicidal uncle, his two sons, and his suffering wife. And he writes straight from the gut, unafraid of the direct pull of honest emotion expressed by so-called ordinary people. Willy Loman, a "low man"—not a god or a king, but an Everyman.

The perceptive English critic Michael Billington wrote with a sense of wonder about *Death of a Salesman* that it "puts an amazing amount of America on to the stage." It tells the story of the last day in the life of an American dreamer, the salesman Willy Loman, yet it disturbs us on many levels. It's a chronicle of one anonymous man's crackup—Arthur Miller's original title of *Salesman* was *The Inside of His Head*. (Thank God he didn't use it.) It's also a domestic tragedy of family life, of guilt and need and primal love, of the yearning between fathers and sons:

"Pop, I'm nothing!" Willy's son, Biff, pleads furiously. "I'm nothing, Pop. Can't you understand that? There's no spite in it anymore. I'm just what I am, that's all."

As played by Brian Dennehy and Kevin Anderson in the fifteeth-anniversary revival of *Salesman* on Broadway, that scene is almost unbearable. Biff breaks down, holding on to his father. "What're you doing?" Willy says, bewildered. "What're you doing? Why is he crying?"

"Will you let me go, for Christ's sake? Will you take that phony dream and burn it before something happens?"

And *Salesman* is, of course, an unapologetic critique of "the wonder of this country"—the pursuit of happiness and the American Dream. The moral seriousness of Arthur Miller—call it conscience—can turn preachy. It's become quite fashionable to glibly patronize his political views as mere polemic or old hat. But who else has written such enduring dramas about capitalist greed *(All My Sons)*, the Communist witch-hunts of the 1950s *(The Crucible)*, or the steep price of the McCarthy era *(A View from the Bridge)*? No, Mr. Miller's moral universe is not so easily dismissed, not so irrelevant as a dated sermon.

In a 1950s essay, he wrote of *Death of a Salesman:* "Willy Loman has broken a law without whose protection life is insupportable if not incomprehensible to him and to many others; it is the law which says that a failure in society and in business has no right to live. Unlike the law against incest, the law of success is not administered by statute or church, but it is very nearly as powerful in its grip upon men."

Willy protests to his son: "I am not a dime a dozen! I am Willy Loman, and you are Biff Loman!" But the prideful Willy never was a success, only a failure. It is why—in Arthur Miller's universe—attention must be paid. "I don't say he's a great man," goes the famously compassionate speech of his suffering wife, Linda. "Willy Loman never made a lot of money. His name was never in the paper. He's not the finest character that ever lived. But he's a human being and a terrible thing is happening to him. So attention must be paid."

"Charley, the man didn't know who he was," says Biff Loman at Willy's grave. He was a sham. But what does this salesman actually sell? Mr. Miller doesn't tell us, and perhaps there's no need. Willy Loman is selling himself— like every salesman, including presidents. Willy himself is the commodity, riding on a smile and a shoeshine—until he's used up and spat out.

Our first sight of Brian Dennehy's salesman is of a shadowy colossus silhouetted in the darkness against the bright headlights of his car. It's a startling, near mythic image, and the heft of the man signals a giant fall. When he lugs his two suitcases, the weary weight of his life hangs in the defeated, exhausted balance.

For those of us who saw Mr. Dennehy as the arriviste merchant Lopakhin in Peter Brook's 1988 production of *The Cherry Orchard,* the poetry within this fine yeoman actor will come as no surprise. Where he touches us so deeply is in his naked emotional rawness. I felt he paced act 1 a little cautiously, as if holding something in reserve for the big arias of act 2. But Mr. Dennehy has produced a monumental performance. He is honest in everything he does—from Willy's utter, tragic bewilderment, to his burning agitation, to his ultimate Lear-like madness in the garden scene when Willy plants seeds in the darkness, pathetically planting a future, some rootedness, some desperate meaning to his futile life.

I much preferred Mr. Dennehy's Everyman to Dustin Hoffman's Dustin Hoffman in the 1984 Broadway production of *Salesman.* The technically brilliant Mr. Hoffman is invariably himself in disguise. But Mr. Dennehy moves us precisely because he's devastatingly real. And nowhere is he more effective than in his tremendous scenes with Kevin Anderson's Biff. The two of them stamp Robert Falls's production with its heartbeat of self-delusion and failure and ferocious love.

The cast is splendid, and my doubts in places aren't decisive. Mr. Anderson's Biff is a most effective, emotionally true performance, but he is almost too much the jock, lacking only the delicacy or refinement that often accompanies fallen favorite sons of rich promise. Elizabeth Franz has been raved about by many of my colleagues, but for my taste her Linda Loman holds too little in reserve, including inner despair. Ms. Franz's Linda is no passive doormat, however. This frail protector-wife could knock her two wastrel sons senseless, and in the "attention must be paid" scene, she practically does, and to devastating effect.

I found Mark Wendland's scenic designs at first too busy (and that neat little Loman kitchen has never been cooked in). Why is the house impressionistic, and the car real? But the revolving set with its gaping dark spaces successfully mirrors the rupture within Willy's psyche, the blur between past and present, until everything floats unhinged in the void between reality and dreams. There is excellent work, too, from lighting designers Michael Philippi and composer Richard Woodbury.

In the end, though, we return to the play, and we are reminded that
Death of a Salesman is arguably the greatest play of the twentieth century. We
know its flaws. And with each throw of the dice, with each new production,
we think what might have been done differently, as we do with a Chekhov
or Ibsen, or any masterpiece.

In many ways, this important production marks a coming home for
Arthur Miller. His plays have been far more celebrated abroad than at home.
The English, in particular, have always valued his narrative form and public conscience. His dramas are a forum for debate. And the English have felt
comfortable with *Death of a Salesman*'s tragedy of the American Dream; it
confirmed a certain anti-Americanism. But post-Thatcherite England has
changed dramatically, becoming Americanized. We are all salesmen now.

So this classic drama speaks to us as urgently as it ever did. And all family wars and disappointments and yearnings are eternal.